# MANDATED REPORTING *of* SUSPECTED CHILD ABUSE

### ETHICS, LAW, & POLICY

# MANDATED REPORTING *of* SUSPECTED CHILD ABUSE

## ETHICS, LAW, & POLICY

### SECOND EDITION

### SETH C. KALICHMAN

American Psychological Association, Washington, DC

Published by
American Psychological Association
750 First Street, NE
Washington, DC 20002

Copies may be ordered from
APA Order Department
P.O. Box 92984
Washington, DC 20090-2984

In the U.K., Europe, Africa, and the Middle East, copies may be ordered from
American Psychological Association
3 Henrietta Street
Covent Garden, London
WC2E 8LU England

Typeset in Goudy by EPS Group Inc., Easton, MD

Printer: Edwards Brothers, Inc., Ann Arbor, MI
Designer (text and cover): Anne Masters, Washington, DC
Technical/Production Editor: Rachael J. Stryker

**Library of Congress Cataloging-in-Publication Data**
Kalichman, Seth C.
    Mandated reporting of suspected child abuse : ethics, law & policy
/ Seth C. Kalichman.—2nd ed.
        p.    cm.
    Includes bibliographical references and index.
    ISBN 1-55798-602-9 (cloth : alk. paper)
    1. Drug abuse—Reporting.   2. Child abuse—Case studies.
3. Child abuse—Law and legislation.   I. Title.
HV8079.C46K35   1999
363.25'95554—dc21                                         99-28737
                                                          CIP

**British Library Cataloguing-in-Publication Data**
A CIP record is available from the British Library.

*Printed in the United States of America*
*Second Edition*

To Syd and Rita B. Kalichman
For everything you have always done,

And

To Moira and Hannah
For your inspiration.

# CONTENTS

Foreword .................................................. xi

Preface ................................................... xiii

Introduction ............................................. 3

I. MANDATED REPORTING: LEGAL, ETHICAL, AND
   PROFESSIONAL ISSUES .................................. 7

Chapter 1   Mandatory Child Abuse Reporting Laws: Origins
            and Evolution ................................. 11
            Evolution of the Mandatory Reporting System .... 12
            State Mandatory Reporting Laws ................ 17
            Opposition to Mandated Reporting ............. 30
            Failure to Report Suspected Child Abuse ......... 33
            Conclusions ................................... 41

Chapter 2   Mandated Reporting as an Ethical Dilemma ........ 43
            Duty to Warn .................................. 44
            Mandated Reporting and Professional Ethics ...... 46
            Confidentiality and Reporting ................... 47
            Informed Consent .............................. 48
            Diluting Professional Roles ..................... 51
            Considerations in Research Settings ............. 53
            Effects of Reporting on Child and Family
              Services ..................................... 55
            Reporting Perpetrators in Treatment ............. 57
            Conflicts Between Reporting Laws and Ethical
              Standards ................................... 61
            Conclusions ................................... 62

Chapter 3   When Professional Hunches Become Reasonable
            Suspicions ........................................   65
                Applying Decision-Making Models to Mandated
                    Reporting ...................................   66
                Utility Models: The Perceived Benefits and Costs
                    of Reporting ................................   66
                Evidence-Based Models: Indicators of Abuse as
                    Reasonable Suspicions .......................   69
                Threshold Models .............................   79
                Conclusions ..................................   91

II. REPORTING SUSPECTED CHILD ABUSE: CASEBOOK
    AND GUIDELINES ........................................   93

Chapter 4   Therapeutic Jurisprudence and Mandated Reporting   97
                Therapeutic Aims of Mandatory Reporting Laws ...   98
                Antitherapeutic Applications of Mandatory
                    Reporting Laws .............................  100
                Coercive Uses of Mandatory Reporting in
                    Therapy ....................................  101
                Therapeutically Applying Mandatory Reporting
                    Laws .......................................  102
                Conclusions ..................................  104

Chapter 5   Unreported Cases of Suspected Child Abuse ........  105
                Case 5.1. Emily: Weighing the Risks and Benefits
                    of Reporting ...............................  105
                Case 5.2. Elizabeth: Pushing Back the Limits of
                    Confidentiality .............................  108
                Case 5.3. Danny: Third-Party Disclosure of
                    Abuse .....................................  110
                Case 5.4. Nathan: Misinterpreting Allegations of
                    Abuse as Psychiatric Symptoms ..............  111
                Case 5.5. Leah: Using the Threat of Reporting to
                    Facilitate Change ..........................  113
                Case 5.6. Mallory: Revelation of Abuse in a
                    Research Setting ...........................  114
                Case 5.7. Stephanie: Therapist Acting as
                    Investigator ...............................  116
                Case 5.8. Nicole: Reporting to Protect All
                    Children ...................................  117
                Case 5.9. Dillon: Waiting Until the Next Time to
                    Report .....................................  118
                Case 5.10. Paige: Walking the Line on Punishment
                    and Abuse .................................  120

Case 5.11. Rita: Responsibilities for Ensuring the
   Report ....................................... 121
Case 5.12. Megan: Suspected Abuse Defined by
   Visible Injuries ............................ 122
Conclusions ................................... 123

Chapter 6    Reported Cases of Suspected Child Abuse .......... 125
Case 6.1. Jake: Suspected Sexual Abuse Reported
   by a Student Intern ......................... 125
Case 6.2. Claudia: Physical Abuse of an Adolescent
   Girl ........................................ 127
Case 6.3. Maria: Sexual Abuse Inflicted by a Fellow
   Professional ................................ 128
Case 6.4. Billy: Reporting Psychological–Emotional
   Abuse ...................................... 129
Case 6.5. Amy: Suspected Neglect in a School
   Setting ..................................... 130
Case 6.6. Sarina: Suspected Sexual Abuse in Foster
   Care ....................................... 132
Case 6.7. Nancy: From Anger to Physical Abuse .. 133
Conclusions ................................... 134

III. MANDATORY REPORTING PRACTICE AND POLICY..... 137

Chapter 7    Guidelines for Reporting Suspected Child Abuse .... 141
Interviewing Children ......................... 143
Informing Parents, Guardians, and Children ...... 145
Preparing for the Report ....................... 146
Reporting Suspected Child Abuse .............. 148
Screening and Initial Risk Assessments .......... 150
Child Protection Investigations ................. 152
Working With Child Abuse Investigators ......... 156
Child Abuse Investigation Findings ............. 157
Reporting Other Vulnerable Populations ........ 159
Conclusions ................................... 160

Chapter 8    Professional Practice and Research ................. 161
Ethical Standards and Mandated Reporting ....... 162
Points of Ethical Consideration in Mandated
   Reporting .................................. 162
Standards, Definitions, and Reporting Thresholds
   Revisited ................................... 165
A Hierarchical Approach to Managing Ambiguous
   Suspicions of Abuse ......................... 166

Professional Training in Child Abuse and
Mandated Reporting ......................... 168
Mandatory Training in Child Abuse Reporting .... 174
Avenues for Future Research ................... 176
Conclusions ................................. 178

Chapter 9    Child Protection Policy ......................... 181
Minimal Reform: Strengthening and Supporting
Existing Systems ........................... 182
Adaptive Reform: Modifying Existing Statutes .... 184
Overhauling Existing Systems ................. 191
Conclusions ................................. 192

References ................................................. 195

Appendix A: Glossary ........................................ 213

Appendix B: Directory of Information Resources ................. 223

Appendix C: Directory of National and State Child Protection
Hotlines ..................................................... 225

Index ...................................................... 227

About the Author ........................................... 235

# FOREWORD

In 1993, Seth Kalichman made an uprecedented effort to combine scientific research, ethical standards, legislation, and case law regarding the mandated reporting of child abuse. The result was *Mandated Reporting of Suspected Child Abuse: Ethics, Law, and Policy*, a thoughtful classic that has proved indispensable not only to working clinicians, but also to attorneys, researchers, law enforcement, and policymakers. Remarkably, 6 years later, Kalichman has taken the landmark *Mandated Reporting* and found ways to improve it.

Much has happened since the original volume appeared. Innovative research has not only increased our understanding of the mandated reporting of suspected child abuse, but has also made us more aware of how complex its issues are, as well as how much we still do not know. Ethical and legal standards have continued to evolve and, unfortunately, sometimes conflict with each other, and policymakers have found new ways to disagree on how to approach the challenges presented by child abuse. For example, one of the most striking recent developments has been the heated controversy over recovered and false memories of child abuse. This controversy has yielded an extreme polarization—on one side sits informed, thoughtful people who, because of their views, have been characterized as supporters of pedophilia and in some cases, as molesters themselves, and on the other sits an equally informed and thoughtful set of people holding different views who are sometimes characterized as hate-filled, pseudoscientific witch hunters and "True Believers."

In this updated edition of *Mandated Reporting*, Kalichman continues to remain unaffected by the venom of controversies inspired by the mandated reporting of suspected child abuse. A scrupulous scholar, he has eschewed selecting or emphasizing studies that support a particular view in favor of examining a full range of data, bringing it to bare on some of the most difficult dilemmas that individual clinicians and society as a whole must confront.

Even those who have but a passing acquaintance with research terminology will probably be familiar with the terms *Type I* and *Type II error*, at least as abstractions. But when applied to mandatory reporting and the attempt to accurately identify instances of child abuse, these two forms of error reflect almost intolerable costs. A false positive (Type I error) may mean that a loving father who has never acted inappropriately toward his daughter may lose his family, his job, his friends, and his reputation. If wrongly convicted, he may also lose his freedom. A false negative (Type II error) may mean that a 4- or 5-year-old girl will be condemned to be violently raped and tortured by her father night after night for years. In this volume, Kalichman has exhibited a great amount of respect for the realities, complexities, and costs of each mandated report of suspected child abuse (whether or not the report reflects actual abuse), as well as each instance in which actual abuse goes unreported.

Kalichman—who has also made outstanding contributions through his books on HIV and AIDS—is the preeminent scholar and researcher in the area of mandated reporting of suspected child abuse. This second edition is an invaluable resource.

Kenneth S. Pope, PhD, ABPP

# PREFACE

*Mandated Reporting of Suspected Child Abuse* provides a comprehensive review of the research findings, ethical issues, and policies related to the mandated reporting of suspected child abuse. In addition, cases collected from clinicians in the field are integrated with theory and research and presented as a casebook. Therefore, by design, the book weaves empirical findings with practice issues and sets an agenda for advances in professional practice, legislative reform, and research. The book was written for professionals who are required to report suspected child abuse, including students, experienced practitioners, and researchers.

The first edition of *Mandated Reporting of Suspected Child Abuse: Ethics, Law, and Policy*, published in 1993, was the product of 7 years of research on professional responses to mandatory child abuse reporting laws. These ideas evolved through collaborative research efforts, discussions at conventions and conferences, and numerous conversations with friends and colleagues. The need for the second edition became clear as new research revealed that multiple factors and multiple decision-making models help to explain the decision to report. Recent changes in reporting laws also demanded an updated edition of *Mandated Reporting*. Unlike the first edition, the second speaks more to general principles of mandatory reporting laws than to the specifics of any given state law. For this reason, the information presented in the second edition will remain more durable over time as mandatory reporting laws continue to evolve. This edition also views reporting laws through the lens of therapeutic jurisprudence, a contemporary legal perspective that has been useful in several areas of mental health law. Therapeutic jurisprudence is the topic of chapter 4, and it is used as a framework for discussing cases of reported and unreported suspected abuse in chapters 5 and 6. Finally, many of the changes included in this edition reflect suggestions and feedback I received from readers of the first edition. For example, the discussion of cases in chapters 5 and 6 now include lessons learned from the experiences of clinicians who have reported and not reported. This edition also includes updated research and an expanded glossary.

There are several people to whom I am indebted for their help with both editions. Linda Steinman and Tony Broskowski contributed to the development of the first experimental studies investigating factors that influence professional reporting decisions. In addition to conducting some of the key studies related to mandated reporting, Ken Pope provided valuable feedback and insights on the first edition. Also, Michael Miller reviewed portions of the first edition and contributed substantive comments. Brian Wilcox encouraged the development of the first edition and provided valuable comments.

The following people contributed to the ideas presented in both the first and second editions: Jeanne Murrone, Arne Gray, Fred Cavaiani, Robert Muckenheim, Allan G. Hedberg, Nancy Townsend, Mary Ellen Luxon, Gary R. Schoener, Jeanne E. Sokolec, Diane Follingstad, Paul Jose, Art Bodin, and several clinicians and researchers who provided cases for the casebook and wished to remain anonymous. Over and above her own contributions to the child abuse reporting literature, Cheryl L. Brosig fueled many of my ideas and provided many comments throughout the first edition. In addition to their support, encouragement, and enthusiasm, Julia Frank-McNeil and Ted Baroody of APA Books provided many excellent ideas for the development and structure of the first and second editions. I am also grateful to Mary Lynn Skutley, Shelly Wyatt, and Rachael Stryker for their work. Finally, the first and second editions of this book would not have been possible without the ideas and encouragement of Moira and Hannah Kalichman, each of whom have inspired the revision and writing.

# MANDATED REPORTING *of* SUSPECTED CHILD ABUSE

## ETHICS, LAW, & POLICY

# INTRODUCTION

Debbie is a 10-year-old girl who lives with her mother, father, and younger brother. Debbie was referred to a school psychologist by her physical education teacher, who became concerned when Debbie refused to change for swimming class. Debbie would not discuss how she was feeling or why she would not participate in swimming. Her teacher told the psychologist that Debbie was behaving differently than usual, and was becoming increasingly more withdrawn from other students. The teacher also said that she was concerned that Debbie may be having problems at home.

During her first session with the psychologist, Debbie was mostly quiet and refused to talk about how she was feeling. When asked about how things were going at home, Debbie started to cry and ran out of the room saying, "I hate them for what they did to me."

Putting yourself in the place of the school psychologist, what is the next thing that you would do? What are the psychologist's options? What actions would be in the best interest of the child? Would this case be required to be reported as a case of suspected child abuse? If so, would the physical education teacher violate the law by not reporting?

Child abuse is one of the great social maladies of our time. In 1997, there were over 3 million children reported as victims of child maltreatment in the United States, representing more than a 40% increase since 1988. Although the majority of reported cases of child maltreatment involve neglect (52%), physical abuse accounts for 26% of reports, sexual abuse accounts for 7%, emotional maltreatment 4%, and 11% of reports concern other forms of abuse and exploitation. The number of deaths that result from child abuse also increased by as much as 8% between 1997 and 1998 (Wang & Daro, 1998). Staggering as these statistics are, they reflect only the surface of the child abuse crisis. Community-based incidence studies have estimated that reported child abuse constitutes only about 40% of all cases (U.S. Department of Health and Human Services [USDHHS], 1988). The prevalence of abuse, coupled with significant budget cuts for child protection and family services, brought the U.S. Advisory Board on Child Abuse and Neglect (1990) to declare child maltreatment a national emergency.

Human service professionals, including psychologists, social workers, teachers, and psychiatrists, are required to report known or suspected child abuse in all states. Approximately half of child abuse reports are filed by professionals—the majority originate from hospitals, schools, day care centers and mental health and social service agencies (USDHHS, 1988). Still, reports of abuse account for only a portion of the abused children that professionals encounter in their services. For example, mandated reporters working in day care centers report less than 12% of cases of suspected child abuse, and professionals in medical hospitals report only 69% of cases. Surveys repeatedly show that one in three professionals who have had contact with suspected child abuse have declined to report. Likewise, the Study of National Incidence and Prevalence of Child Abuse and Neglect found that professionals report only about one third of the 1.2 million cases of suspected abuse (USDHHS, 1988, pp. 6–17).

The decision not to report suspected child maltreatment places professionals at risk for legal and professional sanctions, including fines, licensure suspension, jail sentences, and civil suits. Why, then, do concerned professionals sometimes choose to break the law when it comes to reporting suspected child abuse? What factors contribute to unreported suspicions of abuse? Does the failure to report endanger children or protect them? What can the research literature offer to practitioners who must make the decision to report suspected abuse? How do vague statutes result in over- and underreporting of suspected child abuse? These questions, among others, fuel this book. They also inspire a comprehensive and integrated discussion of mandated child abuse reporting. The focus of this book, however, is not only on the reporting requirements themselves, but also on how reporting functions within service delivery settings and the issues raised by mandatory reporting laws.

This book is composed of three parts. Each part contains three chapters. Part I discusses the problems associated with mandatory reporting laws. As a logical starting point, chapter 1 presents the history and evolution of mandatory reporting laws, as well as an examination of the specific dimensions of current laws and how they vary across states. Chapter 2 discusses mandated reporting as an ethical dilemma, highlighting confidentiality and informed consent, and refers specifically to professional settings in which child abuse is often suspected. Next, using the context of human decision-making models, chapter 3 discusses the dimensions of abusive situations that affect reporting. Part II composes an embedded casebook. Chapter 4 discusses mandated reporting from the perspective of therapeutic jurisprudence and sets a frame of reference for chapters 5 and 6, which present cases of unreported and reported suspected child abuse, including commentaries and lessons learned for each case. Part III focuses on guidelines and strategies for effectively reporting suspected child abuse in practice, as well as suggestions for improving child abuse reporting policies. Finally, three appendixes present a glossary, directories for resources, and a list of hotlines.

# I

## MANDATED REPORTING: LEGAL, ETHICAL, AND PROFESSIONAL ISSUES

# INTRODUCTION

# MANDATED REPORTING:
## LEGAL, ETHICAL, AND
## PROFESSIONAL ISSUES

Child maltreatment is a social malady. It is also a symptom of broader problems. In an effort to address the abuse and neglect of children, contemporary societies have created child protective service systems. Within these systems, professionals are required to report abused children to child protection officials. Such professionals act to identify endangered children, a role that many do not always embrace. Nevertheless, child protection requires identifying, investigating, and intervening with maltreated children and their families, and mandated reports play a crucial role in these processes. Part I is an examination of the history and controversy that surrounds mandated reporting of suspected child abuse. In chapter 1, I review the history of mandatory reporting laws and its implications for human services. Within this historical context, I discuss in chapter 2 the dilemmas posed by mandated reporting. Finally, in chapter 3, I explore professionals' decisions to report suspected child abuse.

# 1

# MANDATORY CHILD ABUSE REPORTING LAWS: ORIGINS AND EVOLUTION

While the medical profession plays a major role in the identification of the battered child and will have a primary role in the alleviation of the consequences of parental abuse and the rehabilitation of the abuser, and while welfare and social workers must play major roles in the resolution of the problem, ultimately the solution must be legal, in the form of legislation and judicial decisions, and the machinery of the state designed for the protection of the child. (McCoid, 1965, p. 3)

It is the policy of the board of education that this school district comply with the Colorado Child Protection Act of 1987. To that end, any school official or employee who has reasonable cause to know or suspect that a child has been subjected to abuse or neglect or who has observed the child being subjected to circumstances or conditions which would reasonably result in abuse or neglect, as defined by statute, shall immediately report or cause a report to be made to the Department of Social Services or local law enforcement agency. (Colorado Board of Education, 1995)

In 1997 over 3 million children were reported for child abuse and neglect in the United States. This number represented a 1.7% increase over the number of children reported in 1996. Child abuse reporting increased 41% between 1988 and 1997 (Wang & Daro, 1998). The majority of cases confirmed by investigation involved child neglect (54%), whereas physical abuse accounted for 22% of confirmed cases, sexual abuse for 8%, and emotional maltreatment for 4%. Other forms of maltreatment represented the remaining 12%. Child fatalities resulting from abuse increased more than 85% between 1985 and 1996 (Wang & Daro, 1998), with trauma being the most common cause of death for children and head injuries being the most common cause of traumatic death in infancy (Duhaime, Christian, Rorke, & Zimmerman, 1998). Staggering as these statistics are, they represent only part of the child abuse problem (Maney & Wells, 1988). Community-based incidence studies estimate that reported child abuse constitutes only about 40% of all actual cases (U.S. Department of Health and Human Services [USDHHS], 1988). The prevalence of abuse, along with reductions in child protection services has caused the U.S. Advisory Board on Child Abuse and Neglect (1990) to declare child maltreatment a national emergency.

In the United States, human service professionals, such as psychologists, social workers, teachers, and psychiatrists, are required to report known or suspected child maltreatment in all 50 states. Approximately 46% of child maltreatment reports are filed by professionals, with the majority originating from hospitals, schools, day care centers, and mental health and social service agencies (USDHHS, 1988). Still, reported cases account for only a portion of the child abuse that helping professionals suspect. For example, day care workers report less than 12% of cases of suspected child abuse, and hospital-based medical professionals report only 69% of suspected cases. Surveys have repeatedly shown that one in three professionals have had contact with at least one case of suspected abuse that they have declined to report (see Table 1.1). Similarly, the National Incidence and Prevalence of Child Abuse and Neglect Study found that professionals reported only about one third of the 1.2 million cases of abuse they suspected (USDHHS, 1988, pp. 6–17). Mandatory reporting laws play a central role in the child protection system, serving as the point of intersection among outlets of children's service, including medical care, mental health, education, and social services. The central role that mandated reporting plays in child protection is apparent in the history of mandatory reporting laws.

## EVOLUTION OF THE MANDATORY REPORTING SYSTEM

Child protection is a relatively recent social concept. Until the 19th century the Western world showed little interest in, and had no policies for, protecting children. Although the child welfare movement originated in 1875 with the advent of the New York Society for the Prevention of Cruelty to Children, it was not until the early part of the 20th century

## TABLE 1.1
### Selected Surveys of Mandated Reporters Who Suspect Abuse and Do Not Report

| Authors | Participants | Percent of professionals not reporting at least one case of suspected abuse |
|---|---|---|
| Swoboda et al. (1978) | 98 Mental Health Professionals | 63 |
| James et al. (1978) | 96 Physicians | 58 |
| Pope et al. (1987) | 465 Psychologists | 61 |
| Pope & Bajt (1988) | 60 Senior Psychologists | 21 |
| Kalichman et al. (1989) | 279 Psychologists | 37 |
| Kalichman & Brosig (1992) | 552 Psychologists | 35 |
| Kalichman & Craig (1991) | 328 Psychologists | 37 |
| Brosig & Kalichman (1992b) | 297 Licensed Psychologists | 39 |
| Kennel & Agresti (1995) | 431 Psychologists | 29 |

| Authors | Participants | Percent of professionals who suspect abuse but do not report |
|---|---|---|
| Finkelhor (1984) | 790 Mandated Reporters in Boston | 36 |
| Kim (1986) | 120 Physicians | 25 |

that child protective services were instituted in the United States (A. Levine & Levine, 1992). The American Humane Association was established in the late 1870s to serve as a national organization concerned with child abuse. Child abuse, however, was given low priority by the association; at the time, infant mortality and maternal health were of much greater concern (A. Levine & Levine, 1992). On the federal level, the 1935 Social Security Act initially funded public welfare for the protection and care of homeless, dependent, and neglected children (USDHHS, 1988). Legislation concerning child welfare focused on willful neglect or failure to provide adequate child care (Maryland Social Services Administration, 1988). Since the inception of the child welfare system, it has been true that any citizen may report known or suspected child abuse to child protection authorities. However, mandatory reporting of child abuse by professionals serving children and families did not become law until the early 1960s (see Exhibit 1.1).

Increased public awareness of child abuse and the civil libertarian social climate of the 1960s set the stage for child protection legislation (National Center on Child Abuse and Neglect [NCCAN], 1979; Newberger, 1983). However, the catalyst for the first generation of child abuse

EXHIBIT 1.1
The Evolution of Mandatory Reporting Laws

| | |
|---|---|
| 1870s | American Humane Association is founded |
| 1875 | New York Society for Prevention of Cruelty to Children is founded |
| 1935 | Social Security Act Welfare for neglected children is enacted |
| 1940s | Early medical descriptions of nonaccidental injuries to infants appear |
| 1962 | Kempe defines the "battered child syndrome" |
| 1963 | Children's Bureau develops model statutes |
| 1965 | The American Medical Association and Program of State Governments propose first statutes |
| 1966 | All states except Hawaii adopt mandatory reporting laws |
| 1974 | Child Abuse Prevention and Treatment Act |
| 1990 | U.S. Advisory Board on Child Abuse and Neglect declares a national emergency |
| 1997 | Over 3 million reports of child abuse filed in the United States |

reporting laws was the establishment of a formal medical profile for abused children. Pediatricians and physicians published a series of clinical reports describing victims of abuse, and the American Academy of Pediatrics held an early symposium dedicated to describing the ailments of battered children. Indeed, as early as 1946, Caffey described combinations of injuries in infants that suggested abuse. These first clinical reports formed much of the groundwork for defining child abuse as a medical problem (for a review, see McCoid, 1965). Kempe, Silverman, Steele, Droegemueller, and Silver (1962) formally described the *battered child syndrome* and published the single most influential report on child maltreatment. As a new medical diagnosis, the battered child syndrome was characterized by "injury to soft tissue and skeleton" (Kempe et al., 1962, p. 105) and accompanied by "evidence of neglect, including poor skin hygiene, multiple soft tissue injuries, and malnutrition" (pp. 105–106). Kempe et al. also provided detailed radiologic features and clinical manifestations that were often discrepant with available information from case histories alone. Thus, the battered child syndrome was objectively defined by several specific features, most of which were relevant to the physical and radiological examination of children.

In addition to providing detailed descriptions of the trauma that characterizes the battered child syndrome, Kempe et al. (1962) referred to the condition as being "inadequately handled by the physician because of hesitation to bring the case to the attention of the proper authorities" (p. 105). Kempe et al. speculated that reluctance among physicians to report suspicious injuries was due to their unwillingness to consider parents as the source of harm. Furthermore, Kempe et al. (1962) stated that "training and personality usually make it quite difficult for [a physician] to assume the role of policeman or district attorney, and start questioning patients as if he (she) were investigating a crime" (p. 107). Kempe et al. (1962) noted that some physicians would ignore any suspicions of abuse despite "obvious circumstantial evidence" (p. 107). Therefore, an agenda was put in motion to establish mandatory reporting laws, and much of what Kempe et al. wrote is reflected in contemporary child abuse reporting statutes.

The battered child syndrome and Kempe et al.'s (1962) comments about physicians' reluctance to report stimulated initiatives to develop mandatory reporting legislation. In 1963, the Children's Bureau of the National Center on Child Abuse and Neglect drafted the first of three model reporting statutes. Two other statutes were drafted in 1965—one proposed by the American Medical Association and the other by the Program of State Governments. By 1966 an unprecedented proliferation of legislation appeared within all of the United States except Hawaii, which followed later. These laws mandated physicians to report suspected child abuse. Soon, reporting laws were established in other countries, including Canada (Walters, 1995), Australia, and New Zealand (Adler, 1995). The first reporting statutes were designed to illuminate cases of the battered child syndrome known to physicians that would be unrecognizable by nonmedical observers (Paulsen, 1967). According to the Children's Bureau statute,

> The purpose of this Act is to provide for the protection of children who have had physical injury inflicted upon them. . . . Physicians . . . should report . . . thereby causing the protective services of the state to be brought to bear in an effort to protect the health and welfare of these children and to prevent further abuses. (Children's Bureau, Principles for Legislation, cited in Paulsen, 1967, p. 15)

With respect to required reports by physicians and institutions, the first statutes specified that

> any physician . . . having reasonable cause to suspect that a child under the age of [the maximum age of juvenile court] brought to him or coming before him for examination, care or treatment has had serious physical injury or injuries inflicted upon him other than by accidental means by a parent or other person responsible for his care, shall report or cause a report to be made in accordance with the provisions of the Act. (cited in McCoid, 1965, p. 20)

Legislative changes subsequently broadened most aspects of these early statutes, including the range of professionals and types of maltreatment meeting legal standards for required reporting. In the late 1960s and early 1970s several groups of professionals were added to the list of mandated reporters. Definitions of abuse were also broadened to include emotional and nutritional maltreatment (Giovannoni, 1989b), as well as sexual abuse and exploitation. Most states dropped the term *serious* as a qualifier of the injuries or harm stated in definitions of abuse. The Child Abuse Prevention and Treatment Act of 1974 defined child abuse and neglect and set the standard for state mandatory reporting laws. The act defined abuse and neglect as

> the physical or mental injury, sexual abuse, negligent treatment, or maltreatment of a child under the age of 18 by a person who is responsible for the child's welfare under circumstances which indicate the child's health or welfare is harmed or threatened thereby as determined in accordance with regulations prescribed. (Child Abuse Prevention and Treatment Act of 1974, Section 3)

States are required to adopt similar definitions of abuse in order to qualify for federal child protection funds. Qualifying definitions of abuse with terms such as *serious injury* resulted in some states' ineligibility for federal support (Daro & McCurdy, 1992; Wells, Stein, Fluke, & Downing, 1989).

Amendments to the act further broadened the types of maltreatment included in definitions of abuse. The Child Abuse Prevention, Adoption, and Family Services Act of 1988 defined maltreatment as

> the physical or mental injury, sexual abuse or exploitation, or maltreatment of a child by a person who is responsible for the child's welfare, under circumstances which indicate that the child's health or welfare is harmed or threatened. (Section 14. Definitions)

States themselves have broadened and expanded their own reporting laws. California, for example, amended its reporting statute more than 15 times in 20 years (Meriwether, 1986). Unfortunately, the expansion of reporting laws has not taken into account the diversity of professionals who have been added to the roster of mandated reporters. Because the battered child syndrome originally described cases that were most likely seen by emergency room physicians, radiologists, and pediatricians, first-generation reporting statutes understandably targeted medical professionals. When reporting laws were expanded to include a range of professionals, there was also an expansion of definitions of abuse and conditions under which reporting was required. But reporting laws do not differentiate between mandated reporters who differ in their professional training, circumstances of practice, and conditions under which suspicions of maltreatment arise. Thus, a single standard for reporting is applied across professions, circumstances, and settings.

Because reporting laws often fail to account for particular circumstances, their uniform application has often been criticized (Ansell & Ross, 1990; Berlin, Malin, & Dean, 1991; J. Jones & Welch, 1989; Newberger, 1983). With few exceptions, reporting statutes place limits on confidentiality and privileged communications. Professional discretion and judgment are rarely given consideration in reporting requirements. As a result, laws that require reporting suspected child abuse and neglect in professional contexts often conflict with basic professional values and ethical principles.

Professional conflicts thus interfere with an adherence to mandatory reporting laws. This creates situations where professionals do not follow the law and therefore, by definition, breach professional ethics (see Figure 1.1).

As a central component of child protective systems, mandatory reporting laws hold individuals responsible for alerting authorities about potential abuse on the premise that maltreated children are too young, too frightened, and too vulnerable to seek their own assistance. There are, therefore, three objectives upon which reporting laws are predicated: (a) Reporting laws are designed to expedite the identification of abused children by the child protection system; (b) reporting laws designate agencies to receive, investigate, and manage cases of child maltreatment; and (c) reporting laws are intended, when appropriate, to mobilize protective services to prevent further abuse and to help preserve family unity and welfare (NCCAN, 1979). Howitt (1992) has noted, however, that there are three general concerns regarding the practice of child protection: (a) concern that lack of involvement will leave children open to abuse; (b) concern that too much involvement will identify abuse when it does not, in fact, exist; and (c) concern about the quality of care provided by child protective systems. These concerns are also at the heart of complications with mandated reporting of suspected abuse.

## STATE MANDATORY REPORTING LAWS

Laws that require professionals to report suspected child abuse aim to increase the number of identified cases of child maltreatment. According to Besharov (1990), reports of child abuse and neglect in the 1980s increased more than 14 times the number reported in the 1960s. This infers that mandated reporting caused the increase in reports. Such causal interpretations, however, may be misleading because they do not take into ac-

*Figure 1.1.* Relationships among professional ethics, confidentiality, child protection, and mandatory child abuse reporting laws.

count the social changes that accompanied child protection legislation, including greater public awareness of child abuse, elevated social consciousness, and the encouragement of all citizens to anonymously report suspected abuse. Although a direct causal link between media and child abuse reports could not be drawn, McDevitt (1996) showed that reports of child abuse increased in conjunction with an increase in the number of news media stories concerning child abuse. In another study, Lamond (1989) investigated an increase in reporting of suspected child sexual abuse in New South Wales, Australia, that followed the enactment of legislation requiring professionals to report suspected child sexual abuse. This research showed that although the overall number of reports remained unchanged during the study period, reports of sexual abuse filed by school personnel increased from 21% to 30%. Schoolteachers reported sexual abuse nearly three times more often after the legislative change, which made teachers the source of almost a quarter of all reports of sexual abuse. Mandatory reporting laws, therefore, seemed to account for the observed increase in reported sexual abuse, despite the many mandated reporters who do not comply with the law (Budai, 1996).

Mandatory child abuse reporting laws invariably share several core components. All reporting laws (a) define abusive situations; (b) delineate reportable circumstances, as well as the degree of certainty that reporters must attain, the age limits of reportable children, and details of who must report; (c) outline the sanctions for failing to report; and (d) provide immunity from civil and criminal liability for reports filed "in good faith." Although most reporting statutes share general features, state-level reporting laws can differ in important ways. The greatest causes of variability among laws are the ways in which abuse is defined and the conditions under which reporting is required. Thus, three elements of reporting laws appear to pose the greatest challenges to professionals: (a) Who is required to report? (b) what is required to be reported? and (c) when is reporting required?

## Who Is Required to Report?

The first laws that required professionals to report suspected child abuse were directed exclusively at medical professionals. This focus, however, was short-lived, and soon a variety of helping professionals were added to the rosters of mandated reporters. One reason for expanding reporting requirements to other professions was that physicians were opposed to being singled out as the sole detectors of child abuse. Among other concerns, physicians did not want to become a mere extension of the legal system. They also felt that parents who were scared of being reported might fail to provide abused children with adequate health. According to the American Medical Association,

> This is a social problem in which the physician plays a part. Visiting nurses, social workers, school teachers and authorities, lawyers, marriage and guidance counselors, and others frequently learn of cases before medical care is demanded or received. To wait until the child requires medical attention is too late. To compel reporting by the physician alone may single him out unwisely. Knowing of this requirement, the parent or guardian may, for his own protection, put off seeking medical care. (American Medical Association, 1964, p. 136)

In response to the concerns of physicians, legislators expanded mandatory reporting laws to include a broad range of human service providers, including those working outside of health-related fields, such as social service workers and teachers. Such expansion continues. For example, several states now mandate commercial film processors to report suspected abuse, and focus specifically on cases of suspected abuse and exploitation indicated by sexually explicit photographs of children. In addition, professionals who care for or supervise children in a variety of settings have been added to the list of mandated reporters. Even animal humane officers have been designated as mandated reporters in some states because of the common association between cruelty to animals and child abuse. In almost every state, mental health professionals, including psychologists, counselors, social workers, and psychiatrists, are required to report suspected abuse. Other professionals who may be required to report suspected child abuse include pharmacists, dentists, and religious healers. Finally, it has become increasingly common for states to require reporting by *any* person who suspects the abuse of a child. When all states are considered, there are nearly 40 different professions named in mandatory reporting laws (Wurtele & Miller-Perrin, 1992).

Research has shown that members of various professions respond quite differently to reporting requirements. In the first study to formally survey professional responses to mandated reporting, psychologists were less knowledgeable about reporting laws than psychiatrists. In turn, psychiatrists were much less knowledgeable than social workers (Swoboda, Elwork, Sales, & Levine, 1978). Psychiatric nurses are more likely to report abuse compared with nonmedically trained mental health workers (Kalichman, Craig, & Follingstad, 1988). Williams, Osborne, and Rappaport (1987) showed that nurses and ministers were more likely to report abuse than family practice physicians and psychologists. These studies suggest differences in compliance with reporting laws among professions and differences in service delivery settings.

Professionals who are required to report suspected abuse are given immunity from civil and criminal liabilities associated with reporting. Mandated reporters are protected when reports are filed in good faith, or in the absence of malicious intent, regardless of whether abuse is substantiated upon investigation. Some states specify that reports must be filed in good faith or without malice, whereas others presume that all reports are indeed filed in good faith. All states, however, provide immunity for reporting suspected child abuse, as required under the Federal Child Abuse Prevention and Treatment Act, which grants "immunity for persons reporting instances of child abuse and neglect from prosecution, under any state or local law, arising out of such reporting" (NCCAN, 1979, p. 10). Immunity from liability due to participation in judicial proceedings resulting from a report is also granted by most states. The intent of immunity is to remove hesitations to report when one is uncertain that abuse has occurred. It is extremely rare for mandated reporters to file reports that are deemed harassing and without just cause (Drake, 1996).

### What Is Required to Be Reported?

A great deal of confusion exists concerning definitions of child maltreatment, much of which is the product of language used for divergent purposes. As a matter of classification, definitions serve diagnostic functions in medicine as well as other human service professions. Diagnosing child abuse offers a range of treatment alternatives. However, medical diagnoses are not necessarily aligned with social service definitions, although the latter functions as a minimum criterion for family intervention (Giovannoni, 1989b), and both medical and social service definitions of abuse may diverge from legal definitions. With respect to legal definitions of abuse, there are three different functions for which abuse is typically defined: (a) criminal acts, (b) determination of child dependency, and (c) identifying cases that warrant reporting. Whereas legal definitions will overlap across these three areas of law, there are often distinguishing characteristics of the law.

Legal definitions of child abuse in reporting statutes often vary considerably. Examining definitions of child abuse shows how some forms of maltreatment are included while others are excluded. For example, Rycraft (1990) found that 40% of state reporting laws did not include poverty-related neglect in their definitions of neglect, 22% did not include emotional maltreatment, 55% omitted educational neglect, and 24% did not recognize medical neglect. Four different types of child maltreatment are most commonly included in reporting laws: physical abuse, sexual abuse, neglect, and emotional maltreatment. Of course, the different types of abuse are not mutually exclusive; sexual abuse includes physical assault and both physical and sexual abuse imply emotional abuse. In addition, approximately 10% of reported child abuse cases fall into an "other" category that may include abandonment and dependency (Daro & McCurdy, 1992). Most states do not distinguish between reporting *abuse* versus *neglect*

(NCCAN, 1979). However, states do define the composition of each of the different types of maltreatment, all of which must be reported. Exhibit 1.2 summarizes common definitions of abuse included in state reporting laws.

Legal definitions of child abuse focus on either the behavior of the abusive adult or the effects of abuse on children (Meriwether, 1986). Focusing on the perpetrator's behavior results in a set of circumstances or behaviors that lead to abusive conditions. For example, intercourse with a child defines abuse based on an act. On the other hand, focusing on the consequences suffered by victims points to signs and symptoms. For example, a child with genital herpes defines abuse based on injuries. In either case, definitions of abuse can be broad, such as the circumstances of abuse and the signs of serious injury, or narrow, such as genital fondling or subdural hematoma. Legal definitions of types of abuse, therefore, represent two dimensions: circumstances of abuse versus signs of abuse, and narrowly defined indicators versus broadly defined indicators.

Legal definitions of abuse frequently describe physical abuse as serious injury by other than accidental means. Specific signs and symptoms are the most common legal definitions offered for serious injury (see Appendix A for a glossary of terms and Appendix B for information resources). For example, one state law includes in its definition of abuse "any case in which a child exhibits evidence of skin bruising, bleeding, malnutrition, failure to thrive, burns, fracture of any bone, subdural hematoma, soft tissue swelling, or death" (NCCAN, 1989, pp. CO-9–10). Narrow definitions leave little ambiguity about reporting requirements, but narrow definitions do not represent the universe of physically abusive situations. In addition, it is impossible for professionals who do not conduct physical examinations to make such fine distinctions. However, abuse may also be broadly defined to encompass a range of unspecified injuries. For example, some states have defined abuse as "harm or threatened harm to a child's welfare by acts or omissions of his/her parent or other person responsible for his/her welfare" (NCCAN, 1979, p. 5). Broad definitions of abuse can be traced back to the earliest state statutes. Legal definitions of abuse, both narrow and broad, appear problematic for mandated reporters (J. Jones & Welch, 1989; S. Smith & Meyer, 1984). Broad definitions of abuse are likely to result in high rates of reporting with many such cases going unfounded (false positives), whereas narrow definitions of abuse reduce the number of false reports but often at the expense of missed cases of abuse (false negatives).

The complexity of defining physical abuse is further illustrated by attempts to delineate serious from less serious injuries. Within the context of reporting laws, some states have specified serious harm as a part of their definition, while others have not made these narrow distinctions. Including the word "serious" in a reporting statute leaves the reporter to determine what constitutes a level of severity that requires reporting (Meriwether,

# EXHIBIT 1.2
## Twelve Common Legal Definitions of Child Abuse

1. Harm or threat of harm to a child's health or welfare through nonaccidental physical or mental injury, sexual abuse or attempted sexual abuse, or sexual exploitation.

2. The physical injury or neglect, sexual abuse, sexual exploitation, or maltreatment of a child by a person who is responsible for the child's welfare under circumstances that indicate that the child's health or that a child has suffered welfare is harmed or threatened.

3. Any nonaccidental physical injury, mental injury, sexual abuse, or sexual exploitation inflicted on a child by anyone legally responsible for the care and maintenance of the child, or any injury that is at variance with the history given. The term *abuse* encompasses both acts and omissions.

4. Any physical injury that is inflicted by other than accidental means on a child by another person. *Neglect* means the treatment or the maltreatment of a child by a person responsible for the child's welfare under circumstances indicating harm or threat of harm to the child's health or welfare. *Severe neglect* includes severe malnutrition, medically diagnosed nonorganic failure to thrive, and intentional failure to provide adequate food, clothing, shelter, or medical care. *Willful cruelty or unjustifiable punishment of a child* means a situation where any person willfully causes or permits any child to suffer, or inflicts thereon, unjustifiable physical pain or mental suffering.

5. An act or omission in one of the following categories that threatens the health or welfare of a child: evidence of skin bruising, bleeding, malnutrition, failure to thrive, burns, fracture of any bone, subdural hematoma, soft tissue swelling, or death. It is also abuse if the history given concerning such conditions is at variance with the degree or type of such conditions or death, or if circumstances indicate that such conditions may not be the product of an accidental occurrence.

6. A child whose physical or mental health or welfare is harmed, or has been threatened with harm, by the acts or omissions that the parent inflicts, or allows to be inflicted upon the child, such as physical or mental injury, which includes injury sustained as a result of excessive corporal punishment, sexual battery, exploitation of a child, or abandonment of a child. Physical injury means death, permanent or temporary disfigurement, or the impairment of any body part. Mental injury means an injury to the intellectual or psychological capacity of a child as evidenced by a discernable and substantial impairment in his or her ability to function within his or her normal range of performance and behavior, with due regard to his or her culture.

7. A child whose parent inflicts, causes to be inflicted, allows to be inflicted or who creates a substantial risk of physical injury by other than accidental means, which ultimately causes death, disfigurement, impairment of physical or emotional health, or loss or impairment of any bodily function.

8. *Battered and abused child* means a child whose parent, or any other person responsible for his or her care or support, has inflicted physical injury, including sexual abuse, other than by accidental means.

9. Inflicts or allows to be inflicted upon such child physical injury by other than accidental means that causes or creates a substantial risk of death, serious protracted disfigurement, protracted impairment of physical or emotional health or protracted loss or impairment of the function of any organ, or creates or allows to be created a substantial risk of physical injury.

EXHIBIT 1.2   (*Continued*)

10. Any physical injury to a child that has been caused by other than accidental means, including injury that appears to be at variance with the explanation given of the injury. Any mental injury observed to cause substantial impairment of the child's mental or psychological ability to function caused by cruelty to the child.

11. Any serious physical or mental injury that cannot be explained by the available medical history as being accidental.

12. The knowing exposure of a child to, or the knowing failure to protect a child from, conditions of brutality and neglect that are likely to cause great bodily harm or death and the knowing use of force on a child that is likely to cause great harm or death, specifically, brutality, abuse, or neglect that in the opinion of experts has caused or will reasonably be expected to produce severe psychosis, severe neurotic disorder, severe depression, severe developmental delay or retardation, or severe impairment of the child's ability to function adequately in his or her environment.

*Note:* State reporting laws are available on the Internet through various legal resources Web sites, such as the Smith Law Firm at http://www.smith-lawfirm.com/mandatory_reporting.htm#StateStatutes.

1986). Thus, judging what constitutes serious and less serious abuse is subjective. For example, in one study, Rosenthal (1988) defined serious injuries as brain damage, skull fracture, bone fracture, dislocated joints, strains, twists, internal injuries, serious burns and scalds, serious cuts, bruises, and welts. Less serious burns, scalds, cuts, bruises, and welts were defined as minor injuries. Although one could argue that such injuries might be amenable to ratings based on subjective impressions for diagnostic staging, without any indication of their reliability or validity, such distinctions remain arbitrary. When physical signs of abuse are visible but their cause is unknown, reporting laws often indicate that the injuries must be considered accidental. Plausible explanations for injuries vary with the complexity of situations and the developmental level of the child. Thus, while on the surface physical abuse appears readily detectable and therefore reportable, suspicions of physical maltreatment are complicated by definition problems.

For the most part, reporting laws rarely define physical abuse by acts or circumstances. States usually do not delineate hitting or beating as acts of abuse, primarily because to do so would be to legislate parental use of discipline. Specifying acts as physical abuse may therefore be viewed as infringing on parental rights (Morris, Johnson, & Chasen, 1985). Along these lines, corporal punishment is not prohibited in any state, and some states specifically exclude corporal punishment from definitions of child abuse. For example, South Carolina law indicated that abuse be excluded when conditions met the following criteria: "Force or violence of the discipline must be reasonable in manner and moderate in degree . . . [it] must not have brought about permanent or lasting damage to the child" (NCCAN, 1979, p. SC-8). It would, therefore, be difficult to define physical abuse by acts alone. Rather, legal definitions of physical abuse apply when punishment is excessive and results in injury or harm, because laws tend to focus on symptoms and signs of abuse.

In contrast to physical abuse, physical signs and symptoms rarely form the basis for legal definitions of sexual abuse. Most reporting laws do not include as part of their definitions of sexual abuse behaviors exhibited by sexually abused children. Rather, legal definitions of sexual abuse rely on situations and exploitative actions. For example, some states define sexual abuse or exploitation as child molestation, immoral or indecent acts performed in the presence of a child, enticing a child for indecent purposes, incest, or the involvement of a child in sexually explicit materials. State laws sometimes specify other detailed acts and situations that constitute sexual abuse. Thus, definitions of sexual abuse, unlike physical abuse, tend to rely on circumstances, situations, and behaviors rather than consequences, signs, and symptoms.

Defining sexual abuse by acts and conditions reflects the circumstances under which sexual abuse is most likely to be detected. As many as 75% of sexual abuse cases present without physical signs of maltreatment (Zielinski, 1992), and approximately 40% of substantiated cases of sexual abuse provide no physical evidence (Adams, 1991; Goodwin, Sahd, & Rada, 1982). Although sexual abuse itself involves the physical violation of children, nonsexual violence co-occurs with sexual abuse in only 5% of cases (Finkelhor, 1985). Unlike the relationship between injuries sustained in physical abuse and corporal punishment, all acts associated with sexual abuse are readily defined as warranting criminal investigation.

Definitions of neglect tend to rely on circumstances and situations in their definitions (Meriwether, 1986). Neglect is most typically defined as a "failure to provide, by those legally responsible for the care of the child, the proper or necessary support, education as required by law, or medical, surgical, or any other care necessary for his or her well-being" (NCCAN, 1979, p. 5). For example, one state defines neglect as the "failure by a person responsible for a child's care to supply a child with necessary food, clothing, shelter or medical care when reasonably able to do so or failure to protect a child from conditions or actions which imminently and seriously endanger the child's physical or mental health when reasonably able to do so" (NCCAN, 1989, p. MN-9). Deprivation, and failure to provide adequate care and supervision, are therefore circumstances encompassed under definitions of neglect. Thus, like sexual abuse, and unlike physical abuse, legal definitions of neglect focus on circumstances and situations rather than signs and symptoms.

Finally, laws define emotional or psychological maltreatment, although often with great ambiguity (Melton & Davidson, 1987). Emotional abuse, like physical abuse, is usually defined on the basis of signs indicative of abuse, rather than abusive situations. Most typically, emotional maltreatment is legally defined as "an injury to the psychological capacity or emotional stability of a child as evidenced by an observable or substantial impairment in his or her ability to function within a normal range of performance and behavior with due regard to culture" (NCCAN, 1979, p. 5). In Florida, for example, mental injury is defined as "an injury to the intellectual or psychological capacity of a child as evidenced by a discernable and substantial impairment in his ability to function within his normal range of performance and behavior" (NCCAN, 1989, p. FL-10). Emotional maltreatment, as defined by law, may pose particular problems for mental health service providers because many of their clinical cases exhibit signs of emotional or mental impairment. In these contexts, therefore, the source, intentions, and conditions related to the impairment are likely to play an important role in identifying children at risk of emotional abuse.

Figure 1.2 presents a succinct two-dimensional representation of legal definitions of abuse. The first dimension, represented along the vertical, involves identifying abuse as signs/symptoms or circumstances/conditions. The second dimension, along the horizontal, represents abuse as specifically/narrowly or vaguely/broadly defined. Usually, reporting laws define physical abuse in terms of specific signs, sexual abuse as specific circumstances, neglect as vague circumstances or conditions, and emotional maltreatment in terms of vague signs. Although states vary with respect to how their definitions of abuse fall along these two dimensions, this repre-

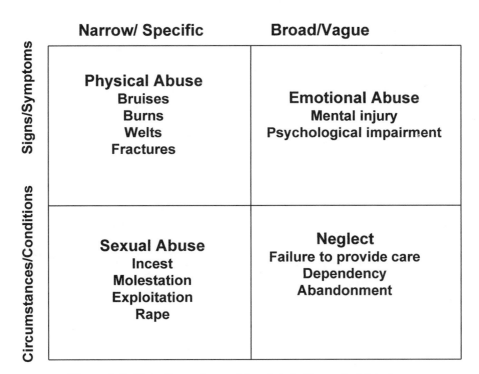

| | Narrow/ Specific | Broad/Vague |
|---|---|---|
| **Signs/Symptoms** | **Physical Abuse**<br>**Bruises**<br>**Burns**<br>**Welts**<br>**Fractures** | **Emotional Abuse**<br>**Mental injury**<br>**Psychological impairment** |
| **Circumstances/Conditions** | **Sexual Abuse**<br>**Incest**<br>**Molestation**<br>**Exploitation**<br>**Rape** | **Neglect**<br>**Failure to provide care**<br>**Dependency**<br>**Abandonment** |

*Figure 1.2.* Two dimensions of legal definitions of child abuse.

sentation shows the major distinctions in conceptualizing legal definitions of child abuse.

Delineating what professionally and legally constitutes child abuse and neglect directly affects whether cases are reported. Although research has found differences in tendencies to report different types of abuse (Giovannoni, 1989b; Kalichman & Craig, 1991; USDHHS, 1988; C. A. Wilson & Gettinger, 1989; Zellman, 1990), there is little research to support the idea that signs or circumstances of different types of abuse, or that narrow or broad definitions of abuse, differentially affect decisions to report. One study has, however, determined relationships between broad/narrow definitions of child abuse with both reporting and substantiation rates. Rycraft (1990) evaluated legal definitions of abuse and found that states with broad and nonspecific definitions have the highest reporting and substantiation rates, and states with narrow and specific definitions of abuse have among the lowest. Rycraft concluded that definitions of child abuse are a determining factor in reporting decisions as well as the final dispositions of reported cases.

## When Is Reporting Required?

Professionals mandated to report child abuse must do so under explicit conditions defined by law. The circumstances that specify when reporting is required are another source of controversy (Brahams, 1988; J. Jones & Welch, 1989; Meriwether, 1986; Wurtele & Miller-Perrin, 1992). State laws, following the first model statutes, do not require reporters to have knowledge or any degree of certainty that abuse has occurred or will occur. Most often, laws use terms such as "reason to believe" or "having reasonable cause to suspect" to describe the conditions required for reporting. However, states that do define conditions for reporting may define suspicion as objectively reasonable, provided it is, "based upon facts that could cause a reasonable person in a like position, drawing when appropriate on his or her training and experience, to suspect abuse" (California Crime Prevention Center, 1988, p. 1). Still, what constitutes reasonable suspicion, as it may be differentiated from clinical hunches, professional impressions, and intuition, remains fuzzy. Understanding reporting laws and their implications for child welfare varies among persons involved in the child abuse reporting and child protection processes (Brooks, Perry, Starr, & Teply, 1994). Deisz, Doueck, George, and Levine (1996) found that the reasonable cause standard for reporting was interpreted differently by mental health professionals and child protection workers. Mental health professionals generally applied more expansive concepts of reportable situations to this standard, whereas child protection workers were more restrictive in their concept of reasonable cause to suspect abuse (M. Levine, 1998).

Qualifying suspicions with the term "reasonable" can imply that reporters are expected to engage in a thoughtful, discretionary process when reporting. Although Kempe et al. (1962) detailed physical and radiological signs of abuse as the basis for reason to believe that physical abuse has occurred, it is far more problematic to define the subjective experiences and perceptions of mental health workers as reasonable suspicions. Here is where we find the major problem in applying legal definitions of abuse that were drafted from medical experiences in nonmedical service settings. Applying reasonable suspicion to sexual abuse, neglect, and psychological–emotional maltreatment is even more complicated. Exhibit 1.3 summarizes 12 common legal definitions of reporting requirements.

The distinction between requirements to report suspicions of abuse as opposed to *reasonable* suspicions of abuse may not result in actual differences in reporting, although empirical data have not been collected on this question. However, language differences can be important in determining liability for failure to report (Meriwether, 1986). Reasonable suspicion denotes an objective standard set by a reasonable person under similar circumstances. It implies reasoned discretion. In contrast, use of terms such as "reason to believe" or "reason to suspect" by themselves imply a subjective impression that helps the reporter to form an opinion (Meriwether, 1986). The more objective the statutory language, the easier it is to enforce penalties for failure to report suspected child abuse.

Outside of the United States, similar language has been adopted in mandatory child abuse reporting laws. For example, in Victoria, Australia, mandated professionals are required to notify Child Protection Victoria if they believe on reasonable grounds that a child has suffered, or is likely to suffer, significant physical harm as a result of physical injury or sexual abuse, and the child's parents have not protected or are unlikely to protect the child from such harm. In such a situation the person must notify Child Protection Victoria of the belief and of the grounds for it as soon as possible. Reasonable grounds may exist where, for example, a child tells the professional that he or she has been physically and sexually abused; someone else, such as a relative, friend, acquaintance or sibling of the child, tells the professional that the child has been abused; the professional's observations of the child's behavior or knowledge of children generally leads him or her to believe that the child has been abused; or the professional observes signs or indicators of abuse.

In contrast to broad requirements to report reasonable suspicions of abuse, which encompass the universe of possible circumstances, some states have retained language used in the Children's Bureau's model statute, limiting the conditions under which reporting is required (Davidson, 1988). For example, in Wisconsin, a professional who has

> reasonable cause to suspect that a child seen in the course of professional duties has been abused or neglected, or having reason to believe that a child seen in the course of professional duties has been threat-

# EXHIBIT 1.3
## Twelve Common Legal Definitions of When Reporting Is Required

1. When a professional, in the performance of occupational duties, has cause to believe that a child has suffered harm as the result of abuse.

2. When a professional has reasonable grounds to believe that a minor is or has been the victim of abuse.

3. When one has reasonable cause to suspect that a child has been abused or neglected.

4. When a professional who has knowledge of, or who observes a child in his or her professional capacity who he or she knows or reasonably suspects has been the victim of child abuse. *Reasonable suspicion* means that it is objectively reasonable for a person to entertain such a suspicion, based upon facts that could cause a person in a like position to suspect child abuse, drawing when appropriate on his/her training and experience.

5. When a professional has reasonable cause to believe a child known to him or her in his or her professional capacity may be an abused or a neglected child.

6. When a person knows or has reason to believe that a child is being neglected or physically or sexually abused, or has been neglected or physically or sexually abused within the preceding 3 years.

7. When any person having reasonable cause to suspect that a child brought to him or her or coming before him or her in treatment, or of whom he or she has knowledge through observation is a neglected child or an abused child.

8. When one has reasonable cause to suspect that a child has been, or may be subjected to, abuse or neglect, or when one observes a child being subjected to harmful conditions.

9. When one knows or has reasonable cause to suspect abuse as a result of information he or she receives in his or her professional capacity.

10. No professional who is acting in his or her professional capacity and knows or suspects that a child has suffered any wound, injury, disability, or conditon of any nature shall recklessly fail to immediately report or cause reports to be made of that knowledge or suspicion.

11. When one has reason to believe a child has had injury or injuries inflicted upon him or her by other than accidental means or where the injury appears to have been caused as a result of physical abuse or neglect.

12. When persons who, in the course of their profession, come into contact with children and have reason to believe, on the basis of their professional training and experience, that a child coming before them in their professional capacity is a victim of child abuse.

*Note:* State reporting laws are available on the Internet through various legal resources Web sites, such as the Smith Law Firm at http://www.smith-lawfirm.com/mandatory_reporting. htm#StateStatutes.

ened with an injury and that abuse of the child will occur shall report (NCCAN, 1989, p. WI-14).

As another example, Mississippi law indicates that a professional

having cause to suspect that a child brought before him or coming before him for examination, care, or treatment, or of whom he has

knowledge through observation is a neglected child or an abused child
. . . shall report. (NCCAN, 1989, p. MS-10)

A number of conditions that may result in suspected child abuse, therefore, fall outside of these narrow reporting laws, including a perpetrator's self-disclosure of abuse, an adult's disclosure that a child is being abused by a spouse, and virtually any other indication of abuse by any other source than the suspected child–victim (Davidson, 1988). Although not required to report under limited conditions defined by law, professionals may, of course, file a voluntary report of suspected child abuse.

Unlimited and limited conditions for required reporting brought Kalichman and Brosig (1992) and Brosig and Kalichman (1992b) to investigate the effects of statutory wording on decisions to report suspected child abuse. In this research, two studies were conducted to directly test two state statutes. In the first statute, reasonable suspicions of abuse required reporting—unrestricted language (Colorado; reasonable cause to suspect that a child has been subjected to abuse or neglect or who has observed a child being subjected to circumstances or conditions which would reasonably result in abuse or neglect). In the second, professionals were required only to report observations of a child suspected of being abused—restricted language (Pennsylvania; that a child coming before them in their professional or official capacity is a victim of child abuse).

In Experiment 1 of Kalichman and Brosig's (1992) research, licensed psychologists from Colorado and Pennsylvania read a case scenario depicting a child in a clinical situation who showed signs of being abused. The psychologists were then asked to read one of the two state reporting laws, either Colorado's unrestricted or Pennsylvania's restricted. Participants twice indicated their tendencies to report—first after reading the vignette and then a after reading the law. In this study, the Colorado and Pennsylvania laws both resulted in significant increases in reporting. Thus, when presented with a child suspected of being abused, both laws prompted professionals to report.

In Experiment 2, Kalichman and Brosig (1992) asked an independent sample of licensed psychologists from the same two states to respond to a case scenario that depicted an adult in a clinical situation who showed signs of being abusive. Once again, the independent sample of practitioners was asked to indicate the likelihood of their reporting the suspected abuse after reading the adult case vignette and then again after reading one of the two same state statutes used in the first study. The results here were dramatically different from Experiment 1. Whereas the Colorado law again resulted in an overall increase in reporting, the Pennsylvania law had the opposite effect. That is, Pennsylvania's law significantly decreased practitioners' tendency to report when the source of the suspected abuse was not the child. Kalichman and Brosig concluded that specific reporting requirements directly affected professionals' decisions to report suspected child abuse. These results were subsequently replicated by Brosig and Kalichman (1992b) in a single study that directly tested a child case against an adult case under each of these same two types of laws.

The Kalichman and Brosig (1992) and Brosig and Kalichman (1992b) studies raise two important points. First, although reporting statutes are often discussed as if they are homogeneous and vague, subtle variations among statutes do appear to have specific effects on mandated reporting. As a result, it is likely that states vary in the types and severity of abuse that enter their child protection systems. States with restricted reporting requirements will be less likely to identify cases where an adult is suspected of being abusive. Second, in contrast to many characterizations of mandated reporters (Kalichman et al., 1988, 1989; Pope & Bajt, 1988; Swoboda et al., 1978), professionals appear sensitive and responsive to reporting requirements. Professionals may always voluntarily report reasonable suspicions of abuse, regardless of the conditions under which they are required to report. Decreased reporting observed in professionals confronted with an adult suspected of being abusive when operating under a statute that restricts requirements to report demonstrates adherence to legal standards by mandated reporters. Thus, when the law is stated in terms that fit the circumstances of a suspicion, professionals tend to comply. This finding is important to the degree that professionals are knowledgeable of the language contained in their reporting law or likely to consult statutory language when deciding to report. However, in the real world, unlike contrived experimental case vignettes, the complexities of conditions under which suspicions arise do not necessarily reflect legal requirements to report. Rather, in practice, cases of abuse interact with a number of factors that make up the context of reporting.

## OPPOSITION TO MANDATED REPORTING

Few clinical issues are the source of as much emotionally charged debate as mandated child abuse reporting. Mandated reporting is often opposed by child advocates, civil libertarian protectors of family rights, and service providers. In general, four key arguments have been waged against mandated reporting: (a) Reporting interferes with child protection; (b) reporting is destructive to helping relationships; (c) reporting is harmful to children and families; and (d) reporting laws are overly vague and unenforceable. Each of these perspectives is discussed below.

### Reporting Interferes With Child Protection

Several critics of mandated reporting argue that reporting requirements have failed in their primary objective to protect endangered children. The purported goal of identifying every possible case of child abuse comes at an expense to the very system designed to help children. From this view, resources expended on investigating reports are understood to be mischanneled and contribute to the gutting of other child abuse prevention and intervention services. For instance, studies show that a majority of child protection workers are unable to provide services in a majority of substantiated cases of child abuse (Meddin & Hansen, 1985). One review of substantiated abuse in New York found that 55% were officially closed the same day that abuse was confirmed (Salovitz & Keys, 1988). According to Besharov (1990), mandated reporting can be destructive to child protective services: "The flood of unfounded reports is overwhelming the limited resources of child protective agencies. For fear of missing even one abused child, workers perform extensive investigations of vague and apparently unsupported reports" (p. 17).

In support of this argument, proponents of repealing mandatory reporting laws also note that two out of three reports of child abuse are not substantiated, again indicating that the net cast to capture child abusers is too broad to be effective. Thus, required reporting ultimately burdens child protection systems and detracts from child protection.

## Reporting Is Destructive to Helping Relationships

Educators, clinicians, and other service providers oppose mandated reporting on the grounds that reporting their clients, including children, breaches confidentiality, and is therefore destructive to their services. Surveys of practicing psychologists show that 31% believe reporting has adverse consequences for their clients and their treatment (Kalichman & Craig, 1991). An extreme perspective on the harmful effects of reporting on services comes from Bollas and Sundelson (1995), who stated that breaches of confidentiality in reporting dismantles the therapeutic relationship in psychoanalysis. Bolas and Sundelson (1995) wrote with reference to free association in psychoanalysis: "Were there to be a restriction in this basic process, that is, if the patient felt that he could safely talk about his neediness but could not discuss sexuality or aggression, then the entire procedure would come to a halt" (p. 61). They also stated, "Psychoanalysis cannot function if the patient does not have complete confidence that what he says to his psychoanalyst is privileged" (p. 59). Bollas and Sundelson held that reporting betrays the therapeutic trust and can cause great harm to persons in therapy. For example, they wrote, "Instead of protection for the patient who discloses his private life to a psychoanalyst, there is protection for the psychotherapist (or anyone else) who makes a report under the law—protection, that is for the informant" (p. 48). Thus, opposition to reporting laws can stem from concerns for the integrity of clinical services.

In addition to concerns for protecting the integrity of services, providers believe that the effects of reporting on therapy can indirectly harm children. For example, when abuse is detected during the course of family therapy, reporting can impair the progress of an intervention that may offer the greatest hope of preventing further abuse. Similarly, reporting in the midst of treating an abusive parent can impede progress. Even more concerning is that mandated reporting may deter perpetrators of abuse from seeking treatment (Berlin, Malin, & Dean, 1991; Kalichman, Brosig, & Kalichman, 1994). Thus, mandated reporting has been criticized for endangering children by interfering with opportunities for effective intervention.

### Reporting Is Harmful to Children and Families

Opponents of mandated reporting state that withholding a report of suspected abuse is justified when it is in the best interest of children and families. This view holds that reporting and investigative procedures are, at best, intrusive and, at worst, coercive. Besharov (1990) stated that "the determination that a report is unfounded can be made only after an unavoidably traumatic investigation that is, inherently, a breach of parental and family privacy" (pp. 13–14). Extending from this perspective is the suggestion that decisions to report suspected abuse should only be considered when there is ample evidence to warrant such reports, rather than reporting when there is reason to suspect abuse. Raising the threshold for when a report should be filed is therefore meant to protect parents and children from an intrusive investigation.

### Reporting Laws Are Overly Vague and Unenforceable

Critics of the statutory language of reporting laws originate from both those who oppose the laws and those who support them. From an opposition perspective, the reliance on subjective impressions for meeting reporting thresholds causes confusion across various professional settings. In particular, mental health professionals express concerns that reason to suspect abuse is insufficient grounds for reporting because they commonly experience many hunches and subjective impressions in the course of providing treatment. The intuitions that mental health professionals use to mindfully guide their decisions could, therefore, easily trigger what would become reflexive reporting. Relying on suspicions to warrant a report is further complicated by the lack of symptom specificity in cases of abuse. A given set of symptoms or circumstances may have a number of alternative explanations other than abuse. As an extreme example of this perspective, Kihlstrom stated that "it is not permissible to infer, or frankly even to suspect, a history of abuse in people who present symptoms of abuse" (cited in Pope & Brown, 1996, p. 95). Similar objections have been raised over the vagueness of legal definitions of abuse (Bourne & Newberger, 1977). Thus, not knowing what constitutes suspected child abuse in a given setting is seen as reason enough not to report.

The vague language of reporting laws has also been criticized for setting an unenforceable standard. Supporters of mandated reporting believe that clearer laws would surely lead to stronger law enforcement. Indeed, the validity of mandatory reporting laws has been challenged on the grounds that they are unconstitutionally vague. This argument stems from a 1926 U.S. Supreme Court ruling:

> That the term of a penal statute creating a new offense must be sufficiently explicit to inform those who are subject to it what conduct on their part will render them liable to its penalties, is a well recognized requirement, consonant alike with ordering notions of fair play and the settled rules of law. A statute which either forbids or requires the doing of an act in terms so vague that men of common intelligence must differ as to its application violates the first essential of due process of law. (*Connally v. General Construction Company*, 1926)

The premise that people should not be held to a vague standard is important to challenge mandatory reporting laws. For example, Michigan's reporting law was challenged for being unconstitutionally vague in *People v. Cavaiani*, a case of a psychologist prosecuted for failure to report (see discussion in the following section). Thus, even for those who would otherwise support mandatory reporting laws, broad language and vague definitions make the laws difficult to enforce and, therefore, of limited use in protecting children.

## FAILURE TO REPORT SUSPECTED CHILD ABUSE

There have been several professionals held legally responsible for failure to report suspected child abuse. Although their cases are often discussed to teach professionals to approach reporting with caution, they also illustrate some important elements of reporting requirements and how suspected child abuse can remain unreported. Decisions not to report can occur when professionals suspect abuse but are uncertain of its occurrence. However, most cases of professionals who are held accountable for not reporting involve mandated reporters who appear to have had some degree of knowledge of abuse beyond reasonable suspicion. It is important to note that controversies surrounding these cases are not so much about *what* constitutes child abuse, but rather *when* the law requires reporting. Is reporting in the best interest of children? And when are social service interventions warranted?

In most states, failure to report suspected child abuse by a mandated reporter is a misdemeanor and can carry penalties of a fine and a possible jail sentence. Professionals who fail to comply with mandatory reporting statutes may also face sanctions that suspend or revoke their professional licensure (S. Smith & Meyer, 1984). In addition to criminal charges and professional disciplinary actions, there is also the possibility for civil action against the professional (Knapp, 1983; Mazura, 1977; Paulsen, 1967). In this sense, failure to report suspected child abuse may be viewed as a case of failure to diagnose (S. Smith & Meyer, 1984). Under standards of professional malpractice and negligence per se, failure to comply with a statutory mandate could result in civil liability. Indeed, several cases of civil liability have occurred with respect to the failure to report suspected child abuse (Bross, 1983; Knapp, 1983; Meriwether, 1986; Paulsen, 1967).

Cases of unreported suspected child abuse by mental health professionals have received a great deal of attention (i.e., Buie, 1989; Denton, 1987a, 1987b). These cases serve many purposes in our understanding of the role that mandatory reporting laws play in mental health practice. However, the lack of appellate decisions in this area has resulted in a dearth of case law available on mandated reporting. The following six cases illustrate the potential repercussions for failing to report suspected child abuse.

### Landeros v. Flood

Landeros v. Flood (1976) is a classic case of a court treating a failure to report as malpractice. In this case, a physician failed to diagnose and report an incidence of the battered child syndrome. The case involved an 11-year-old girl with multiple body bruises and broken bones, most of which were consistent with Kempe et al.'s (1962) description of battered children. The hospital that treated the child released her without having conducted a full radiological examination. Within only a few weeks of the prior injuries the child was taken to a second hospital. There, the child presented with traumatic blows to the eye, several bites on her face, and burns on her hand. A physician at the second hospital diagnosed child abuse and filed a report. The physician who treated the girl at the first hospital was subsequently deemed negligent for failing to diagnose and report. Negligence directly followed from the statutory mandate to report. In addition, subsequent injuries that occured close in time to a failed report, as in the case of Landeros, could have been prevented by reporting immediately (Besharov, 1986b).

### People v. Cavaiani

One of the first criminal cases of failure to report was People v. Cavaiani (1988, 1989), a case that involved a family counselor who had been treating a couple and their 15-year-old daughter. The girl's stepfather had been reported and investigated for sexually fondling her prior to starting therapy. The mother had moved out of the home with her daughter after the acts of sexual abuse were initially reported. The therapist had been referred by the local child protection service agency to help resolve family problems related to the abuse. During the course of therapy, many of the family's issues subsided and the family reunited to resume their life together. The family moved to a new county, but remained near enough to the therapist to continue their treatment.

Shortly after moving, as therapy was nearing termination, the girl's mother called the therapist and told him that her daughter was once again accusing her stepfather of sexually molesting her. The therapist immediately arranged an appointment for that day to interview the girl. During the interview, the girl stated that her stepfather touched her, but she was vague in describing what had actually happened. When asked if she felt threatened staying home, the girl said that she felt safe. Ultimately, the therapist doubted the girl's statements because she could not provide details of what had happened and because she had been angry with her stepfather a couple of days earlier. The therapist also interviewed the stepfather that same day. He adamantly denied touching his stepdaughter again. He did admit the previous acts, but claimed that he had done nothing of the sort since that time.

Cavaiani considered the situation carefully. Knowing that the stepfather would probably be arrested because of his previous record with the department of social services, the therapist felt that reporting would be destructive to the family and reverse much of the progress they had made in therapy. Cavaiani decided not to report, and the alleged abuse became the focus of a renewed course of family therapy.

Within 2 weeks of interviewing the girl and stepfather about the most recent abuse allegation, the child repeated her accusations to her schoolteacher. Also a mandated reporter, the teacher told the girl that she should talk about the situation with her school counselor, who, in turn, reported the situation to the social services department in the family's new county of residence. After receiving this report, the child protection agency arrested the stepfather on the basis of his previous record in the neighboring county. Subsequently, Cavaiani was arrested for failure to report suspected child abuse.

Cavaiani's attorney challenged the constitutionality of the state reporting statute on the grounds that its language was excessively vague and thus violated rights of expression. Although a lower court found the statute unconstitutional, the Michigan State Supreme Court would not hear the case unless Cavaiani was first found guilty of failure to report. After a jury trial, Cavaiani was acquitted of the charges, making the case against the statute unable to proceed further.[1]

## People v. Gray

In *People v. Gray* (Denton, 1987b; see also Newman, 1987), a psychologist with an established practice had been seeing a family where the parents sought treatment for help with their 13-year-old adopted son. Although the boy had been a part of this family since the age of 3, the family had difficulty with him throughout, and none of its members felt that he had really bonded with them. The boy's behavior was frequently described as uncontrollable. He acted aggressively toward other children, including his siblings.

In their efforts to manage his behavior, the boy's parents resorted to using time-outs as both a threat and actual means of punishment. They placed the boy in a furnished but secluded area of the house when his behavior was out of control, but this punishment was not effective. Eventually, the boy was spending as many as 7 days at a time in seclusion, with the exception of his going to school, eating meals, and bathing. The parents felt that their actions had become excessive and wanted help in finding more effective and humane ways to deal with their child. The parents sought help from a psychologist, Dr. Gray, who focused on parent-skills training and developing an appropriate behavior-management program for the child.

The psychologist was aware of the mandatory reporting requirement in his state and had reported suspected abuse on numerous other occasions. However, Gray believed that there were limited resources available to the child protective team and that their investigative procedures had the potential to be aversive to children and families. Therefore, Gray chose not to report, believing that his decision was in the best interest of the child. He reasoned that this was the most ethical course of action.

Within a few months of treatment, a neighbor filed a report of suspected child neglect concerning the family with the local department of social services. During the course of the investigation, agency employees interviewed Gray, who offered his full cooperation. The social service agency substantiated that child maltreatment had taken place and proceeded to place the two adopted children, one of whom had not been implicated in the maltreatment, in foster care. Subsequently, a district court judge ordered that the children remain in foster care pending further investigation. This same judge subsequently issued a warrant for Gray's arrest on charges of contributing to the delinquency of a minor. Just 3 days later,

---

[1]Details of this case have been constructed from Denton (1987b), personal communications with F. Cavaiani, and briefs from *People v. Cavaiani* (1986).

the same judge signed two more warrants for Gray's arrest for failure to report suspected abuse.

Gray was arrested in the midst of a therapy session with a different family. The assistant district attorney in the case was quoted in a local newspaper as saying that the arrest was intended to "teach professionals a lesson" (*Durham Morning Herald*, cited in Newman, 1987). The case went to trial after Gray refused to settle out of court. Although the judge dropped the contributing to delinquency charges, Gray was found guilty on one count of failure to report suspected abuse. The judge stated, "A psychologist shouldn't be the omnipotent one who decides totally what's in the child's best interest" (*Durham Morning Herald*, cited in Newman, 1987). The judge ruled that general misdemeanor penalties applied, including a $200 fine. He also issued a Prayer for Continued Judgement, or the removal of the case from court records. Although Gray wanted to appeal the decision, this was not possible because he was not actually convicted of the offense. Gray therefore refused to pay the fine. This forced a conviction that allowed him to appeal the case. Gray was sentenced to 1 month in jail and 1 year of supervised probation, although the judge suspended the jail sentence. Eventually, Gray appealed his case, but the appeal was dismissed by a higher court.[2]

### People v. Hedberg

In *People v. Hedberg* (Ebert, 1992), a 7-year-old girl living with her mother and stepfather was being treated for a number of behavioral problems, including aggressiveness, lying, acting out oppositionally, and achieving only minimal progress in school. She also began inserting toys and other objects into her vagina. The girl frequently experienced encopresis and enuresis. In addition, she had developed several health-related problems that were being treated by a pediatrician, including body rashes and urinary tract infections.

The family constellation in this case was complex. The girl's mother had gone through a difficult divorce 3 years earlier, and conflicts persisted at the time of her daughter's treatment. The girl lived with her stepfather and with her mother, who had custody of her. The girl's biological father had also remarried. Both parents regularly disputed custody and the girl's mother opposed the father's visitation rights.

Through a court referral to assist in settling the custody dispute, Hedberg was consulted to mediate the resolution and treat the child. During this time, the child lived for brief periods with each parent in an effort to

---

[2]Details of this case have been constructed from three primary sources: Denton (1987a), Gray (1987), and personal communication with Arne Gray (July 15, 1992).

establish a visitation agreement. As treatment, which included working with the parents on appropriate child-management practices, positive discipline procedures, and age-appropriate expectations, progressed, the child's behavior and school problems improved. During this time, the girl became somewhat more partial to living with her father, who quickly opened his home to her.

Six months into treatment, the mother phoned Hedberg and said that her daughter told her that the girl's stepfather "stuck his finger up my butt" in the middle of the night. The girl followed this statement by saying, "now I can go live with Daddy." The girl's mother told Hedberg that the girl made the remarks during a time that she had been playing with a neighbor boy who accused his own stepfather of a similar act that resulted in his living with his father. The girl knew of these events and their outcome, and her mother told Hedberg that she believed her daughter was motivated by these events to falsely accuse the stepfather of molestation.

The mother brought the girl to see Hedberg and the daughter recounted the story to him. This angered her mother, who still did not believe her daughter's accusation. Her mother then explained that it was common for her husband to check the girl's bed for wetness because of the enuresis and to assist her to the bathroom at night. In an interview with Hedberg, the child did not describe any acts of penetration. The girl did say that she had wet the bed the evening of the alleged abuse and went to the bathroom to clean up. The child also told Hedberg that she was not frightened of her stepfather. Hedberg assessed her motivations and discerned that no one had told her what and what not to say to him. The child could not provide details of what had happened that night, other than general statements about touching, which presumably happened while she slept.

The girl's father and stepmother were advised of the girl's statements. Neither of them believed them to be true. They agreed to observe the girl when she was visiting and to watch for new problems. The girl's pediatrician was consulted to examine her, and reported no indications of sexual abuse. The child did not mention the abuse again for 2 months and did not report any further indications of molestation.

Two months after the original allegation, the child made similar statements to her teacher, alleging that her stepfather had touched her in sexual ways. The girl's mother informed Hedberg of the new allegation, but again, denied its validity. Because the remarks were made to a person who did not have any input into the custody decision, Hedberg decided to take action. He called the stepfather, who categorically denied the allegation. He then proceeded to notify all parents that the incident was being reported to the state office of social services and filed a report.

Social services eventually substantiated sexual abuse by the stepfather and informed local police. The stepfather was subsequently arrested, at which time he pled guilty to one count of child molestation. Hedberg was also arrested for failure to report suspected abuse. Although he did in fact report the case, the district attorney premised the case on the earlier signs of abuse that went unreported. The case went to trial and Hedberg's defense was based on a hierarchy of abuse symptoms that a number of other psychologists stated would not have constituted reasonable cause to suspect abuse. Hedberg also used the literature on false allegations of abuse in custody disputes as a part of his defense. Ultimately, he was acquitted.[3]

### State Licensing Board v. Johnson

Dr. Johnson started treatment with a 4-year-old girl who was referred for therapy by her mother, who complained that her daughter was oppositional, aggressive, hitting her stepfather, refusing to sleep alone, and complaining of stomachaches. The mother also said that she had seen her daughter inserting tissues into her vagina. The girl stated that her father cleaned her using tissues and was only doing what he did. Although hygiene was a plausible explanation for these occurrences, Johnson considered the possibility of the girl being sexually abused. The child, who was mostly nonverbal during treatment, did not offer any statements indicative of sexual abuse. Johnson interviewed the child, asked direct and indirect questions, and requested an interview with her father so that he could conduct an assessment of potential abuse.

Soon after, the girl's mother claimed that her daughter was making little progress and abruptly terminated treatment. Following termination of treatment, the child continued to experience serious behavior problems and the family relationships deteriorated further, ultimately involving allegations of sexual abuse filed by the mother against the biological father. This occurred within the context of a heated custody battle over the child. The court appointed a second psychologist to conduct an independent assessment as part of the custody proceedings. In his own evaluation, the second psychologist learned that the girl had been inserting pens and pencils into her vagina. He immediately reported the family to the local child protection agency. He also filed a complaint against the first psychologist, Johnson, with the state's Board of Professional Regulation. Although the authorities were aware that Johnson did not report, charges for failure to report suspected abuse were not brought against him. The board did move toward suspending his license to practice psychology; however, Johnson

---

[3]Details of this case were gathered from Hedberg (1992) and Ebert (1992), and through court transcripts.

was also fined and required to attend a series of continuing education courses geared toward the assessment and treatment of abused children.[4]

## State of Washington v. Motherwell, Hedley, and Menosnides (1990; see also MacDonald, Hill, & Li, 1993)

Louis Menosnides was a staff counselor at an independent church. Although he was not ordained, he provided pastoral counseling to a large congregation. Menosnides was counseling a couple who had been separated. The couple had two boys, ages 5 and 8, and a girl, age 4. One of the reasons the mother was seeking separation from her husband was because she believed the children's father had repeatedly hit the two boys on the buttocks with enough force to cause bruises. The father hit the boys because he believed that they had knocked out their sister's front teeth. Menosnides did not report the allegation of abuse to child protective services. Instead, he conducted couples counseling with the mother and father. Eventually, the couple divorced, after which the mother filed charges of assault against the father for the injuries he inflicted on the boy. The father was tried and acquitted in the assault case. However, during the course of the investigation and trial, the county prosecutor's office learned that the allegations of abuse had been disclosed in counseling. The prosecutor therefore charged Menosnides with failure to report suspected child abuse under Washington state law.

In a separate case, a second counselor from the same church was charged with failure to report suspected abuse. In this instance, Motherwell, a counselor and supervisor at the counseling center, had been counseling a couple with marital difficulties. The woman told Motherwell during their first session that she believed that her husband had sexually molested their daughter. Motherwell advised the woman to report her husband to child protective services, but he did not file a report himself. The mother subsequently testified in the case against her husband and during her testimony she referred to her telling Motherwell about the abuse in their counseling session. The father pled guilty to charges of indecent liberties, and the county prosecutor's office filed criminal charges against Motherwell for failure to report suspected child abuse.

Both counselors were convicted for failing to report suspected child abuse. Both also appealed the case to the Washington State Supreme Court, which subsequently upheld the convictions. Thus, these counselors

---

[4]Information regarding this case was collected through personal communications. The case was handled in an administrative hearing of a state licensing board and is therefore not a matter of public record. However, the psychologist who was the subject of the case provided his permission to use the case for education and research. Names and other identifying information are altered to protect the identity of the psychologist and others in the case.

working in pastoral care and religious services were not protected by rules of privileged communication offered to ordained clergy.[5]

## Summary of Cases

These cases, in which psychotherapists have been charged with failure to report suspected child abuse, share several features in common. In each case, a mandated reporter was told of an abusive situation either through a verbal disclosure or description of the child's conditions. The professionals were also aware of the mandatory reporting law in their state and had previous experience with the child protection system. In two cases, Cavaiani and Hedberg, additional mandated reporters were aware of the potential abuse, but were not charged with failure to report. It was usually the case that the professionals involved were found not guilty of failure to report. These cases serve to illustrate how legal standards of reasonable suspicion fail to translate to professional settings, particularly those of psychological assessment and psychotherapy. Vague legal thresholds for reporting often leave mandated reporters to define their own professional standards. Professionals generally believe that their actions are ethical and their decision making is sound. How mandated reporting fits within professional ethics codes and a detailed account of report decision-making processes are the subject of chapter 2.

## CONCLUSIONS

Mandatory reporting laws were enacted to require physicians to report injuries they might otherwise not acknowledge as possible abuse. In this respect, mandated reporting has been successful. Since the first reporting laws went into effect in the United States, Canada, Australia, New Zealand, and elsewhere, increases in reporting rates have occurred. In fact, the rise in reports in the United States has exceeded the child protection system's resources. Following the intent of the original reporting statutes, more recent and broader statutes have resulted in even greater increases in reporting.

The problem with mandatory reporting laws is their application in mental health service settings without regard to the nature of these services. The settings and relationships within which suspected child abuse occurs in mental health services are qualitatively different from those of emergency medicine and pediatrics, the original targets of mandatory reporting legislation. Mental health professionals, and other nonmedical human service professionals, are unlikely to detect the battered child syn-

---

[5]Details of this case were abstracted and paraphrased from MacDonald, Hill, and Li (1993).

drome, although it is likely that they may be exposed to those circumstances that raise suspicions of child abuse. In addition, mental health
professionals frequently rely solely on their observations of behavior in
making determinations about child abuse. Concerns about privacy, trust,
and respect play crucial roles in mental health professionals' dissatisfaction
with mandated reporting. Vague statutory language generalizes across many
nonabusive situations encountered by the typical mental health professional.

Despite difficulties posed by required reporting, few people have suggested a complete reversal of reporting legislation that would allow professionals full discretion when reporting suspected abuse. Rather, many observers have called for legislative reform that will clarify definitions of abuse
and neglect, as well as the circumstances that warrant reporting (J. Jones
& Welch, 1989; Melton & Davidson, 1987; S. Smith & Meyer, 1984).
Others have suggested that professionals working with families to stop
abuse should not be required to report (Ansell & Ross, 1990). Still others
have called for allowing professionals with expertise in child abuse greater
flexibility in reporting (Finkelhor & Zellman, 1991). Finally, some have
claimed that the current laws would adequately function only if the child
protection system had sufficient resources to manage the large volume of
reports. Given the complexity of these issues, it is unlikely that a single
answer will address the roles of mandated reporters. Rather, a combination
of changes seems necessary, such as clarification of the laws and a greater
social commitment to protecting children.

Mandated reporters view the welfare of children and families as their
greatest consideration when deciding to report suspected child abuse. Reporting suspected child abuse is typically a thoughtful process, with consideration given to the situation, previous reporting experiences, and family
circumstances. Professionals will most likely do what they believe is in the
best interests of those they serve. Providers who are fully aware of their
legal obligation to report suspected abuse, however, may choose not to
report when they believe that doing so is unethical.

# 2

# MANDATED REPORTING AS AN ETHICAL DILEMMA

I find it difficult to report abuse. On the one hand, I feel I must report quickly if a child is in danger. But on the other hand, reporting disrupts treatment, ruins relationships among family members, and the child protection system often acts punitively, even if the family is making therapeutic progress. I often struggle not knowing if abuse has occurred, especially when I have young children as clients. (Survey participant, Kalichman & Brosig, 1993)

The decision to report suspected abuse is a tough one. Reporting can disrupt therapy and damage rapport with clients. However, I feel protection of the child is my highest priority. In most cases I have been involved with, I have been able to work through the family's anger toward me by careful explanation of my ethical and legal responsibilities. (Survey participant, Kalichman & Brosig, 1992)

Requirements to report suspected child abuse stem from two broader professional obligations: the duty to protect and the duty to warn. Professionals must protect those they serve from potential harm. Physicians and other providers, for example, must report violent injuries, such as those sustained by gunshot, knifing, poisoning, and any other wounds believed to result from suspicious acts. Often, reports of domestic violence are also required. Health care providers must report several diseases to public health officials. Mandatory reporting laws exist to protect the public. Reporting potential child abuse does not require informed consent and reporting laws supercede assurances of professional confidentiality. Laws that require reporting suspected child abuse therefore occur in a broader context of standards for protecting vulnerable persons from harm. This chapter discusses mandated reporting as an ethical dilemma, including the array of factors that create conflict in decisions to report suspected child abuse.

## DUTY TO WARN

Mandated reporting of suspected child abuse occurs within the context of professional obligations to protect persons from harm. Professionals are bound to a protective duty through ethical codes, standards of practice, and the law. Aside from required reporting of suspected child abuse, professionals must report suspected elder abuse and abuse of disabled persons (see Exhibit 2.1). For example, in New Jersey, abuse of adults is defined as "the willful infliction of physical pain, injury, or mental anguish; unreasonable confinement; or the willful deprivation of services which are necessary to maintain a person's physical and mental health" (Wulach, 1998). In New York, however, reporting adult abuse is required only when it occurs within nursing homes or residential care facilities (Wulach, 1993). In California, institutionalized elder abuse is broadly defined to include assault, deprivation of food or water, sexual assault, negligent care, abandonment, fiduciary abuse, and isolation, all of which require reporting (Caudill

### EXHIBIT 2.1
### Types and Indicators of Elder Abuse

| Forms of Elder Abuse | |
| --- | --- |
| Physical abuse | Psychological/emotional abuse |
| Financial abuse | Neglect |
| Self-neglect | Abuse from the caregiver |

| Possible Indicators of Physical Abuse | |
| --- | --- |
| Cuts, lacerations, puncture wounds | Bruises, welts, discoloration |
| Any injury incompatible with history | Unattended injury |
| Poor skin condition or poor skin hygiene | Absence of hair |
| Hemorrhaging below scalp | Dehydration or malnourishment |
| Weight loss | Burns |
| Soiled clothing or bed | |

| Possible Indicators of Psychological/Emotional Abuse | |
| --- | --- |
| Helplessness | Hesitation to talk openly |
| Implausible stories | Confusion or disorientation |
| Anger | Fear |
| Withdrawal | Depression |
| Denial | Agitation |

& Pope, 1995). The duty to report therefore extends to other vulnerable populations, and many of the principles of mandated reporting of suspected child abuse extend to these other situations.

Because reporting suspected child maltreatment involves breaking confidentiality to protect vulnerable persons, reporting requirements fall under the rubric of the duty to protect (Besharov, 1986b; Newman, 1987). Obligations to warn third parties of potential danger has been widely debated, particularly with reference to the case of *Tarasoff v. Board of Regents of the University of California* (1976; Koocher, 1988). The case of *Tarasoff* is widely discussed and has had substantial effects on mental health law. Stone (1976) summarized the core characteristics of *Tarasoff* as follows:

> In the fall of 1969, Prosenjit Poddar, a citizen of India and a naval architecture student at the University of California's Berkeley campus, shot and stabbed to death Tatiana Tarasoff, a young woman who had spurned his affections. Poddar had been in psychotherapy with a psychologist at the university's student health facility, and the psychologist had concluded that Poddar was quite dangerous. This conclusion stemmed from an assessment of Poddar's pathological attachment to Tarasoff and evidence that he intended to purchase a gun. After consultation with appropriate colleagues at the student health facility, the psychologist in question notified police both orally and in writing that Poddar was dangerous. He requested that Poddar be taken to a facility to be evaluated for civil commitment under California civil commitment statutes. The police allegedly interrogated Poddar and found him rational. They concluded that he was not really dangerous and secured a promise that he would stay away from Ms. Tarasoff. After his release by the police, Poddar never returned for further psychotherapy and two months later he killed Ms. Tarasoff. (Stone, cited in Keith-Spiegel & Koocher, 1985, p. 62)

Psychologists are obligated to warn third parties of known dangers when such persons can be identified. In the case of children, warnings are given to child protection agencies that act on behalf of children. Protecting intended victims from harm is, therefore, what connects mandated reporting and the duty to warn (Besharov, 1986b; Bross, 1983).

Duty to warn is also the mechanism that pits professional standards of confidentiality against the necessity of protecting others. It is in this sense that reporting suspected child abuse is considered a special case of duty to warn. Reporting abuse necessarily involves breaching confidentiality and preventing personal harm, and thus places legal constraints on professional actions. Reporting also appears most akin to duty to warn when the source of the information is an adult suspected of being abusive, and where potential harm may come to a third party. Also, like other types of duty to warn, reports of suspected child abuse can be used in prosecution of a crime (Leong, Eth, & Silva, 1992). In contrast to other instances of duty to warn, however, a child welfare agency receives the warning and responds on behalf of the child. Mandatory reporting is also different from most other cases of duty to warn because reporting suspected abuse is, for the most part, a legal obligation with ethical implications; most other situations of duty to warn are ethical obligations with legal implications.[6]

## MANDATED REPORTING AND PROFESSIONAL ETHICS

Human service professionals in general, and mental health practitioners in particular, frequently experience mandated reporting of suspected abuse as an ethical dilemma. For example, a national survey of American Psychological Association (APA) members showed that conflicts over client confidentiality were the most frequently encountered ethical dilemmas, constituting 18% of all ethically questionable situations, with reporting suspected child abuse being among the most common (Pope & Vetter, 1992). These results mirrored those of an earlier national survey of psychologists, in which 45% indicated that breaking confidentiality to report suspected child maltreatment was common, and 35% stated that it was ethically questionable to do so (Pope, Tabachnick, & Keith-Spiegel, 1987). Similarly, S. L. Green and Hansen (1989) found that reporting suspected child abuse was the most ethically significant clinical situation experienced by family therapists.

Although many professionals have identified mandated reporting as an ethical dilemma, there is often a discrepancy between what professionals believe they should do and what they say they would do in such situations (T. S. Smith, McGuire, Abbott, & Blau, 1991; Wilkins, McGuire, Abbott, & Blau, 1990). Professionals who believe that they know the ethical course of action when faced with an ethical dilemma take few steps to resolve the conflict between what they should do and would do (T. S. Smith et al., 1991). It is their internal standards and the demands of particular situations that influence professional decisions to act against ethical guidelines. However, unlike many other ethical dilemmas, such as knowledge of an impaired colleague or engaging in a dual relationship, acting outside of mandated child abuse reporting involves breaking the law. This sets child abuse reporting apart from most other ethical dilemmas.

Mandated reporting becomes an ethical dilemma when there are conflicts among serving the best interest of children, professional standards, ethics, and the law. Reporting is also complicated by the fact that breaching confidentiality and breaking the law constitute unethical behavior (Bersoff, 1975). Professionals may also perceive reporting as an unnecessary threat

---

[6]Some states have enacted statutes that mandate the duty to warn third parties and police of serious threat of physical violence against a reasonably identifiable victim. For example, California enacted such a statute, California, Section 1. Section 43.92.

to the integrity of their clinical services (Newberger, 1983). Human service professionals can find themselves in the precarious situation of seeking information to justify reporting, despite the fact that the law does not require them to do so, and that such actions may compromise their roles as helping professionals. Thus, there are three principal ethical concerns that arise from mandated reporting: breaching confidentiality, perceived adverse consequences of reporting, and the potential to dilute professional roles.

## CONFIDENTIALITY AND REPORTING

In professional practice, assurances of privacy and confidentiality are regarded as necessary for the development of therapeutic relationships (Heymann, 1986; S. Smith & Meyer, 1984). Confidentiality allows for the revelation of the most private information, and maintaining confidentiality is well recognized as a standard of professional conduct. According to the APA,

> Psychologists have a primary obligation to respect the confidentiality of information obtained from persons in the course of their work as psychologists. They reveal such information to others only with the consent of the person or person's legal representative, except in those unusual circumstances in which not to do so would result in clear danger to the person or to others. Where appropriate, psychologists inform their clients of the legal limits of confidentiality. (APA, 1990, pp. 392–393)

Revisions of the *Ethical Principles of Psychologists and Code of Conduct* of the APA (1992) retained this standard, stating, "Psychologists have a primary obligation and take reasonable precautions to respect the confidentiality rights of those with whom they work or consult, recognizing that confidentiality may be established by law, institutional rules, or professional or scientific relationships" (APA, 1992, Standard 5.02). In addition, it stated that "psychologists disclose confidential information without the consent of the individual only as mandated by law, or where permitted by law for a valid purpose" (Standard 5.05a).

Confidentiality is commonly defined as "the general standard of professional conduct that obliges a professional not to discuss information about a client with anyone" (Keith-Spiegel & Koocher, 1985, p. 57). Confidentiality is an ethical concept and should not be confused with privileged communication, a legal concept that refers to "the quality of certain specific types of relationships that prevent information, acquired from such relationships, from being disclosed in court or other legal proceedings" (Keith-Spiegel & Koocher, 1985, p. 58).

Privileged communication statutes protect the confidentiality of patients and clients when professionals are called to testify in legal proceedings. All states have some form of privileged communication protected by law, and privileged communications with mental health professionals are protected under specified conditions in most state and federal laws (Knapp & VandeCreek, 1997). For example, the U.S. Supreme Court ruled in *Jaffee v. Redmond* (1996) that communications between psychotherapists and their clients are protected by privilege in federal courts under specified conditions (DeBell & Jones, 1997). However, state and federal laws recognize mandated reporting of suspected abuse as an exception to privileged communication, with most states providing explicit exceptions for child abuse and neglect (Glosoff, Herlihy, Herlihy, & Spence, 1997). The waiver of confidentiality is, however, apparently limited to the need for filing a report. As shown in the California Supreme Court ruling in *People v. Stritzinger* (34 Cal. 3d 505, 1983), mental health professionals must waive confidentiality to report suspected abuse, but information sought in subsequent inquiries by police and child protection workers may remain protected under privileged communications statutes (see Caudill & Pope, 1995).

## INFORMED CONSENT

Professional standards in mental health practice specify that information revealed by clients should remain confidential, and that, when appropriate, persons should be informed of the legal limits of confidentiality. Specifically, the *Ethical Principles of Psychologists and Code of Conduct* (APA, 1992) states,

> Psychologists discuss with persons and organizations with whom they establish a scientific or professional relationship (including to the extent feasible, minors and their legal representatives) (1) the relevant limitations on confidentiality, including limitations where applicable in group, marital, and family therapy, or in organizational consulting; and (2) the foreseeable uses of the information generated through their services. (Standard 5.01a)

Similarly, the *Ethical Code of Social Workers* states that "the Social Worker should inform clients fully about the limits of confidentiality in a given situation, the purpose for which information is obtained, and how it may be used" (National Association of Social Workers, 1980, pp. 5–6). Informing persons about the limits of confidentiality, however, creates practical challenges. Clinicians must simultaneously avoid undermining the concept of confidentiality and uphold their obligation to share information with social service agencies responsible for intervening on behalf of children (Taylor & Adelman, 1989). Although providing informed consent is an essential aspect of treatment, several studies have shown that informing clients of the limits of confidentiality is not consistently practiced (Butz, 1985; Keith-Spiegel & Koocher, 1985; Kelly, 1987; Koocher & Keith-Spiegel, 1990; Stadler, 1989).

For example, Baird and Rupert (1987) found that only 50% of practicing psychologists surveyed informed their clients of the limits of confidentiality, and 12% usually told clients that everything discussed in treatment would remain confidential. Doueck and Levine (in press) found that a majority of therapists felt uncomfortable discussing limited confidentiality with clients and that many opted to discuss confidentiality without discussing its limits. Therapists were also inclined to discuss the limits of confidentiality at a later point in therapy, only after establishing a relationship and trust with the client. Issues of inhibiting a client's willingness to disclose under the pretense of limited confidentiality are clearly a major consideration for many clinicians. As noted by M. Levine (1993), informed consent is complicated by mandated reporting:

> Most therapists feel an ethical responsibility to inform a client of the limits of confidentiality. Informing the client is an act that respects a client's autonomy. Enhancing autonomy is certainly a therapeutic goal, but the reporting mandate complicates the effort to meet the duty to inform. (p. 722)

Clients, no matter what their age, have a right to be informed of the limits of confidentiality before they disclose information in confidence. Informing minors about limited confidentiality, however, is complicated by their willingness to discuss issues that could anger their parents. In one survey, Beeman and Scott (1991) found that 70% of practicing psychologists obtained informed consent from adolescent clients, including consent for limited confidentiality. Beeman and Scott also found that professionals viewed limiting confidentiality as the single most important element of informed consent for both adolescents and adults. However, treating minors requires parental consent, and this raises the possibility of parents interfering with the treatment process, especially when the parent is abusive. Parents may badger a child about what he or she is saying in therapy, or tell a child that the social service workers will take him or her away for telling family secrets. Still, professionals state that including limited confidentiality in informed consent is necessary and has the potential benefit of enhancing a sense of autonomy that can help build therapeutic relationships (Beeman & Scott, 1991).

Psychologists who have previously experienced problems resulting from breached confidentiality are more likely to inform clients about limited confidentiality compared with those psychologists who have not experienced such problems (Baird & Rupert, 1987). In one survey, 59% of practicing psychologists believed that their clients were at least somewhat aware of professionals' requirements to report suspected child abuse (Brosig,

1992). This finding suggests that professionals may not believe it is necessary to inform clients of limited confidentiality with respect to mandated reporting. Although there are no standards for informing clients of limited confidentiality, there are some noteworthy suggestions.

The *Ethical Principles of Psychologists and Code of Conduct* (APA, 1992) states that informing persons of confidentiality and the limits of confidentiality should occur at the outset of professional and scientific relationships. Specifically, the code states, "Unless it is not foreseeable or is contraindicated, the discussion of confidentiality occurs at the outset of the relationship and thereafter as new circumstances may warrant" (Standard 5.01b). Keith-Spiegel and Koocher (1985) agreed with this position, suggesting that professionals discuss the limits of confidentiality as early in relationships as possible, such as during initial interviews. They also advise that possible breaches of confidentiality be carefully considered by professionals and openly discussed with clients.

Statements of limited confidentiality included in informed consent vary among individual professionals and professional settings, and are influenced by the characteristics of clients. Taylor and Adelman (1989) provided an example of a verbal explanation for exceptions to confidentiality that may be appropriate to use with children and adolescents:

> Although most of what we talk about is private, there are three kinds of problems you might tell me about that we would have to talk about with other people. If I find out that someone has been seriously hurting or abusing you, I would have to tell the police about it. If you tell me you have made a plan to seriously hurt yourself, I would have to let your parents know. If you tell me you have made a plan to seriously hurt someone else, I would have to warn that person. I would not be able to keep these problems just between you and me because the law says I can't. (Taylor & Adelman, 1989, p. 80)

Taylor and Adelman (1989) have also suggested that limits of confidentiality be framed to emphasize what can be discussed confidentially in order to facilitate open sharing of information.

Keith-Spiegel and Koocher (1985) and Wilcoxon (1991) noted that clients may best be informed of limited confidentiality in writing. A good example is a pamphlet created by the Judge Baker Children's Center in Boston titled *Privacy and Confidentiality in Mental Health Services*. Among 11 other circumstances that involve limited confidentiality, including situations of duty to warn and child custody, the pamphlet states,

> If the clinician, in his professional capacity, has reasonable cause to believe that a child under the age of eighteen years is suffering serious physical or emotional injury resulting from abuse inflicted upon the child (including sexual abuse), or from neglect (including malnutrition), or who is determined to be dependent upon an addictive drug

at birth, the clinician is required to report information to the Massachusetts Department of Social Services. (p. 4)

An alternative procedure is to provide a signed informed-consent form at the outset of treatment to describe all of the conditions and expectations of treatment, including limited confidentiality and appropriate releases of information. With respect to child abuse reporting requirements, a statement such as the following can be included:

> What is discussed in therapy is confidential unless and until you give consent to its release, with two exceptions: I will need, and am compelled by law, to inform an appropriate other person(s) if I hear that you are in danger of hurting yourself or someone else, and if there is a reasonable suspicion that a child has been abused. (California State Department of Social Services, 1991, p. 24)

Like a pamphlet, an informed-consent form should detail the conditions of treatment to avoid later misunderstandings. Although pamphlets and forms can be of great use in structuring information and ensuring that all relevant points are covered, they do not necessarily replace a frank discussion of confidentiality and its limits (Pope & Vasquez, 1991). Open discussions allow the professional to assess the recipient's understanding of confidentiality, and to invite questions and comments.

## DILUTING PROFESSIONAL ROLES

Medical and mental health care professionals evaluate clients to diagnose clinical conditions and to determine an appropriate course of treatment. In the case of child abuse, however, diagnostic decisions also carry reporting responsibilities. Thus, human service professionals often find themselves acting in the dual role of diagnostician and investigator (Giovannoni, 1989b). Human service professionals are primarily concerned with the welfare of those they serve, and so reporting suspected child abuse is most compatible with their helping role when reporting is in the best interest of their client.

Although they are not required to have knowledge of abuse to report, professionals tend to feel obligated to seek further information prior to reporting suspected child abuse. In one survey, 57% of licensed practicing psychologists indicated that they believed they had at least some ethical responsibility to find information that supported the occurrence of abuse prior to reporting (Kalichman & Brosig, 1993). In addition, psychologists who have not reported suspected child maltreatment are more likely to believe that they have an investigative role in determining abuse before reporting. However, professionals who have reached a level of reasonable suspicion but have not reported because their suspicions lack evidence are not, in fact, complying with reporting laws. Thus, gathering evidence of abuse is not a role expected of mental health professionals.

Role conflict occurs when expectations of two or more roles are incompatible with one another (Kitchener, 1988). Professionals may experience conflicts between their perceived responsibilities as mandated reporters and their roles of helper, service provider, and keeper of sensitive information. Despite the fact that mandatory reporting laws require reasonable suspicions of abuse, and that immunity is granted to mandated reporters, professionals are often compelled to obtain some degree of certainty before reporting abuse (Kalichman et al., 1989). The need to seek out further information before reporting is likely to be motivated by (a) beliefs about the effects of investigations on families and professional services (Zellman, 1990), and (b) the simple desire to be right when reporting.

Professionals whose duties do not include investigative roles may confuse their professional identity when they seek information about abuse to justify reporting. Role diffusion therefore causes conflict in reporting decisions. In addition, because most practitioners have not acquired adequate investigative skills, they may be overstepping boundaries of competence by doing so. *The Ethical Principles of Psychologists* (APA, 1992) states that "psychologists recognize the boundaries of their competence and the limitations of their techniques. They only provide services and only use techniques for which they are qualified by training and experience" (p. 390). Similarly, the APA ethics code states that services are provided within competence based on "education, training, supervised experience, or appropriate professional experience" (1992, Standard 1.04a). Seeking to validate abuse is a specialized area of forensic evaluation, and requires specific skills and training (Conte, 1992). Thus, therapists who investigate abuse when existing signs have surpassed a reasonable suspicion are usually functioning outside of their professional competence.

The potential role conflicts that reporting suspected child abuse could cause for professionals were discussed in the earliest days of mandated reporting. Kempe et al. (1962) stated that physicians would be reluctant to take on a police function by investigating abuse, noting that the training and character of physicians would make them unwilling to question parents about possible criminal behavior. Because these observations predated reporting laws, and because of the influence that Kempe et al. had on the design of reporting laws, requirements to report reasonable suspicions of child maltreatment relieve professionals of the duty to seek information before reporting. The intent of the law is to identify a maximum number of abuse cases. In doing so, however, the law allows practitioners to maintain their professional stance. Limiting professional roles to those defined by one's training and the expectations of one's clients will minimize role conflict and confusion (Melton & Limber, 1989).

Diluting professional roles in managing cases of child abuse, however, is not unique to the experience of mandated reporters. Child protection service workers often experience similar role conflicts seen in mandated reporters. Police, for example, whose principal roles are investigative, frequently focus their attention on determining criminal intent, despite the requirement that reasonable suspicions be reported (Willis & Wells, 1988). Child protection workers can also experience conflict between their roles as investigators and social service providers (Cook, 1991). It is therefore important to recognize the potential role conflicts that occur in cases of child abuse across professions.

Role diffusion is minimized first by defining duties that fall within a professional's capacity and then limiting one's practice to those activities. In the case of practicing psychologists, for example, roles should be limited to one of evaluator, therapist, researcher, or, if employed in such a capacity, investigator (Melton & Limber, 1989). When child abuse is suspected it is within the scope of practitioners' roles to report. Suspicions of abuse in the professional context may be subtle, often resembling clinical hunches or intuitions (J. Jones & Welch, 1989). However, standards for reporting reasonable suspicions imply a degree of discretion and evaluation. It is within practitioners' roles and duties to follow up suspicions with queries for evaluation or treatment. Probing into important life events is a regular and frequent practice in treatment. However, seeking additional information outside of treatment, or delaying reporting with the intent of gathering more information at a later time is precarious. Aside from being in violation of the law, it goes beyond professional roles of evaluator, therapist, or researcher.

## CONSIDERATIONS IN RESEARCH SETTINGS

Researchers often guarantee that sensitive information will remain confidential in order to help participants feel comfortable in revealing personal and sensitive information. Procedures to ensure confidentiality are therefore considered essential to the collection of valid research data (Turner, 1982). Similar to suspicions of abuse within clinical settings, challenges to confidentiality occur in research settings. Contrary to researchers beliefs that they are not mandated reporters (Kinard, 1985), the law rarely excludes researchers from reporting requirements (Liss, 1994). Thus, to the extent that research fits within the definition of professional activities, the law includes health-related researchers as mandated reporters.

The APA Ad Hoc Committee on Child Abuse Policy (L. E. Walker, Alpert, Harris, & Koocher, 1989) noted the conflict that researchers may experience in reporting suspected child maltreatment:

> Gaps in knowledge and need for further research in the area of child abuse and neglect are considerable. Particular tensions involve efforts

by investigators and institutional review boards to protect the privacy and social rights of research participants, while also remaining appropriately responsive to legal reporting requirements. (p. 12)

Thus, similar to clinical settings, confidentiality in research requires balancing rights to privacy, child protection, and legal obligations.

Abuse is discovered in research settings under a variety of conditions where a child is believed to suffer abuse (Kinard, 1985) or an adult is thought to perpetrate abuse (Kalichman, 1991). In either case, professional ethics state,

> Information obtained about research participants during the course of an investigation is confidential unless otherwise agreed upon in advance. When the possibility exists that others may obtain access to such information, this possibility, together with the plans for protecting confidentiality, is explained to the participant as a part of the procedure for obtaining informed consent. (APA, 1990, p. 395)

In research where the discovery of an abusive situation is likely, such as research in delinquency, domestic violence, or studies of perpetrators or victims of abuse, informed consent would most likely include limits to confidentiality regarding suspected child maltreatment. However, other situations that involve contact with children or adults, particularly when sensitive information is collected in confidential settings, can reveal circumstances that suggest abuse. It is in these situations where an unexpected discovery of abuse occurs that the researcher is usually faced with breaching confidentiality. Thus, information gained in research poses similar ethical challenges as that found in clinical practice. For example, it is common for depression researchers to identify participants with suicide intentions. This requires a protocol for breaking confidentiality to report and refer.

The APA recognizes the complexity of standards of confidentiality in situations where abuse is suspected. According to the APA's Ad Hoc Committee on Child Abuse Policy (L. E. Walker et al., 1989),

> There was unanimous agreement that the APA should have a clearer policy that strongly supports the basic principle that the social policy of protecting children from the enormous damage to a child's physical and mental well-being and subsequent development inflicted by abuse outweighs the important social policies supporting the protection of confidentiality of the therapy relationship and protection of the projected disruption of the therapy relationship that can result from such mandatory reporting. (L. E. Walker et al., 1989, p. 4)

Similar sentiments are found in APA's Standards for Confidentiality in Research. As the Committee for the Protection of Human Participants in Research stated,

> The protection afforded research participants by the maintenance of confidentiality may be compromised when the investigator discovers

information that serious harm threatens the research participant or others. The obligation to make this information known to research participants, their associates, or legal authorities nonetheless creates an ethical dilemma in consideration of the promised maintenance of strict confidentiality. (APA, 1982, p. 72)

Researchers, however, may fear that informing study participants of their duty to report could reduce willingness to participate, or encourage participants to lie in response to questions related to child abuse (Sieber, 1994). In fact, researchers may avoid asking questions directly related to child abuse and other situations that require reporting, simply to avoid detailed discussions of limited confidentiality. Alternatively, researchers may apply for a Federal Certificate of Confidentiality when the reason for not reporting disclosed abuse is compelling. A Federal Certificate protects confidentiality in research settings and supercedes state laws and court orders.

To summarize, the experience of reporting suspected abuse as an ethical dilemma is directly tied to two central issues of confidentiality. First, confidentiality constitutes a core component of the value system ascribed to by human service professionals and researchers with human participants. Second, the role that professionals believe confidentiality plays in the quality of their work can exert enormous influences on reporting decisions. Among other things, reporting decisions are affected by the degree to which breaches in confidentiality are perceived to have adverse affects on professional duties.

## EFFECTS OF REPORTING ON CHILD AND FAMILY SERVICES

There is a clear expectation that human service professionals will act in the best interest of those they serve. Therefore, if reporting suspected child abuse is perceived as deleterious to the progress of professional services, it should be expected that providers will hesitate to report (Newberger, 1983). Because confidentiality is heralded as a necessary element of helping relationships, professionals have been advised to err on the side of maintaining confidence by not disclosing private information (Watkins, 1989). Professionals have also been told to consider a range of options in place of reporting, despite their legal duty to report (Ansell & Ross, 1990). Cautions against reporting stem from beliefs that reporting will cause more harm than not reporting.

Reporting dilemmas are partially fueled by the conflict between doing what is best for clients, families, and treatment, on the one hand, and acting in accordance with the law, on the other. Conflicts about reporting occur when the law is seen as a threat to the interests of children and families. Surveys of professional psychologists have shown that concerns about potential adverse effects on therapy influence reporting. Kalichman et al. (1989) found that 42% of licensed psychologists surveyed believed that reporting suspected abuse has negative consequences for the progress of family therapy. In another study, nearly one third of licensed psychologists rated safeguarding the process of therapy as an important consideration in reporting decisions (Kalichman & Craig, 1991). One participant in the Kalichman and Craig study commented, "If a family makes a commitment to treatment following a disclosure of abuse, I typically will not report unless the family drops out of treatment or fails to make use of treatment. I feel there is more to be gained therapeutically this way." These same sentiments were held by some professionals arrested for failure to report suspected abuse discussed in chapter 1.

The experience of reporting child abuse can also affect subsequent decisions to report. Kalichman and Craig (1991) found that psychologists who reported abuse perceived the adverse effects of their report on the progress of therapy, whereas the effects of the report on the child, family, and abuse patterns were understood to be positive. One third of participants in the study believed their report of abuse had harmful affects on therapy.

Not all research, however, supports the concern that perceived adverse effects on therapy influence reporting. Brosig and Kalichman (1992b) found that protecting children and one's own clinical judgment were rated as more important influences on reporting than were concerns about therapy in decisions to report suspected abuse, whereas lacking evidence of abuse was more important than therapy concerns in decisions not to report. Thus, although different factors are weighed in decisions whether to report suspected child abuse, concerns of interrupting services are not the most important in either case.

In Brosig and Kalichman's (1992b) study, practicing psychologists who had both reported and withheld reporting cases of suspected child abuse rated their perceptions of the effects of both decisions on the child, family, outcome of therapy, and the maintenance of trust in therapy. The study found that there were no differences in relative perceived effects of reporting and not reporting on the child and outcome of therapy. However, reporting was perceived as more damaging to families and trust in therapy than was not reporting. Of interest is that treatment outcome and trust in therapy were seen differently. This suggests that different dimensions of treatment may be differentially affected by reporting.

M. Levine and Doeuck (1995) provided the most complete accounts of clinicians' perceptions of the effects of reporting on therapeutic relationships. Through a careful analysis of in-depth interviews with mental health providers, Levine and Doeuck found that reporting poses the greatest threat to treatment when professionals view their report as resulting in insufficient action to protect the child named in the report. Among the factors that ultimately influenced outcomes of reporting were (a) the proximity of the potential abuser to the therapeutic relationship, (b) whether the client was an adult or child, (c) how the report was presented to the client, (d) whether the case involved divorce and child custody disputes, (e) the client's level of involvement in making the report, and (f) the nature of the alleged abuse. Levine and Doeuck also noted that the outcomes of reporting can be negative or positive for therapeutic relationships. Reporting can result in a sense of betrayal, a breakdown in trust, and discontinuing treatment. On the other hand, reporting can strengthen therapeutic alliances, express care for the child, model good parenting, bring a new focus to therapy, control abusive behavior, and increase access to needed services. The outcomes a provider anticipates will depend on their beliefs about child protective services and their own first-hand reporting experiences.

## REPORTING PERPETRATORS IN TREATMENT

Suspicians of child abuse can arise when the source is a child–victim or an adult-perpetrator, as well as a third party. The implication of informed limits of confidentiality differ under each of these circumstances. For adults receiving treatment, hiding abuse can stem from fear of investigation and involvement of the state. On the other hand, perpetrators may admit abuse as an integral part of their treatment. Informing and receiving consent that information volunteered in treatment about previous acts of abuse will require reporting is both an ethical and a legal standard (Miller & Weinstock, 1987; Weinstock & Weinstock, 1989). Informed consent regarding limited confidentiality may, however, induce fear and avoidance among perpetrators. Mandatory reporting laws may therefore discourage abusers from seeking treatment, potentially causing more harm than good (Berlin et al., 1991; Miller & Weinstock, 1987; S. Smith & Meyer, 1984; Weinstock & Weinstock, 1989).

Some state reporting statutes have included provisions that were sensitive to treating perpetrators by providing professionals with reporting discretion (Heymann, 1986). For example, at one time the state of Maine permitted mandated reporters to fully utilize their professional discretion to report information that emerged during the course of treatment:

> This subsection does not require any person to report when the factual bases of knowing or suspecting child abuse or neglect came from treatment of the individual for suspected child abuse or neglect, the treatment was sought by the individual for a problem relating to child abuse or neglect, and, in the opinion of the person required to report, the child's life or health is not immediately threatened. (NCCAN, 1979, p. 10)

Maryland's law had also provided professional discretion when there was progress toward successfully ending potential risks of abuse or if it was believed that reporting would interfere with victims or perpetrators who might otherwise seek assistance:

> A person required to notify and report under the provisions of this section need not comply with the notification and reporting requirements of this section if: (1) Efforts are being made or will be made to alleviate the conditions or circumstances which may cause the child to be considered a neglected child and it is concluded by the health practitioner . . . that these efforts will alleviate these conditions or circumstances; or (2) The health practitioner . . . believes that the notification and reporting would inhibit the child, parent, guardian, or custodian from seeking assistance in the future and thereby be detrimental to the child's welfare. (NCCAN, 1979, pp. 9–10)

In the same statute, Maryland also specifically exempted psychiatrists treating pedophiles from reporting suspected abuse:

> A health practitioner who specializes in the psychiatric treatment of pedophilia is not required to report sexual abuse if . . . reason to believe that a child has been subjected to sexual abuse is based exclusively on a report made to the health practitioner . . . (who) is providing psychiatric treatment to the individual for the purpose of curing the individual's pedophilia. (NCCAN, 1989, p. MD-13)

Both Maine and Maryland, therefore, had reporting statutes that provided professionals with discretion and placed reporting decisions within the context of professional services. However, these two statutes underwent substantial reform in the late 1980s, with both laws broadened to better address who is required to report. For example, the amended statute in Maryland reads that "all professionals and nonprofessionals are now required to report suspected neglect as well as suspected abuse" (Maryland Social Services Administration, 1988, p. 4).

After the legislative changes in Maryland, one study reported adverse effects of the new law on the treatment of perpetrators of sexual abuse. Berlin et al. (1991) found that the rate of perpetrators' self-disclosures of sexual abuse at their treatment centers changed dramatically as a result of the new reporting laws. From 1984 to 1987 Berlin et al.'s patients disclosed some 89 acts of sexual abuse during the course of treatment. However, after legislative reform in 1988 and 1989, the number of self-disclosures dropped to zero. Berlin et al. (1991) expressed alarm at this trend, claiming that "children at risk were not being identified by the disclosures of adult patients regardless of whether mandatory reporting was in effect. In this sense, mandatory reporting failed to achieve its desired intent of identifying and helping abused children" (p. 453). The findings of Berlin et al. echo concerns that laws inhibiting offender treatment put children at increased risk (Kelly, 1987; Priest & Wilcoxon, 1988; Weinstock & Weinstock, 1989).

Berlin et al.'s (1991) experience of Maryland's legislative changes were not, however, universal (Kalichman, 1991). Although disclosures of abuse by repeat sexual offenders (55% of which were pedophiles) ceased at this particular treatment center, reports of sexual abuse actually increased in Maryland almost 7% from 1988 to 1989 (see Figure 2.1). Also, in contrast to the findings of Berlin et al. are studies that show that receiving informed consent about the limits of confidentiality has little if any impact on a client's willingness to self-disclose (Muehleman, Pickens, & Robinson, 1985). These conflicting data point to Berlin et al.'s clinical setting as a special case, rather than as a general failure of unlimited reporting requirements. However, Berlin et al.'s experience does illustrate the far-reaching effects of a single legal standard on diverse professional settings. Researchers studying mothers who are not the subject of an abuse investigation suggest that limits of confidentiality do not pose a significant barrier to seeking treatment (Gustafson, McNamara, & Jensen, 1994). Limited confidentiality will therefore have different effects on different client populations.

Adults who are ordered by courts for treatment present a number of additional complicating factors. Because therapists tend to insist on admitting abusive behavior as a precondition for successful treatment, court-

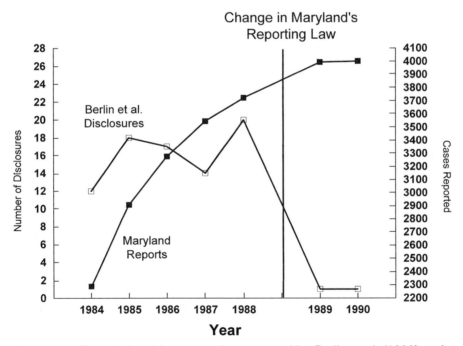

Figure 2.1. The relationship among data reported by Berlin et al. (1990) and the number of cases of sexual abuse reported during Maryland's legislative change. Adapted with permission provided from the American Psychiatric Association, 1993.

ordered clients are often placed in a position where their constitutional rights may be violated. Specifically, the Fifth Amendment states that "no person . . . shall be compelled in any criminal case to be witness against himself." M. Levine and Doherty (1991) detailed the conditions under which an alleged perpetrator's rights may be placed in jeopardy. They showed that by refusing to admit abuse an adult can be held accountable for failing to comply with treatment, whereas admitting abuse can be used as evidence against them in criminal and child custody cases. Thus, when cases are progressing through the legal system, issues of confidentiality and disclosures of abuse are complicated by additional constraints and consequences for disclosing abuse.

Although surveys have shown that professionals perceive reporting as disruptive to therapy and that mandatory reporting laws may impede treating perpetrators, little research has addressed the effects of reporting on human services. In one qualitative evaluation of clinical cases of child maltreatment, Harper and Irvin (1985) found that when cases of abuse were reported in the context of ongoing therapy, clients were unlikely to terminate treatment. Another study that used a stronger retrospective methodology also examined the effects of reporting suspected abuse on the progress of psychotherapy. Watson and Levine (1989) identified 65 cases of reported abuse from a child and adolescent outpatient psychiatric clinic. Reports tended to occur early in the course of treatment. More than 12% were reported at the initial interview, and 50% of reports occurred within the first 3 months of therapy. A careful review of these cases, including a look at client dropout rates and the quality of client–therapist relationships, showed that most cases of mandated reporting did not have adverse effects on the therapeutic alliance. In fact, Watson and Levine found that the majority of cases were unchanged as a result of the report, and nearly one third of cases showed positive changes attributed to reporting. In a quantitative follow-up survey of psychotherapists, Steinberg, Levine, and Doeuck (1997) found that the strength of the therapeutic alliance before reporting was closely associated with a positive outcome from reporting. Watson and Levine also demonstrated that the cases that were least affected by reporting were those where the suspected abuser was not the client in treatment, but rather a third party.

Watson and Levine (1989) interpreted their findings by suggesting that "it is trust, not absolute confidentiality that is essential for the psychotherapeutic relationship. Trust may develop or be maintained even though confidentiality cannot be guaranteed or has been breached" (p. 255). These findings and conclusions supported Harper and Irvin's (1985) suggestion that psychotherapy can benefit from reporting abusive behavior, despite breaching confidentiality. Similar conclusions were reached in a separate study that used detailed qualitative analyses of several clinical cases of reported abuse (M. Levine, Anderson, Terretti, Sharma, et al., 1991; M. Levine, Anderson, Terretti, Steinberg, et al., 1991).

The implications that reporting can convey trust also suggest that not reporting could have negative effects on client perceptions of therapeutic relationships (Van Eenwyk, 1990). Because professionals believe clients are aware of reporting requirements (Brosig, 1992), their knowledge that a professional who suspects abuse and chooses not to report can be interpreted as an unwillingness to get involved (Helfer, 1975). Thus, reporting suspected child abuse can mean as much potential benefit as harm to therapeutic processes. Relative effects of reporting on treatment relate to the manner in which clients are informed of the limits of confidentiality, the sources of information leading to the suspicion, the quality of therapeutic alliance prior to reporting, and the degree to which reporting processes are integrated into therapy.

To summarize, little evidence exists to support the popular perception that reporting child abuse has detrimental effects on the quality and efficacy of professional services. In fact, studies specifically addressing these issues in clinical settings find that reporting sometimes benefits the treatment process. Still, the lack of research in this area and on the known importance of confidentiality in therapeutic relationships suggests that conclusions are tentative. Reporting suspected child abuse is an ethical problem for reasons outside of its effects on service delivery, such as conflicts that arise between reporting laws and ethical standards.

## CONFLICTS BETWEEN REPORTING LAWS AND ETHICAL STANDARDS

In the case of mandated reporting, standards of confidentiality are limited by law. Given that a substantial number of professionals do not report child maltreatment even when they are fairly certain of its occurrence points to a conflict between standards of ethical conduct and adherence to the law. *The Ethical Principles of Psychologists and Code of Conduct* (APA, 1992) recognizes the potential for such conflict:

> In the process of making decisions regarding their professional behavior, psychologists must consider this [APA] Ethics Code, in addition to applicable laws and psychology board regulations. If the Ethics Code establishes a higher standard of conduct than is required by law, psychologists must meet the higher ethical standard. If the Ethics Code standard appears to conflict with the requirements of law, then psychologists must make known their commitment to the Ethics Code and take steps to resolve the conflict in a reasonable manner. (p. 1598)

Psychologists and other professionals are expected to resolve legal–ethical conflicts to the higher standard of ethical conduct. Not reporting suspected child abuse has been discussed as the higher standard of behavior under some circumstances. Choosing not to report suspected abuse can therefore be considered an act of civil disobedience. Pope and Bajt (1988) found that it is common for experts in ethics to violate mandatory reporting laws. This included 21% of participants refusing to report suspected child abuse. Commenting on Pope and Bajt, Ansell and Ross (1990) argued that failure to report is a viable option for ethical professionals concerned with the welfare of children. In response to Ansell and Ross, Kalichman (1990) suggested that, although problematic, mandatory reporting laws are the law and thus offer no alternative to reporting. However, Kalichman failed to discuss civil disobedience as a viable option in professional conduct. As stated by an anonymous commentator,

> We psychologists seek to help the individuals who seek our services. We may care deeply about the welfare of children and the world in general. In fact, we hope that in the long run our work will help others as well as the client. But at those focused, intense times when we are working with clients, we may not be able to be effective agents of the state or help abused children in accord with recent laws that do not place what we view as a sufficiently high value on confidential psychotherapy. (Anonymous, 1992, p. 3).[7]

Thus, failure to report under some circumstances can be viewed as a higher ethical standard than obeying reporting laws (Wells, 1988).

Civil disobedience as a part of the democratic process, however, is a public statement of unjust policy, as opposed to private actions in the service of a profession. For failure to report to be a statement of civil disobedience, professionals would need to openly criticize reporting laws, not just fail to report. Publicly challenging reporting laws has become more common, but no such objection has proceeded through the courts. Ultimately, resolving conflicts between ethical standards and the law requires clarifying ethics codes, greater advocacy, and legislative reform.


## CONCLUSIONS

Mandatory reporting laws limit the degree to which practitioners can exercise professional judgment when facing suspected child maltreatment. Ethics codes and professional guidelines have done little to assist mandated reporters. For example, suggesting that professionals "take steps to resolve the conflict [between ethics and the law] in a reasonable manner" (APA, 1990, p. 1598) leaves mandated reporters pretty much on their own. Few psychologists receive training in managing reports of suspected child abuse (Kalichman & Brosig, 1993). In addition, mandated reporting rarely re-

---

[7]The author wished to remain anonymous because of local controversy surrounding mandated reporting. However, the paper was graciously volunteered.

ceives more than one or two pages of coverage in even the most authoritative ethics books. Where, then, do professionals turn when facing difficult cases of suspected child abuse?

As an ethical dilemma, mandated reporting may not differ from other ethical dilemmas. For instance, consulting with a colleague about the situation should be the first action when reporting conflicts arise. Discussing the circumstances of suspected abuse with a colleague brings in a second and perhaps more objective perspective. More than 80% of practicing psychologists discuss cases of suspected child abuse with colleagues (Kalichman & Brosig, 1993). In fact, professionals who discuss cases with colleagues are much more likely to report suspected child abuse. This suggests that such input helps clarify ambiguities.

Almost invariably, mandated reporters reflect on the perceived welfare of children, families, and privacy rights in their reporting decisions. Professionals, of course, want their reports of abuse to be as accurate as possible to minimize the potential adverse effects of reporting. Thus, higher levels of discretion may be one reason for higher substantiation rates observed in reports filed by mandated reporters (Eckenrode, Powers, Doris, Munsch, & Bolger, 1988; Giovannoni, 1989b). Despite what the law requires, professionals tend to reach a greater level of certainty about abuse than what they would consider to be a reasonable suspicion. Conflicts among reporting reasonably suspected child abuse, protecting children, maintaining confidentiality, protecting the integrity of professional services, and acting within professional roles are complex. A closer examination of professionals' decision-making processes concerning reporting may, therefore, be of use in understanding these conflicts.

# 3

# WHEN PROFESSIONAL HUNCHES
# BECOME REASONABLE SUSPICIONS

I feel that professionals need to be reasonably sure before reporting. A skilled professional should be able to achieve this through insights derived from interviews with the child and family, as well as by observing any marks, physical signs, or psychological symptoms. (Survey participant, Kalichman & Brosig, 1992)

I have trouble with the subtleties of language of the laws, aside from the ethical issues. I tend to over report [sic]. I feel I do not need to make the final judgement about abuse, and would rather err on the side of false positives. (Survey participant, Brosig & Kalichman, 1992b)

Mandated reporters set personal standards for when to report and when not to report suspected child abuse. The law implies a degree of discretion in reporting, insofar as reporting is required when one has *reasonable* suspicions of abuse. Human service professionals are known to engage in decision-making processes when confronted with signs of child abuse (Finkelhor & Zellman, 1991). Professionals, particularly those who provide treatment and evaluation services, frequently experience intuitions or hunches in the course of their duties. The difficulty professionals experience in distinguishing between clinical impressions and reasonable suspicions of abuse accounts for many failures to report (J. Jones & Welch, 1989). This chapter discusses mandated reporting from the professionals' perspective and reviews deliberation processes as well as the factors that influence the decision to report.

## APPLYING DECISION-MAKING MODELS TO MANDATED REPORTING

Among the available models of human decision making, three appear most relevant to mandated reporting. First, *utility models* stress the relative costs and benefits of making critical decisions. In mandated reporting, professionals weigh perceived pros and cons when determining whether to report suspected child abuse. This suggests the applicability of utility models. *Evidence-based models* have also been important in understanding mandated reporting. In evidence-based models, professionals are influenced by the quality of evidence for abuse and the degree to which the available evidence matches legal standards for reporting. Finally, *threshold models* suggest that mandated reporters set internalized standards for when they will report. Evidence for abuse is placed on a subjective continuum of indicators of abuse. Thus, utility, evidence-based, and threshold decision-making models offer different perspectives on how professionals determine when to report suspected abuse. All three can be synthesized to provide a more comprehensive view of report decision making.

## UTILITY MODELS: THE PERCEIVED BENEFITS AND COSTS OF REPORTING

An array of outcomes follows both reporting and not reporting suspected child abuse. The relative benefits and costs associated with reporting decisions vary with the circumstances of suspected abuse. For example, the relative costs associated with not reporting increase when abuse is perceived as severe, because professionals hold child protection as their primary concern (Brosig & Kalichman, 1992a). How professionals weigh the potential outcomes of reporting suspected child abuse illustrates their basic assumptions about the probable outcomes of reporting. Professionals have identified a number of perceived outcomes associated with reporting and not reporting suspected child abuse, and these perceptions exert considerable influence on reporting decisions.

### Benefits and Costs of not Reporting Suspected Abuse

Benefits that can result from not reporting suspected abuse center around protecting confidentiality in both treatment and research. Professionals have widely discussed and researched the potential impact of reporting on therapeutic relationships. In one study, 31% of practicing psychologists surveyed perceived reporting to have harmful affects on the course of treatment (Kalichman & Craig, 1991). Negative perceptions will likely motivate professionals to hold back from reporting, despite evidence that reporting can have minimal adverse affects on treatment and can even be positively integrated into professional relationships (Harper & Irvin, 1985; M. Levine, Anderson, Terretti, Sharma, et al., 1991; M Levine, Anderson, Terretti, Steinberg, et al., 1991; Watson & Levine, 1989). Therefore, when professionals believe that unreported suspicions of abuse will result in child protection, preservation of the family, and progress in therapy, their tendency will be to not report. However, unreported suspected child abuse comes with its own perceived costs.

One set of potential costs of underreporting abuse is the legal consequences for professionals who do not report. Failure to report suspected child abuse is typically a misdemeanor that may carry a fine and possible jail term. In addition, professionals who do not report suspected abuse face potential civil suits and actions from licensing boards. Although these outcomes have become increasingly more publicized and likely in recent years, there is evidence that potential legal problems resulting from reporting decisions are of little concern to most professionals. For example, nearly one third of practicing psychologists indicate that avoiding legal problems is not important in their decisions to report suspected abuse, making it among the least influential factors in their reporting decisions (Brosig & Kalichman, 1992b). Fear of legal consequences for not reporting is usually ranked lowest among factors taken into consideration by professionals when deciding to report (C. A. Wilson & Gettinger, 1989). However, avoiding legal problems is more important to professionals who have consistently reported suspected abuse compared with those who have at some point not reported (Kalichman & Brosig, 1993). Thus, a subset of professionals may be motivated to report by their concerns about breaking the law. However, Kalichman and Brosig also found that concerns about legal problems that result from not reporting are of little importance relative to other situational factors. Therefore, the most severe personal consequence for failure to report is among the least important in professionals' decision making.

Another potential cost associated with not reporting suspected abuse is the possibility of continued or recurrent child abuse—a factor that weighs heavily against all other considerations. When professionals do not report suspected child maltreatment it is most likely because they believe the risks of future abuse are minimal. However, little is known about the accuracy and the limitations of professionals' estimations of a child's risks for abuse. In addition, treatment resistance among perpetrators and a high risk for recidivism further raise the costs for unreported suspected abuse.

## Benefits and Costs of Reporting

Many of the benefits of reporting child abuse are complimentary to the costs of not reporting. For example, reporting is often associated with the cessation of abuse. If nothing else, child protection system interventions can reduce risk for children with respect to further abuse. The prospect of stopping abuse is thus a strong motivation for professionals to report (Finlayson & Koocher, 1991). Kalichman and Craig (1991) found that 83% of licensed psychologists believed that reporting abuse had been helpful in stopping abuse. Because the intent of mandatory reporting laws is to protect children, stopping abuse should be the expected outcome of reporting, and it is clearly the most beneficial.

Reporting suspected child abuse also carries the additional benefit of not breaking the law, eliminating the possible legal retributions associated with not reporting. Professionals who report suspected abuse are also protected against legal repercussions when abuse is not substantiated. Reporting abuse can also cause families to face the abusive situation in therapy and work toward a resolution of family conflicts. As discussed in chapter 2, M. Levine and Doueck (1995) summarized the potential benefits of reporting to therapy. An additional and rarely discussed benefit of reporting is the potential for increases in public trust of professionals. In a broader sense, public perceptions of professional credibility can be enhanced when professionals adhere to the law (Kalichman, 1990). Professionals may also be perceived as caring and willing to risk getting involved throughout the reporting process (Watson & Levine, 1989). Finally, children can feel protected by professional involvement.

There are, however, potential costs associated with reporting suspected child abuse. Professionals who report suspected maltreatment bring an overburdened and underresourced child welfare system to intervene in abusive situations. Regardless of how efficiently a child protection investigation may proceed, it will introduce a new dimension to the ongoing process of treatment within which the suspicion occurred. Investigations may become yet another distraction for treatment-resistant families, acting as a means of avoiding family conflicts that contribute to abuse. The threat of removing a child from a home is another real potential cost of reporting. Of the physicians sampled by James, Womack, and Strauss (1978), one third believed that reporting would be harmful to families or that there are better ways to handle cases of child abuse without reporting. In addition, nearly one third of practicing psychologists believe that reporting is harmful to psychotherapy, and 13% believe reporting is harmful to families (Kalichman & Craig, 1991). As noted by the U.S. Advisory Board on Child Abuse and Neglect (1990),

> In many communities, timely investigation of reports of suspected child maltreatment does not occur. Failure to conduct timely investigations

|  | **Costs** | **Benefits** |
|---|---|---|
| **Reported** | Disrupting treatment<br>Relying on CPS to handle cases<br>Family must face CPS investigation | Stopping abuse<br>Upholding the law<br>Maintaining trust |
| **Not Reported** | Potential for further abuse<br>Liability for failure to report | Maintaining confidentiality<br>Protecting the child from system |

*Figure 3.1.* Costs and benefits of decisions to report suspected child abuse. CPS = child protective services.

and then to provide services when imminent risk is determined or a post-adjudication treatment plan is developed has serious repercussions. Professionals who serve children and families often fail to report suspected cases of child maltreatment because they have no confidence in the capacity of CPS [child protective services] to respond appropriately (p. xiii).

Figure 3.1 summarizes the costs and benefits for outcomes of reporting and not reporting suspected child abuse. Outcomes vary with different circumstances of suspected abuse and are weighed differently under various conditions. The relative weight of these potential outcomes has a direct effect on the decision criteria professionals use to report. The benefits of reporting suspected child abuse weigh heaviest when maltreatment is most likely occurring. On the other hand, when abuse is more questionable, the benefits of not reporting are greatest. It is along these lines that professionals appear to subjectively define what constitutes reasonable suspicions of child abuse and whether they should report.

## EVIDENCE-BASED MODELS: INDICATORS OF ABUSE AS REASONABLE SUSPICIONS

Evidence-based models of report decision making emphasize the factors that influence reporting. For example, Willis and Wells (1988) developed a model for understanding police officers' compliance with mandatory child abuse reporting laws. They differentiated between legal and extralegal factors related to reporting. Among legal factors relevant to police work, Willis and Wells included the severity of abuse as it is related to legal definitions of abuse, organizational policies, and individual officer's knowledge of reporting laws. Among extralegal factors were (a) characteristics of officers, such as length of service, education, attitudes, and marital and

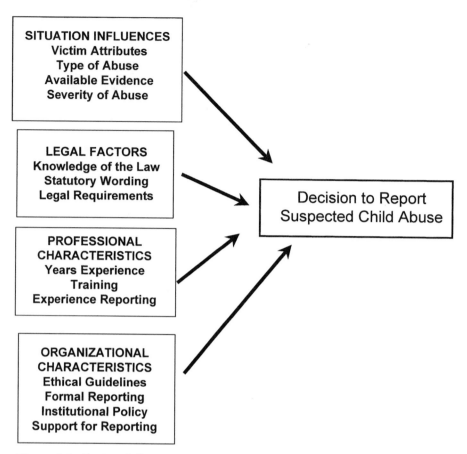

*Figure 3.2.* Factors influencing professionals' decisions to report child abuse.

parenting status; (b) situational factors, including victim and perpetrator social class; (c) organizational factors, including formal reporting procedures and institutional support for reporting; and (d) officer attitudes and experiences regarding reporting, including experiences with child welfare agencies and beliefs about the outcome of reporting. Willis and Wells framed their model on the premise that police frequently underreport suspected child maltreatment and confront reporting decisions from a crime-fighting perspective, one that focuses on severity of abuse and criminal intent.

Brosig and Kalichman (1992a) adapted Willis and Wells' (1988) model to structure practicing psychologists' reporting decisions. This model highlighted legal requirements, clinician characteristics, and situational factors related to reporting. Together, the models of Willis and Wells, and Brosig and Kalichman, encompass most of the factors identified in reporting decisions. An integration of the models proposed by Willis and Wells (1988) and Brosig and Kalichman (1992a) is presented in Figure 3.2. The components of the model represent major influences on reporting decisions, including characteristics of the situation, legal requirements to report, individual characteristics of the mandated reporter, and organizational structures that may facilitate or inhibit reporting. These models provide frameworks for summarizing factors that are associated with reporting decisions.

The uncertainty of when to report is the principal reason for failure to report suspected child abuse. Clear indicators of abuse usually include bruises, cuts, burns, and other signs of physical injury, as well as verbal disclosures of abuse made by children and adults. However, subtle signs and indirect communications can suggest abuse and cause confusion in determining when a report should be filed. Unfortunately, many signs associated with child maltreatment overlap with clinical conditions that do not involve abuse (Herrenkohl & Herrenkohl, 1979). A comprehensive review of the literature on the effects of child abuse is beyond the scope of this chapter (see Finkelhor, 1987; Kendall-Tackett, Williams, & Finkelhor, 1993; C. E. Walker, Bonner, & Kaufman, 1988; Wurtele & Miller-Perrin, 1992). Concerns about initial, or proximal, effects are paramount in evidence-based models, with less consideration to the long-term, or distal, effects of child abuse. Evidence-based models also set external criteria for reporting, usually relying on legal standards for defining when abuse occurs. Below are brief summaries of common proximal signs of child abuse that constitute the bases for reporting in evidence-based models.

### Sexual Abuse and Exploitation

In mental health settings, actions and situations clinically define sexual abuse. For example, Roane (1992) found that more than one third of boys who had been sexually abused had experienced oral–genital contact, anal penetration, or fondling, and that children, more often than not, experienced more than one act of sexual abuse. However, because mental health professionals do not perform physical examinations, they can become aware of such acts only through verbal disclosures. Sexually descriptive statements by children are the single best indicator of sexual maltreatment (Adams, 1991; Herbert, 1987). Still, only about one third of sexual abuse cases involve verbal accounts from children, and girls are more likely to disclose sexual abuse than boys (Herbert, 1987; Sebold, 1987). In fact, disclosures implicating sexual abuse of boys usually originate from a third party, such as a neighbor, friend, or nonabusive family member (Reinhart, 1987). There are many reasons for a lower rate of disclosure of sexual abuse among boys, including homophobia and misguided beliefs that boys cannot be victims of sexual abuse (Roane, 1992).[8] Thus, for both girls and boys,

---

[8]More than 90% of boys who are sexually abused are victimized by men (Finkelhor, 1984; Reinhart, 1987).

suspected sexual abuse often results from means other than verbal disclosures.

Despite their importance for confirming sexual abuse, physical signs of sexual abuse are less common than verbal statements (Conte, Sorenson, Fogarty, & Rosa, 1991). Most sexually abused children, including those who experience vaginal or anal penetration, are asymptomatic upon physical examination (Adams, Harper, & Knudson, 1992; Ellerstein & Canavan, 1980; Reinhart, 1987). Even in the case of medical examinations, using such techniques as the colposcope—an instrument that provides binocular magnification of the vaginal canal—physical signs are not definitive when they are present because there are no established standards for anatomical findings (Adams, Philips, & Ahmad, 1990). But even when physical signs of sexual abuse are present, they are hidden from nonmedical professionals. Rather, complaints of discomfort associated with physical trauma of sexual abuse should be enough to raise suspicions. Complaints of pain or irritation in the anal or genital region, painful urination, and bleeding are signs of sexual abuse, although these symptoms may be caused by other conditions (Adams, 1991). Medical examination is necessary, however, to determine the nature of such physical symptoms.

Because verbal disclosures of sexual abuse occur in a minority of cases and physical signs of sexual abuse are rarely identified by mental health professionals, suspicions of sexual abuse usually occur as a result of child behaviors and emotional reactions. Sexualized acting-out can be a salient indicator of sexual abuse and is among the most frequent symptoms exhibited by sexually abused children (Kendall-Tackett et al., 1993). In both boys and girls, such behaviors include excessive masturbation, masturbating in front of others, and sexually touching other children or adults (Adams, 1991; Browne & Finkelhor, 1986; Herbert, 1987; Roane, 1992). Friedrich et al. (1992) found that behaviors related to sexual self-stimulation, sexual aggression, gender role behaviors (i.e., cross-dressing), and behaviors that involve personal boundaries (i.e., touching and rubbing against others) occur with greater frequency among sexually abused children relative to nonabused children. Goldston, Turnquist, and Knutson (1989) found that 24% of sexually abused girls excessively masturbated, 17% masturbated in public, and 11% sexually experimented with peers. These rates were substantially higher than those among members of a nonsexually abused clinical sample. Sexual acting out is more likely after longer periods of abuse and therefore may not be apparent in cases involving few episodes of abuse (Roane, 1992). Sexually acting out is not, however, specific to sexually abused children (Herbert, 1987), and sexually abused children are likely to act out in nonsexual ways (Browne & Finkelhor, 1986; Kendall-Tackett et al., 1993). Combinations of behavioral signs have not, therefore, been demonstrated as valid indicators of child sexual abuse (M. Levine & Battistoni, 1991).

There have been a number of attempts to identify valid emotional responses to sexual abuse. Among some of the more common findings are high rates of depressive symptoms in sexual abuse victims (Adams, 1991; Browne & Finkelhor, 1986; Goldston et al., 1989; Kendall-Tackett et al., 1993). In addition, symptoms of anxiety, withdrawal, shyness, and sleep disturbance are frequently observed in victims of sexual abuse (Adams, 1991; Browne & Finkelhor, 1986; Herbert, 1987). Extreme fearfulness is also common in sexually abused children, with as many as 83% of victims presenting fearful responses across a variety of situations (Browne & Finkelhor, 1986). Nightmares and diffuse symptoms of anxiety are also common to survivors of sexual abuse (Krugman, 1990; Mannarino & Cohen, 1986). The affective–emotional responsiveness of sexual abuse victims tends to be restricted in range or flat in tone as a result of trauma (Kendall-Tackett et al., 1993). Sexually abused children are also described as having a low sense of self-esteem, although not necessarily to a greater degree than nonabused children (Browne & Finkelhor, 1986; Kendall-Tackett et al., 1993). Again, clinically distressed children who have not been sexually abused present a similar range of emotional disturbances.

Symptoms of sexual abuse are difficult to interpret because they overlap with symptoms of living in dysfunctional but nonabusive families. Children's reactions to parental conflict, marital violence, separation, and divorce resemble many of the signs of distress described in sexually abused children (Graham-Bermann, 1998; Margolin, 1998). This is particularly true of children in families involved in custody disputes (Eastman & Moran, 1991; Paradise, Rostain, & Nathanson, 1988; Weissman, 1991). Finkelhor (1987) discussed a number of family constellations common to families of child sexual abuse, such as having only one biological parent in the home, parents who use punitive discipline or are physically abusive, and children who believe their parents are unhappy. In addition, more than 40% of sexually abusive families have violent conflicts between parents. Thus, most of the vague signs of anxiety and depression, in the absence of corroborating indicators, are unlikely to lead to strong suspicions of sexual abuse. Finally, the large number of children who have been sexually abused who do not present any signs of abuse reminds us that an absence of indicators cannot rule out the occurrence of sexual abuse (Gomes-Schwartz, Horowitz, & Cardarelli, 1990).

Definitions of sexual abuse have also been broadened to include a range of exploitative relationships that adults may have with children. For example, child pornography is often included under definitions of sexual abuse. The use of the Internet to engage children in sexual communications and to transmit child pornographic material is also included in sexual abuse definitions. The United States Customs Service has declared the following statement in response to child sexual exploitation and child pornography over the Internet:

We are looking for offenders that possess, trade, distribute and/or produce pictures that visually depict a minor engaging in sexually explicit conduct. Please do not forward these suspected child pornography pictures/images to us as the transmission and/or forwarding of child pornography images is a violation of U.S. Law. Instead, please document the picture's description for us and anything else pertaining to the source (i.e., E-mail address, Internet protocol address, website URL, name and location of chat room, etc). We only investigate based on the limits of the law and the legal definitions of child pornography violations.

Similarly, states are passing Internet legislation as part of child protection initiatives (e.g., http://www.treas.gov). Legal responses are likely to continue to broaden as technology advances and predators gain increased access to children.

**Physical Abuse**

In contrast to sexual abuse, physical abuse usually involves physical signs specific to the abuse. The most common physical sign of child abuse is soft-tissue damage, specifically bruises and welts. Burns and scalds are less common, occurring in less than 10% of abuse cases (Haughton, 1977). Bone fractures and internal injuries are also common in physical abuse of younger children, but these injuries are seen more often in emergency rooms than they are observed by mental health professionals. Finally, shaken baby syndrome is the cause of death in the majority of nonaccidental infant fatalities (Duhaime et al., 1998). Because injuries may not always be apparent, verbal disclosures also play an important role in suspected physical abuse.

As was the case with sexual abuse, acting-out behaviors can be indicators of physical abuse. However, the behaviors acted out are more likely to involve acts of violence, particularly hitting other children, including peers and siblings (Ammerman, Cassisi, Hersen, & Van Hasselt, 1986; Hoffman-Plotkin & Twentyman, 1984). Physically abused children also tend to display more disruptive behaviors than other children, although not necessarily more so than children from nonabused but distressed families (Gelardo & Sanford, 1987). Longer term signs of physical abuse also point toward aggressive behavior. Engfer and Schneewind (1982) found a modest but significant pattern of physical abuse in the development of conduct disorder. Similarly, the rate of physical abuse histories in juvenile delinquents is substantially higher than among nondelinquent children (Lewis, Shanok, Pincus, & Glaser, 1979). Thus, as was the case in sexual abuse, acting out may be indicative of physical abuse. Aggressive acts, however, are not specifically associated with physical abuse victims.

Emotional responses associated with physical abuse can also raise suspicions of maltreatment. For example, physically abused children tend to present signs of social maladjustment across developmental periods. Maltreated infants tend to be unattached to their parents and abused children are generally less prosocial than their nonabused peers (Ammerman et al., 1986). Physically abused children hold negative self-perceptions and low self-regard, although not necessarily lower than other children receiving clinical services (Oates, Forrest, & Peacock, 1985). It is also common for physically abused children to experience somatic symptoms of anxiety and in some cases symptoms that resemble posttraumatic stress disorder (A. H. Green, 1983). Intellectual impairment and academic deficits are also frequent characteristics of physically maltreated children, and often result from damage to the central nervous system caused by the abuse. However, the direction of these relationships has not been demonstrated, so it is possible that cognitive deficits exist before the occurrence of abuse (Ammerman et al., 1986; Gelardo & Sanford, 1987).

## Neglect

Unfortunately, there is little information available regarding the identifiable signs of child neglect independent of physical abuse. Neglect in infancy may result in nonorganic failure to thrive (Gelardo & Sanford, 1987). However, the characteristics of neglect in later childhood are less defined. Malnutrition, lack of adequate clothing, poor hygiene, inadequate health care, unsafe living conditions, and periods of being left without supervision are all circumstances regarded as child neglect (C. E. Walker et al., 1988). Still, these circumstances must be viewed in the context of cultural expectations and values, and the inextricable relationship between neglect and poverty.

Social withdrawal characterizes the behavior of neglected children (Hoffman-Plotkin & Twentyman, 1984). Children who suffer neglect are also likely to present internalized emotional symptoms as well, such as anxiety and depression (Gelardo & Sanford, 1987). Again, these symptoms are common in nonneglected children who are experiencing other clinical problems. Thus, suspicions of neglect with sufficient evidence for reporting requires awareness of the child's life circumstances and parental behaviors, usually through observation, home visits, or the child's description of their living situation (Meriwether, 1986).

## Psychological–Emotional Abuse

Among the different types of child abuse, emotional maltreatment is the vaguest and most poorly defined (Garbarino, Guttman, & Seeley, 1986; Melton & Corson, 1987). Much of the confusion about psychological–

emotional abuse stems from the poor reliability of definitions and the variable signs of abuse across different circumstances and developmental periods (Melton & Corson, 1987; Melton & Davidson, 1987). Brassard and Gelardo (1987) noted seven conditions of emotional abuse, five of which were also discussed by Garbarino (1987): (a) *Rejecting*—treating a child in a secondary fashion, or refusing to respond to a child's needs; (b) *degrading*—name calling and public humiliation; (c) *terrorizing*—threatening with harm, or forcing the child to witness violent acts; (d) *isolating*—locking a child away in closets or rooms alone, or denying him or her access to relationships; (e) *corrupting*—teaching or encouraging antisocial acts or beliefs, such as aggression or substance abuse; (f) *exploiting*—using for self-gain at the child's expense; and (g) *denying emotional responsiveness*—ignoring a child's initiatives and needs for affection and emotional contact. Likewise, Melton and Davidson (1987) suggested that the following factors contribute to emotional abuse: rejection, intimidation, humiliation, hostile or violent acts that produce fear or guilt, lack of nurturance, lack of acceptance, and damage to psychological and intellectual capacity. Definitions of emotional abuse can also include isolation.

Baily and Baily (1986) empirically defined emotional maltreatment on the basis of expert responses to a series of brief vignettes depicting a spectrum of potentially abusive situations. Examples included when the parent shows no attachment to the child and fails to provide nurturance; exposes the child to maladaptive and harmful influences; confuses the child's sexual identity; does not permit the child autonomy or independent learning; and regularly denigrates and ridicules the child, stating, without foundation, that he or she reminds everyone of a person who is totally offensive and unacceptable to the family. These descriptions move us closer to an operational definition of emotional abuse.

Also falling within the scope of emotional abuse is the witnessing of domestic violence. Children exposed to family conflict experience an array of symptoms that are indistinguishable from other sources of emotional abuse. These include attention deficits, externalizing and internalizing behavioral problems, symptoms of anxiety, difficulties in school, and social incompetence (Holden, Geffner, & Jouriles, 1998). Children who witness spousal abuse show both short-term and long-term adverse effects. Witnessing greater degrees of violence results in increased trauma for the child (Margolin, 1998).

Although the circumstances of emotional abuse are now better understood, there is little information concerning the signs of emotional abuse exhibited by children. Behaviors that are self-destructive, aggressive, or incorrigible may be taken as signs of emotional abuse (Melton & Davidson, 1987). Thus, similar to physical neglect, when suspicions of emotional maltreatment occur, they have probably resulted from verbal disclosures of the child's circumstances or from direct observations of emotional abuse.

To summarize, physical signs and direct verbal disclosures of abuse, although not specified by law, would invariably constitute reasonable suspicions of child abuse and provide ample evidence for reporting. Behaviors, on the other hand, overlap substantially with other, nonabusive clinical problems commonly seen in children. Although sexual and aggressive acting out may be indicative of child abuse, children who exhibit these problems are not always maltreated. Exhibit 3.1 presents behaviors that are commonly thought of as indicators of abuse but that overlap considerably with each other and with non–abuse-related clinical problems. However, child behavior problems that form the basis for reporting suspected child abuse could lead to substantiated cases. For example, Giovannoni (1989a) found that in 20% of substantiated cases of child sexual abuse, reporting was initiated by behavioral problems. Generalized and diffuse symptoms of depression and anxiety result in the highest rates of false identifications in the absence of other signs of abuse. Figure 3.3 presents a dimensional representation of maltreatment indicators as they may be related to each other in the context of reporting.

Given the chronic psychological sequelae of child abuse, it is likely that child–victims respond to abuse and neglect with some degree of trauma (Gelinas, 1983; A. H. Green, 1983). In this sense, symptoms of post-traumatic stress disorder (PTSD) may provide a unifying construct for symptoms of abuse, including nightmares, somatic anxiety, fearfulness, and withdrawal. Although abused children may not be diagnosed with PTSD, symptoms of the disorder suggest abuse in the absence of alternative explanations. Family history and social context contribute to the interpretation of nonspecific signs of abuse. For example, children in the midst of custody battles should be expected to present signs of trauma.

Reporting suspected abuse is similar to other types of diagnostic decisions. Although one third of mandated reporters indicated their leaving suspected child maltreatment unreported, Muehleman and Kimmons (1981) proposed that most professionals will immediately report when they believe circumstances warrant it. Muehleman and Kimmons suggested that professionals surpass a critical degree of suspicion, or a reporting threshold, prior to reporting. Others have made similar observations regarding the accumulation of perceptions and judgments to trigger reporting decisions (Herzberger, 1988; Wells, 1988). Support for a threshold model of reporting decisions is also found in experimental vignette studies that show cumulative effects of salient indicators of abuse on reporting tendencies (Brosig & Kalichman, 1992a; Kalichman et al., 1989). Thus, as evidence of abuse increases, professionals become more inclined to report, as would be expected when surpassing a reporting threshold.

## EXHIBIT 3.1
### Behaviors Often Considered Indicative of Child Abuse

#### Sexual Abuse

Reluctance to change clothes in front of others
Withdrawal
Unusual sexual behavior and/or knowledge beyond developmental expectation
Poor peer relationships
Avoidance or seeking out of adults
Manipulation
Self-consciousness
Problems with authority and rules
Eating disorders
Self-mutilation
Obsessive cleanliness
Use of alcohol and/or other drugs
Delinquent behavior, such as running away from home
Extreme compliance or defiance
Fearfulness or anxiousness
Suicidal
Promiscuity
Engagement in fantasy or infantile behavior
Unwillingness to participate in sports acitvities
Academic problems
Enuresis

#### Physical Abuse

Wariness of adults
Extreme aggression or withdrawal
Dependent or indiscriminate attach-ments
Discomfort when other children cry
Drastic behavior change when not with parents or caregiver
Manipulation
Poor self-concept
Delinquent behavior, such as running away from home
Use of alcohol and/or other drugs
Self-mutilation
Fear of parents, of going home
Overprotection of or overresponsibility for parents
Suicidal gestures and/or attempts
Behavioral problems at school

#### Emotional Abuse

Overeagerness to please
Dependence on adult contact
Understanding of abuse as being warranted
Changes in behavior
Excessive anxiety
Depression
Unwillingness to discuss problems
Aggressive or bizarre behavior
Withdrawal
Apathy
Passivity
Unprovoked fits of yelling or scream-ing
Inconsistent behavior at home and school
Running away from home
Suicidal gestures and/or attempts sui-cide
Low self-esteem
Inability to sustain relationships
Unrealistic goal setting
Impatience
Inability to communicate or express his or her feelings, needs, or de-sires
Sabotage of his or her chances of success
Lack of self-confidence
Self-depreciation or negative self-image

# THRESHOLD MODELS

According to evidence-based models, reporting decisions occur in response to indicators of child abuse and evidence that varies across dif-

| | Low Specificity | Moderate Specificity | High Specificity |
|---|---|---|---|
| Sexual Abuse | Anxiety Depression Low self-esteem Social maladjustment | Sexual acting out | Complaints of Genital or Anal Discomfort Detailed Verbal Account |
| Physical Abuse | Anxiety Depression Low self-esteem Social maladjustment | Aggressive acting out | Bruises, Welts, Burns Verbal Account of Abuse |
| Neglect | Anxiety Depression Low self-esteem Social maladjustment | Social withdrawal | Inadequate clothing Poor hygiene Leaving child unsupervised Malnutrition Failure to provide medical care |
| Emotional Abuse | Anxiety Depression Low self-esteem Social maladjustment | Verbal Account of Humiliation Rejection Degradation Terrorizing | Observation of Humiliation, Rejection, Degradation, Terrorizing |

| Lenient Criteria | Strict Criteria |
|---|---|
| Low ReportingThreshold | High ReportingThreshold |
| High False Detection Rate | High Correct Detection Rate |

*Figure 3.3.* Dimensional representation of indicators of abuse in relation to the context of report decision making.

ferent types of abuse (Crenshaw, Crenshaw, & Lichtenberg, 1995). Threshold models go beyond evidence-based models by recognizing a continuum of abuse indicators. Threshold models also differ from evidence-based models because they stress the importance of subjective internalized standards for determining when to report. Subtle signs of abuse may be slightly suggestive, whereas more salient indicators of abuse offer stronger suspicions or knowledge of abuse. In threshold models, a continuum of abuse indicators is an example of a subjectively scaled probability estimate (Swets, 1992). In other words, indicators of child abuse are cumulatively evaluated through observation and perhaps through formal assessment measures. Professionals must rely on observations to identify abuse because of the lack of validated assessment tools relevant to detecting child abuse. Therefore, direct and skilled observations of children and families are the best available methods of detecting indicators of child abuse that ultimately compose a continuum of reporting criteria, or thresholds.

## Empirical Support for Threshold Models

Finlayson and Koocher (1991) have provided some of the strongest support for reporting threshold models. In their study of child psychologists they showed that clinical signs specific to sexual abuse were significantly more likely to be reported than diffuse and nonspecific signs. Finlayson and Koocher demonstrated incremental increases in reporting that directly reflected signs of sexual abuse. The findings demonstrated that clinicians view suspicions of abuse along a continuum, with a "mere hunch" representing one end and "absolute knowledge" representing the other. This innovative study led Finlayson and Koocher to conclude that reporting decisions are complicated by the need for professionals to determine what constitutes a reporting threshold, or a level of reportable suspicion.

A formal analysis of reporting decisions requires quantifying several parameters, including an index of abuse indicators, values for the costs of an incorrect report, benefits of a correct report, and the base rate of abused children in a given setting (Swets, 1992). Unfortunately, our understanding of child abuse is not at a point where formal analyses are feasible. The costs and benefits of correct and incorrect reports are difficult to determine, and vary according to local resources, quality of protective services, and the context within which abuse is suspected. Although a formal analysis of reporting decisions is not possible, reporting accuracy may be improved to the extent that the process of report decision making is made explicit (Swets, 1992). According to threshold models, reporting, like other diagnostic decisions, involves setting a decision criteria, evaluating the probability of outcomes, and evaluating the costs and benefits of decision outcomes.

Several lines of evidence show that professionals are more likely to report after they have observed a combination of child abuse indicators. For example, Kalichman et al. (1988) found that 89% of mental health professionals who chose not to report a case of suspected abuse stated that their lack of confidence that abuse was occurring was the most important factor in their decisions to report. Certainty in abuse is also a reliable predictor of decisions to report among mandated reporters in Canada (Beck & Ogloff, 1995). Other studies have also found that reporting abuse is closely associated with available evidence for abuse (Camblin & Prout, 1983; Finlayson & Koocher, 1991; Watson & Levine, 1989). Overall, confidence in the occurence of abuse is closely associated with tendencies to report (Kalichman & Craig, 1991; Saulsbury & Campbell, 1985), and confidence is determined by observed indicators of abuse. Figures 3.4 and 3.5 illustrate the relationship among indicators of abuse, levels of suspicion, and reporting thresholds for both physical and sexual abuse, respectively.[9]

Experimental analog studies (Brosig & Kalichman, 1992a) have demonstrated several factors that influence reporting decisions. Studies that present mandated reporters with case scenarios and ask them to respond

---

[9] This discussion is limited to signs of abuse presented by children. Although the appearance and behavior of adults-perpetrators can cause suspicions, such suspicions are usually less ambiguous because they tend to be based on verbal disclosures. In addition, few, if any, reliable characteristics of abusive adults are known (Giovannoni, 1989b).

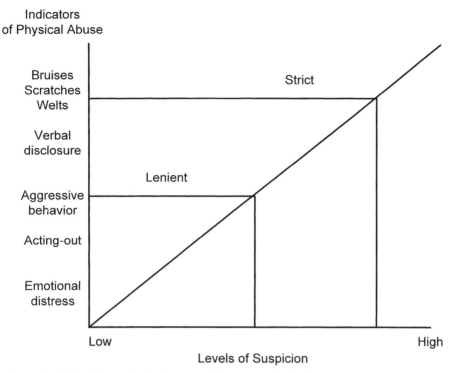

*Figure 3.4.* Decision criteria for reporting suspected physical abuse as a function of levels of suspicion and indicators of abuse.

with their inclination to report have found that approximately one third of professionals decline to report the depicted abuse. Reporting in these studies varies depending on an array of manipulated factors. Although limited with respect to external validity, these studies illustrate the relative salience of various situations and indicators of child abuse. The sections below briefly review the findings from experimental vignette studies as they relate to threshold models of reporting decisions.

## Characteristics of Abuse

Vignette studies have consistently shown that professionals are more inclined to report specific and salient indicators of abuse than ambiguous clinical symptoms. Signs of physical abuse, such as bruises or marks, rather than a child's behavior, significantly increase tendencies to report. In one study of practicing psychologists, 97% of participants indicated that they would report a child who had visible bruises that they believed to be caused by abuse (Kalichman & Craig, 1991). These results were strikingly different from those obtained in other vignette studies that presented less specific signs of abuse. Thus, as suggested by Muehleman and Kimmons (1981),

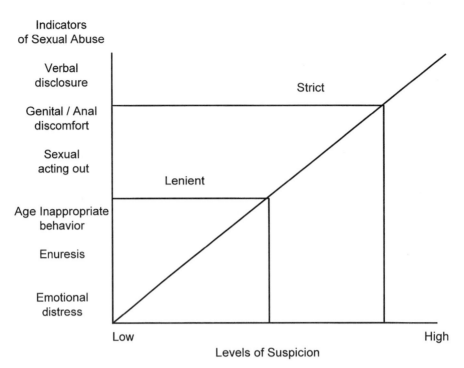

*Figure 3.5.* Decision criteria for reporting suspected sexual abuse as a function of levels of suspicion and indicators of abuse.

under some conditions, such as when abuse seems most probable, almost all professionals will report. Severe signs of abuse are also most likely to be reported (S. L. Green & Hansen, 1989; Zellman, 1990).

Verbal disclosures are more influential than other indicators of abuse. The majority of professionals say they will report when a child states that he or she has been physically or sexually abused. One study showed that psychologists tend to report when there is a direct communication alleging sexual abuse. Ninety-seven percent of participants indicated that they would report a hypothetical case when there was a verbal statement of abuse, as compared with only 14% when indicators of sexual abuse were less direct (Finlayson & Koocher, 1991). Verbal statements indicative of abuse influence the decision to report because they cannot be attributed to other problems and do not allow room for competing explanations (Finlayson & Koocher, 1991).

In a clinically derived model of sexual abuse, Sink (1988) categorically defined verbal disclosures as the most direct communication of sexual abuse, and declared disclosures as a stronger indicator than sexualized play, symptoms of posttraumatic stress, enuresis/encopresis, and other signs of generalized emotional distress. Similar to when a child speaks of abuse, reporting tendencies increase when an adult verbally discloses having abused a child (Kalichman & Brosig, 1992a; Zellman, 1992). Reporting is also likely in response to a third party's disclosures, such as when a non-abusive parent or a friend of the abused child provides information to a mandated reporter (Kalichman et al., 1988).

Although verbal disclosures and direct communications undeniably implicate abuse, verbal statements of abuse occur less frequently in professional settings than do more subtle and indirect signs of child abuse. The cognitive and emotional capacities of people to label abusive situations are complex and vary across developmental periods (Reppucci & Haugaard, 1989). Children, for example, are most likely to refuse to discuss abuse when questioned (Pierce & Pierce, 1985). A child who later recants his or her allegations further complicates verbal disclosures. Professionals clearly reduce their tendencies to report when a child withdraws statements of abuse (Zellman, 1992; Zellman & Antler, 1990), despite the fact that it is common for abused children to do so. In one study, Attias and Goodwin (1985) showed that nearly one third of mandated reporters would not report after a child recanted a statement of being sexually abused, despite high substantiation rates of recanted allegations (D. P. H. Jones & McGraw, 1987). Professionals, therefore, rely on some assurance that their report of abuse will be independently verified upon investigation.

In practice, suspected child abuse arises in the context of more complicated circumstances rather than any single factor. The effect of abuse indicators on reporting decisions varies with the age of the child (Kalichman & Craig, 1991; Kalichman & Brosig, 1992; USDHHS, 1988). Younger children are more likely to be reported than older children (Jackson & Nuttall, 1993; Kennel & Agresti, 1995). This may be attributed to the fact that caseworkers devote a greater amount of attention to younger children in child protective services (Freeman, Levine, & Doueck, 1996).

Family ethnicity and social class have also been shown to influence reporting (Newberger, 1983). In a study of pediatricians, Turbett and O'Toole (cited in Giovannoni, 1989b) found that scenarios in which African American children suffered severe injuries were almost twice as likely to be considered abused when compared with White children with severe injuries. Similar results were found for children from low-income families compared with higher income families, suggesting that sociocultural biases may directly affect reporting decisions. Comorbidity of parental mental health problems can also play a role in reports of suspected abuse. Wolock and Magura (1996) found that parents were much more likely to be reported repeatedly for suspected abuse if they were substance abusers. Specific types of abuse are also differentially reported (Beck & Ogloff, 1995; Nightingale & Walker, 1986; USDHHS, 1988; Wilson & Gettinger, 1989; Zellman, 1990). Sexual and physical abuse are reported more often than emotional abuse or educational neglect is reported.

## Legal Considerations

Knowledge, understanding, and interpretations of reporting laws affect reporting thresholds (Muehleman & Kimmons, 1981). Mandated reporters' interpretation of the law creates a context for judging specific characteristics of abuse. When confronted with a child suspected of being abused, mandatory reporting laws appear to sensitize reporters enough to lower their reporting thresholds and report more often (Kalichman & Brosig, 1992). On the other hand, when an adult is suspected of being abusive, the law can either decrease or increase reporting thresholds, depending on its standards. Statutory language of mandatory reporting laws can therefore form part of the context affecting report decision-making thresholds.

To summarize, a continuum of abuse indicators influences professionals' suspicions, thereby constituting the dimension along which reporting decisions are made. The point at which indicators of child abuse are interpreted as reasonable suspicions of abuse is when reporting is most likely triggered. The concept of a reporting threshold is useful in explaining individual differences in reporting suspected abuse. Professionals are likely to use a range of report decision criteria. A closer examination of report decision criteria further illustrates individual variations in reporting.

## Lenient Decision Criteria—Low Thresholds

When professionals require only a minimal level of suspicion to report, they have exercised lenient decision criteria, and illustrate a low reporting threshold. Children with unexplained changes in behavior and children who appear emotionally distressed, or present with unexplained anxiety and somatic disturbances, are examples of such cases. For instance, one experimental study presented practicing psychologists with the following case vignette:

> Imagine yourself as a therapist in the following situation:
> You have been working with a 7 year old girl, Lynn, for two sessions. Her school guidance counselor who has noted that Lynn has been lying to her teachers, fighting with her peers, and not completing her homework assignments referred her to you. Her counselor also indicates that one of Lynn's girl friends told her that Lynn's step-father [sic] loses his temper at home and hits Lynn. During the first two sessions, your focus has been on evaluating Lynn's problems and developing goals for therapy. Lynn has been somewhat shy and withdrawn in your sessions, which has made rapport building slow. Despite this, you feel you are beginning to gain Lynn's trust.
> At the start of your third session you notice that Lynn seems more tired than usual and her appearance is disheveled. When you ask her how she's feeling, she breaks down crying and refuses to talk with you

further. After ending this session, you reflect back on the case and decide to phone her parents for a family session, but there is no answer at home. (Brosig & Kalichman, 1992b, pp. 8–9)

In a similar study regarding sexual abuse, Finlayson and Koocher (1991) presented the following scenario with a 7-year-old girl:

During the child interview, Anne appears listless, and sad. She seems disinterested in many toys in your office. Anne is polite and compliant. She offers brief responses to your questions about school, and home. You ask Anne about her stomach pain, and she responds, "It feels like someone is stabbing me." You ask her if she has any worries or concerns, and she states, "I worry about what will happen to my sister if I die." You ask Anne to tell you more about that, and she states, "I'm the only one who can take care of my sister." She becomes quiet and withdrawn and you are unable to elicit further information from her. (pp. 466–467)

Although the symptoms presented in these two cases may indicate abuse, they may also be attributed to circumstances unrelated to abuse. This would be the most likely explanation for not reporting these cases. Although signs of abuse that result in reasonable suspicions are required to be reported, studies have consistently shown that professionals are unlikely to report vague circumstances suggestive of abuse (Brosig & Kalichman, 1992a; Finlayson & Koocher, 1991).

The mandatory reporting system, by design, accepts a high false-positive rate to detect a maximum number of abused children. The objective of the reporting system is to cast a wide net to capture as many cases of abuse as possible (Besharov, 1986a, 1990; Hutchison, 1993). Language such as "mandatory reporting of reasonable suspicions of child abuse" helps to ensure that there will be a high proportion of actual cases within a large number of suspicions. Requiring the reporting of subtle signs of abuse aims toward early intervention and the possibility of minimizing later abuse and limiting the potential for more intrusive state responses (Bourne & Newberger, 1977). Low reporting thresholds also result in fewer false rejections—cases where abuse is actually occurring, but goes unreported. Thus, lenient criteria are sensitive to detecting abuse, but are not specific to cases of abuse. Low reporting thresholds result in a proportion of reported cases where abuse is not occurring, such as those when a child has been accidentally injured or is merely emotionally distressed.

Finkelhor (1990) noted that the mandatory reporting system is similar to other social structures that weigh the benefits of correct detection against costs associated with incorrect decisions. Finkelhor discussed due process in the criminal justice system as a social structure analogous to child protection. In the case of the criminal justice system, rates of reported crimes are higher than are the number of arrests, which are higher than the number of criminal convictions. This situation is similar to the ratio of reported-to-substantiated cases of child abuse. Finkelhor noted that the conviction rate of 55% for all violent crimes approximates the substantiation rate for child abuse. He also pointed to the stringent standards of the child welfare system to explain low rates of substantiation. It is unlikely that child abuse will be substantiated in a family where maltreatment has not occurred, because substantiation relies on evidence. In fact, errors are more likely to occur in the opposite direction: failing to validate the occurrence of abuse. High rates of reporting are partially attributable to broad language in reporting laws. Finkelhor explained in detail the causal relationship between social tolerance for high rates of arrests to ensure public safety and the rationale for lenient child abuse reporting criteria prescribed by law.

Indicators of abuse are different from, although not independent of, the severity of abuse. Therefore, reporting occurs in response to both serious and less serious cases of child abuse. Few states have statutes that limit reporting to serious child abuse (Daro & McCurdy, 1992). Bourne and Newberger (1977) described the rationale for required reporting of nonserious abuse:

> The family situation in which a child suffers non-serious harm is not only not "ideal," it is quite oppressive, albeit without danger to life and limb of the child. The child will consistently suffer specific, demonstrable physical or emotional harm, even though such harm does not . . . present a "substantial risk that the child will immanently [sic] suffer" such severe harm. (p. 674)

From this perspective, suspicions of child abuse are serious enough to surpass lenient reporting thresholds.

The greatest concern with setting low reporting thresholds is the costs of false-positive reports. There are several costs associated with false positives, including the utilization of scarce child protective service resources for investigations that may otherwise be used for services. Reporting can burden underresourced child protection systems and therefore actually do more harm than good (Besharov, 1986a).

When reports are made in the context of treatment, many professionals believe that services are disrupted as a result of the reporting. In addition, families may experience abuse investigations as intrusive (Besharov, 1986a; Meriwether, 1986; Newman, 1987). There are many anecdotal accounts of families who have experienced child abuse investigations as traumatic (Besharov, 1990; Faller, 1985). According to Besharov (1978),

> A report of known or suspected child abuse or neglect sets in motion an unavoidably stressful investigation which may lead to the removal of a child from his home and the stigmatization of a family within its community. The benign purposes and rehabilitative services of child

protective agencies do not prevent them from being unpleasant and sometimes destructive—though well meaning—coercive intrusions into family life. (p. 461)

There is, however, mixed evidence to support the idea that reporting is always an adverse process. In fact, some evidence exists to support just the opposite. For example, as discussed earlier, a survey of family reactions to social service agency involvement following reported suspected child abuse suggested that investigations are not intrusive to families and can be generally positive (Fryer, Bross, Krugman, Denson, & Baird, 1990). False positives are likely to be tolerated when there are few negative effects of reporting.

Of course, low reporting thresholds also result in fewer overlooked victims of child abuse. Failure to detect abuse or neglect when it has actually occurred risks continued abuse, further family deterioration, and failure to protect children. Low reporting thresholds reduce the high costs associated with unidentified child abuse.

To summarize, lenient decision criteria, or low reporting thresholds, are based on the rationale of maximizing the detection of child abuse. This perspective is related to the fail-safe approach associated with engineering decisions that relies on the premise that when abuse is present, the probability is very high that it will be detected. The cost of a missed case of abuse, including the possibility of continued abuse, is weighed heavily against reporting a case in which abuse is not substantiated. Low thresholds accept the costs of overreporting in order to minimize underreporting.

## Strict Decision Criteria–High Thresholds

Narrow interpretations of legal language such as "reasonable suspicion of abuse" set the standard for strict reporting criteria. As previously discussed, mandated reporters tend to report when there are salient signs of child abuse. Two case examples of salient signs of abuse that would be reportable even under the strictest criteria are presented in vignettes used in research. In both cases, the majority of professionals indicated that they would report. Kalichman and Craig (1991) provided the first example:

Imagine yourself as a therapist in the following situation. You have been working with a 7 year old girl, Kim, for two sessions. Her school's principal[,] who became aware that Kim was lying to teachers, becoming socially withdrawn and getting into fights[,] referred her to you. In addition, one of Kim's friends had told a teacher that Kim was being physically abused at home.

During your first two sessions with Kim, she remained somewhat shy and withdrawn, which made rapport building slow. However, during your third session you notice that Kim has a bruise on the left side of her face and one on her left arm. When you ask her about the bruises, she breaks down crying and refuses to talk with you any further. After this session, you decide to call Kim's parents and ask them to come in for a family session. After answering the phone and listening to your explanation for the request to come in, Kim's step-father [sic] states that he believes that the problem is with Kim and refuses to come in for the session. (p. 85)

Finlayson and Koocher (1991) used a scenario in their study of professionals' reporting of suspected sexual abuse that led to similar findings. The following case of a 7-year-old girl was presented to suggest salient signs of sexual abuse:

> During the child interview, Brenda is nervous and shy. You ask Brenda about what is worrying her, and she tells you, "I can't tell you." You ask her if she can show you in a drawing. She proceeds to draw a picture that appears to be two naked people. You ask Brenda to tell you about the picture and she says, "He's hurting her." You ask her to tell you more and she says "He's peeing on her." You ask her to identify the characters in the picture and she states, "That's my daddy and that's me, and sometimes my daddy pees on me." She proceeds to cry and is unwilling to talk anymore. (p. 466)

Psychologists interpret reasonable suspicions of abuse as a hierarchy of indicators of abuse. Kalichman and Brosig (1993) showed that the most common interpretations of reasonable suspicions of abuse encompassed verbal disclosures of abuse or apparent physical signs, such as bruises. Behavioral indicators are far less frequent bases for reporting reasonable suspicions of abuse, and only 14% of psychologists indicated that "a suspicion alone" is equivalent to a "reasonable suspicion." These findings support Besharov's (1990) assertion that "behavioral indicators are not, in themselves, grounds for a report" (p. 141). Professionals therefore interpret a narrow range of signs, symptoms, and circumstances as reasonable suspicions of child abuse. These findings support Finlayson and Koocher's (1991) observation that professional and legal standards for reasonable suspicion are not one and the same. It appears that the term "reasonable" exerts influence over professionals' interpretations of legal standards for reporting.

Professionals with a history of reporting suspected child abuse are less likely to believe that subjective suspicions alone constitute reasonable suspicions and are less likely to report (Kalichman & Brosig, 1993; Kennel & Agresti, 1995). This finding shows that professionals who have not reported abuse set more stringent standards for defining reportable suspicions. Thus, individual differences in professionals' interpretations of what constitutes reasonable suspicions partially determine the degree to which they adhere to mandatory reporting laws.

Advocates for setting stricter reporting criteria emphasize the potential adverse consequences of overreporting. For example, high rates of unsubstantiated reports that result from low thresholds can overburden the child protection system and potentially interfere with the efforts of child protective services (Besharov, 1986a, 1990; Eckenrode et al., 1988). In addition, unnecessary investigations may have negative consequences for children and families (Newberger, 1983), and reporting may interfere with the treatment of perpetrators (Berlin et al., 1991; Weinstock & Weinstock, 1989). Establishing higher thresholds for reporting minimizes the potential for adverse outcomes by simultaneously lowering rates of reporting and decreasing the number of false-positive cases.

To balance the low threshold for initiating a report of suspected abuse, the child protection system sets higher thresholds for investigating reports. Case screening is based on the rationale that there are reports that do not warrant or allow for investigation. For example, 25% of child protection agencies screen out cases with incomplete information, 43% screen cases where the perpetrator is not named, and 50% require details concerning acts of abuse (Wells et al., 1989). Thus, the less specific the information contained in a report, the less likely it will be investigated (Wells, Downing, & Fluke, 1991). High reporting thresholds are likely to result in reports that meet screening criteria because they are more likely to include details regarding evidence of child abuse. In this sense, high thresholds reduce

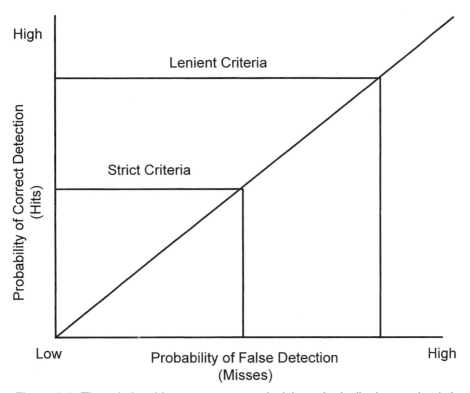

*Figure 3.6.* The relationships among report decision criteria (lenient and strict) and probable outcomes (hits and misses).

burdens placed on the child protection system. The potential cost of high thresholds, however, is a greater number of false negatives, or missed cases of child abuse.

High thresholds are primarily set to minimize the number of false positives. By reporting only cases with salient evidence of child abuse, professionals will report fewer cases where abuse has not occurred. Under high thresholds, mandated reporters can have greater confidence that their report will be investigated and substantiated. However, high reporting thresholds also result in higher rates of incorrect rejections, or abuse that is not reported.

In summary, strict criteria, or high reporting thresholds, result in fewer incorrect reports of abuse, but with increased chances for failing to report abuse. An example of high reporting thresholds is provided by the strict criteria used in research for hypothesis testing, in which more conservative criteria provide greater confidence that a result has not been observed by chance. The relative differences between strict and lenient reporting cri-

## Strict Criteria / High Threshold

|  | Reported | Not Reported |
|---|---|---|
| **Not Abused** | 0 | 240 |
| **Abused** | 10 | 50 |

## Lenient Criteria / Low Threshold

|  | Reported | Not Reported |
|---|---|---|
| **Not Abused** | 45 | 195 |
| **Abused** | 45 | 15 |

*Figure 3.7.* Hypothetical example of the number of cases detected from reports using high and low reporting thresholds.

teria are represented in Figure 3.6, which shows that relative rates of correct classifications (hits) and misclassifications (misses) vary as a function of decision criteria. The relative advantages and disadvantages of low and high reporting thresholds are left for mandated reporters to reconcile.

To illustrate the difference between lenient (low-threshold) and strict (high-threshold) reporting criteria, consider the report decision making of a child-clinical psychologist working in a pediatric setting. Suppose a psychologist evaluates 6 children per week, or approximately 300 children per year. Assume that there is a base rate of 20% of children who are victims of abuse in the particular setting where the evaluations are conducted. This means that the clinician is likely to see about 60 abused children per year. If the psychologist uses strict reporting criteria, and reports only those cases that involve physical signs of abuse or verbal disclosures of abuse, it is expected that 10%, or 6 of the cases will be reported. Although abuse will most likely be substantiated in these cases, 54 abused children go undetected. In contrast, consider a psychologist who uses lenient reporting criteria and reports subtle signs of abuse, such as social withdrawal or acting out behavior. This lower threshold results in the reporting of 75%, or 45 cases of actual abuse. However, there may be as many cases reported in which the children were not abused (see Figure 3.7). Thus, an optimal reporting threshold lies between these two extremes. It is one that catches a maximum number of cases while minimizing the number of false reports.


CONCLUSIONS

The optimal criteria for knowing when to report suspected child abuse depends on the situation. One key factor is the base rate of abuse among children and perpetrators in a given context (Swets, 1992). Settings with many abused children benefit more from low thresholds because lenient criteria result in a greater number of reports, and, therefore, capture an optimal number of cases. In contrast, settings with fewer abused children or perpetrators benefit from high threshold because strict criteria will reduce the number of false-positive cases. Unfortunately, it is difficult to determine the effects of base rates on professionals' decisions because little is known about the relative base rates of child abuse across service delivery settings.

An examination of the relative costs and benefits of reporting suspected child abuse shows that the costs of reporting can be minimized while the benefits are maximized. Among the potential costs of reporting, professionals have consistently pointed to breaches in confidentiality as their greatest concern. This potential cost can be reduced through sensitive informed-consent procedures that include limits of confidentiality. Assuming proper informed consent, breaches in confidentiality are consistent with professional roles and responsibilities. Costs of reporting can also be minimized by openly discussing the report with children and parents. The aftereffects of breached confidentiality are minimized when explanations are tied to previously discussed limits of confidentiality that make clear how the present circumstances fall within these constraints (Taylor & Adelman, 1989). Informing families why the report is necessary and what they can expect from an investigation, and assuring them that they will receive the reporter's support throughout the investigation, can help maintain trust and bring reporting into the context of a therapeutic relationship (Racusin & Felsman, 1986; Watson & Levine, 1989). Reporting can send a message of care, concern, and support to families. Treating suspected abuse seriously communicates the importance of stopping abuse. Thus, professionals can build a context that reduces the potential costs of reporting.

Interpreted in its broadest sense, legal standards for reasonable suspicions of abuse pose lenient decision criteria—low reporting thresholds. Behavioral signs of abuse, emotional reactions, somatic distress, and indirect communications may be considered reportable. In contrast, narrow interpretations of reasonable suspicion sets strict criteria and high reporting thresholds, under which only salient signs of abuse and direct communications are reportable. Indicators of child abuse that exceed high reporting thresholds are likely to be reported by most professionals. How a professional interprets the legal standard "reasonable suspicion" is then the hinge upon which reporting decisions rest. What is reported depends on what signs of abuse are observed, the family contexts within which they occur, and the circumstances under which the report is made. Nevertheless, many mandated reporters still choose not to report when indicators surpass reporting thresholds. Cases of both reporting and not reporting suspected child abuse illustrate decision-making processes across professional settings.

# II

# REPORTING SUSPECTED
# CHILD ABUSE:
# CASEBOOK AND GUIDELINES

# INTRODUCTION

## REPORTING SUSPECTED CHILD ABUSE: CASEBOOK AND GUIDELINES

Each case of suspected child abuse poses unique circumstances and challenges. Yet, there are common themes that link together many cases of suspected child abuse. Each case, for example, requires mandated reporters to (a) set a personal standard for reporting, (b) establish strategies for managing breaches of confidentiality, and (c) serve the best interests of children and families. Much can be learned by examining various cases of professionals who have reported and not reported suspected child abuse. Part II provides a casebook of mandated reporting of suspected child abuse. In chapter 4 I briefly set up a framework for examining cases of suspected abuse and review the principles of therapeutic jurisprudence—a perspective that emphasizes the therapeutic potential of mental health law. In chapters 5 and 6 I present cases of suspected child abuse that were not reported and cases that were reported, respectively. The need for a casebook that illustrates conflicts in reporting suspected child abuse was first recognized by the APA's Ad Hoc Committee on Child Abuse Policy (L. E. Walker et al., 1989). It was suggested that a casebook would be useful to individual practitioners confronting reporting decisions, and that an objective review of cases could also support policy initiatives to address issues in mandatory reporting.

This casebook illustrates abuse across a variety of professional circumstances and settings. The case vignettes are followed by a brief analysis of issues involved in the reporting decisions. These cases of unreported and reported suspected abuse were collected from professionals working in children's mental health services. The cases have been carefully disguised to protect the identity of persons involved.

# 4

# THERAPEUTIC JURISPRUDENCE AND MANDATED REPORTING

Therapeutic jurisprudence is a discipline that looks at the therapeutic impact of the law on various participants involved. Legal rules, legal procedures, and roles of legal actors constitute social forces that often produce therapeutic or antitherapeutic consequences; therapeutic jurisprudence challenges us to reduce antitherapeutic consequences, and to enhance therapeutic consequences, without subordinating due process and other justice values. (Shiff & Wexler, 1996, p. 291)

Mandatory reporting laws are intended to protect children from suffering abuse and neglect. The extent to which they help to achieve this goal, however, depends entirely on the actions of mandated reporters and agencies that receive their reports. Indeed, mandated reporting can have adverse effects on children and families that cue in direct opposition to their therapeutic intent. Legal scholars and social researchers have espoused a perspective for analyzing the law in terms of its potential benefits and peril. Therapeutic jurisprudence focuses on the law's impact on emotional well-being and mental health; the law, in this case, can operate much like a therapeutic agent. Therapeutic jurisprudence examines the law with respect to its capacity for healing and assisting persons. Although there are many value systems, such as equality and dignity, that can be used to judge the social worth of any given law, therapeutic jurisprudence emphasizes therapeutic values in its sociolegal analyses (Small, 1996). According to Wexler (1993), the law

> is a social force that sometimes produces therapeutic and antitherapeutic consequences, and therapeutic jurisprudence involves "the use of social science to study the extent to which a legal rule or practice promotes the psychological or physical well-being of the people it affects." (Slobogin, cited in Wexler, 1996, p. 831)

Therapeutic jurisprudence evolved out of mental health law, particularly the scholarly analysis of civil commitment proceedings, insanity defenses, and conditional releases in insanity cases. Applications of therapeutic jurisprudence have, however, been broadened to include several facets of mental health and family law. For example, therapeutic jurisprudence has been helpful in interpreting and applying duty to warn statutes in mental health settings (Wexler, 1979), patient's rights to refuse mental health treatment (Winick, 1994), and protections of provider–client privileged communications (Winick, 1996). In each instance, the law itself is analyzed to discern its therapeutic aims, assess its progress in meeting its aims, and establish procedures to maximize the law's therapeutic effects. With regard to duty to warn, for example, Wexler (1995) illustrated that the purposes of duty to warn policies stemming from *Tarasoff v. Board of Regents of the University of California* are geared toward protecting public safety, not enhancing the effectiveness of psychotherapy. Duty to warn requirements can be applied in ways that will reduce their potential harm to psychotherapy, while also protecting the public. Therapeutic jurisprudence therefore offers a point of view that can improve the application of laws, particularly those that have implications for emotional and mental health. It is apparent that mandatory reporting laws fall well within the scope of analysis offered by therapeutic jurisprudence.

This chapter uses the broad lens of therapeutic jurisprudence to reexamine mandatory reporting laws, focusing on both antitherapeutic and therapeutic applications of the law. By adopting the point of view offered by therapeutic jurisprudence, mandatory reporting laws can be applied to gain their optimal benefits and to minimize their potential harm. Therefore, this brief overview of therapeutic jurisprudence as applied to mandatory reporting laws foreshadows the evaluation of suspected child abuse cases discussed in chapters 5 and 6.

## THERAPEUTIC AIMS OF MANDATORY REPORTING LAWS

Murray Levine (1993) was among the first scholars to analyze mandatory reporting laws from the perspective of therapeutic jurisprudence. As Levine concluded, mandatory reporting laws aim to (a) restore family competence and eliminate maltreatment, (b) restore children to a renewed family environment, and (c) provide or refer families for mental health services. Thus, reporting suspected abuse should lead to actions that meet the therapeutic aims of the law, most notably child protective services and related treatments. Budget cuts in social services have nearly gutted most child welfare and child protective services. However, even with the dearth of services available through child protection agencies, mandated reporting offers therapeutic value through the application of the law itself.

In the absence of adequate services, child protection via mandated reporting can occur through investigation and intervention. The report itself can serve as a catalyst for therapeutic gains by sending a message of protection to a child—showing that adults can protect children by taking actions on their behalf. Reporting can also warn adults that their behavior is neither ignored nor condoned. By filing a report of suspected abuse, it is also possible to motivate searches for help, as well as behavior changes in abusive adults. A report of suspected child abuse could open access to social services and place external constraints and contingencies on abusive behavior. The extreme end to reporting suspected abuse can, of course, mean the removal of a child from an abusive or negligent home. Although even the tempory removal of a child from his or her parents carries multiple threats of harm, removal effectively brings an end to abuse at that point in time—the primary aim of mandatory reporting laws. According to M. Levine and Doueck (1995), there are four therapeutic applications of mandatory reporting laws:

*Reporting to enhance child safety.* M. Levine and Doueck (1995) noted that clinicians would report abuse to alert authorities and trigger intervention. Indeed, many professionals report because they expect that a child will be removed from his or her home and placed in protected care. Mental health professionals can therefore consider treatment a long-term solution, but few consider counseling and therapy as a sufficient means of protecting an endangered child.

*Reporting to show support for a client.* Therapists may report abuse when it comes to light in treatment, even when the abuse occurred a long time ago. Reporting can make a statement to a client that the therapist cares and has taken the disclosure of abuse seriously. In these cases, the report can serve to foster the therapeutic alliance and enhance trust. However, reporting past abuse, or filing a stale report, contributes to an already jammed protective system and will unlikely trigger a response from child protection workers (M. Levine & Doueck, 1995).

*Reporting to lessen client resistance.* Reporting can be used in therapy to challenge a client's denial of abuse. The report itself becomes a reality for a client. The power of the law can also help motivate clients to engage in therapy and reduce their resistance.

*Reporting to help a client maintain self-control.* The power of reporting can be used as an external control on impulsive behavior. Therapists can communicate their views on reporting and inform their clients when they believe reporting will be necessary. Therapy can then be directed at helping the client gain sufficient self-control to stay well within that threshold (M. Levine & Doueck, 1995).

Therapeutic values are apparent in the structure and language of mandatory reporting statutes. Child abuse reporting laws typically define abuse to emphasize its adverse effects, highlighting the therapeutic value of stopping abuse. The therapeutic intent of mandatory reporting laws is to capture as many cases of child abuse as possible, even at the expense of disrupting mental health services. Indeed, far more reports are received than cases are substantiated. In 1997, for example, there were over 3 million cases of child abuse reported, but only about 1 million substantiated. The law also requires that an investigative arm of the child protection system evaluate reports to determine the occurrence of abuse. This allocation of responsibilities between mandated reporters and child protection workers helps to reduce the policing roles of mandated reporters and minimize adverse effects of reporting on mental health services. In addition, mandated reporters cannot be held liable for reporting suspected abuse, again removing barriers to reporting. The law does not, however, offer guidance for reporting to promote its therapeutic intent. Mandated reporters are left to themselves to figure out how best to report and how to apply the law therapeutically.

## ANTITHERAPEUTIC APPLICATIONS OF MANDATORY REPORTING LAWS

Mandatory reporting laws can have adverse effects and can diminish their own therapeutic potential. For example, mandatory reporting laws can cause mandated reporters to avoid issues of abuse so that they do not have to deal with reporting. Knowing that they must report suspected abuse, professionals may not probe certain areas in questioning, or may not ask detailed questions to gain information needed for a report. In a sense, professionals realize that if they do not learn of the abuse, they can then avoid dealing with reporting. Similarly, mandatory reporting laws can steer abusers away from treatment because abusers know that if they are discovered they will be reported. These effects of mandatory reporting laws are clearly paradoxical; they can actually result in failure to identify abused children.

Another antitherapeutic application of mandatory reporting laws involves their potential conflict with individual rights to protect against self-incrimination—rights protected by the Fifth Amendment of the United

States Constitution. It is generally considered essential for persons to admit abuse for psychotherapy and counseling to progress. Admitting abuse, however, can serve as the basis for filing a report to child protective services, and the report may be used as evidence in the investigation of abuse. Fifth Amendment rights are not violated when clients who admit abuse are receiving voluntary care. However, when clients are receiving court-ordered or involuntary treatment and they are compelled to admit abuse, protections against self-incrimination may have, in fact, been violated (M. Levine & Doherty, 1991). The Fifth Amendment specifies that a person shall not be compelled in a criminal case to be a witness against himself or herself and prohibits officials from bending a person's will to resist confessing a crime. Thus, when in court-ordered treatment, an alleged abuser must decide whether to admit abuse in order to cooperate with treatment or to not admit abuse and be considered uncooperative. Pressure to admit abuse in involuntary treatment can be quite substantial, with potential implications for child custody, child removal, and other adverse consequences. Under these conditions, admitting abuse may indeed be in violation of one's constitutional rights. Therefore, involuntary treatment cannot stipulate that persons admit abuse, and there must not be any explicit threat of legal consequences for not admitting abuse (M. Levine & Doherty, 1991). Requiring admissions of abuse to achieve successful treatment and then reporting the admission to child protective services is more likely to achieve antitherapeutic effects.

Mandatory reporting laws are also potentially antitherapeutic when their application creates conflicts with professional ethical standards. As previously discussed, mandated reporting can cause significant tension among maintaining confidentiality, trust in the therapeutic relationship, and obeying the law. Although receiving informed consent relieves some of this tension, limited confidentiality itself can have antitherapeutic effects, particularly in the treatment of perpetrators who will fear admitting abuse in treatment (Berlin et al., 1991). Mandatory reporting laws will therefore fail to meet their therapeutic potential and increase their antitherapeutic effects when they constrain openness and a sense of safety in therapeutic relationships.

## COERCIVE USES OF MANDATORY REPORTING IN THERAPY

Mandatory reporting laws can be used coercively in therapeutic relationships. The rule of law is designed to manipulate and shape social behavior through means such as conformity, deterrence, and maintaining social order. The law can also be used as a tool to persuade behavior in therapeutic contexts. Anderson et al. (1993) identified a number of ways that mandated reporters have used reporting requirements to achieve therapeutic ends. The power of reporting laws to control parental behavior was a resource for professionals, who manipulated the law to their own advantages. For example, therapists stated that they sometimes used reporting laws to promote changes in the family system by forcing a crisis in the family, propelling them forward in therapy. In this manner, reporting laws can be used as an instrument or catalyst in therapy. Anderson et al. also found that therapists used the threat of reporting suspected abuse to coerce engagement in the therapeutic process. For example, some therapists delayed reporting under the condition that their client continued attending therapy. The consequences of reporting were also used to coerce clients into addressing issues in treatment that they were previously avoiding or denying. Mandated reporting can be used to force people into treatment, such as occurs in involuntary treatment. In these cases therapy primarily serves as a monitoring function, and becomes an arm of the child protection system (Anderson et al., 1993). Reporting could therefore become a coercive instrument for setting limits in therapy, with the aim of protecting children. Finally, it was also found that clients sometimes used reporting laws to their advantage. For example, therapists and counselors had been manipulated to report a case of suspected abuse in an effort to accuse a third party of abuse in child custody and visitation cases.

Mandatory reporting laws can therefore be skillfully applied to enhance their therapeutic potential. Doueck and Levine (in press) found that therapists had used reporting laws to positively affect relationships with clients, obtain social services for families and children, increase trust with clients, keep clients in treatment, and model good parenting. Reporting also had therapeutic value when it opened channels for revealing and discussing unhealed experiences of abuse. Doueck and Levine found that reporting allowed therapists to emphasize the destructiveness and seriousness of abuse, and to potentially mobilize treatment. The coercive use of mandatory reporting laws can, therefore, have therapeutic or antitherapeutic intentions, applications, and outcomes.

## THERAPEUTICALLY APPLYING MANDATORY REPORTING LAWS

The perspective offered by therapeutic jurisprudence emphasizes that the law should be applied to optimize personal and social welfare, while minimizing potential harm. It is helpful to reconsider cases of suspected child abuse that have gone unreported as well as cases that have been reported, focusing on alternative actions that could enhance therapeutic outcomes. Wexler (1979, 1993) outlined a framework for how therapists can skillfully apply their duty to warn under the *Tarasoff* ruling in order to gain maximum therapeutic advantages. Wexler noted that *Tarasoff* is trig-

## EXHIBIT 4.1
### Five Key Considerations in Applying Mandatory Reporting to Maximize Its Therapeutic Advantage

Focus on the child
Identify acceptable courses of action for reporting
Gain acceptance for reporting
Elicit concern for the child and gain consent for reporting
Break confidentiality without breaking trust

gered by a client's threat of violence against an identifiable person. This suggests that the duty to warn could play out through the following steps: (a) placing attention on the potential victim and the environment within which abuse occurs (Hutchison, 1990); (b) seeking an acceptable means of alerting the potential victim about the threat of potential violence; (c) moving the therapist to seek resolution of the threat of violence in a manner that is most acceptable to the client, and therefore, least disruptive to the therapeutic relationship; (d) eliciting concern from the client for the potential victim; and (e) gaining consent for warning the potential victim without violating trust and damaging the therapeutic alliance. Wexler's framework is easily adapted to the duty to warn that is discharged through mandatory reporting laws.

Exhibit 4.1 summarizes five key considerations in therapeutically applying mandatory reporting laws. In reporting suspected child abuse, mental health professionals should shift their focus to the child and his or her risks for abuse. When the client is the child suspected of being abused, this shift will be away from a presenting problem and toward the suspected abuse. However, focusing on the abuse does not mean abandoning the issues that were the focus of treatment. Rather, this creates more of an interactionist perspective that takes all of the actors and the environment into consideration (Hutchison, 1990).

Reporters must also determine their optimal means for reporting suspected abuse. Circumstances and constraints of reporting vary with each case of suspected child abuse. This suggests that professionals should adjust their reporting strategies in order to meet the needs of situations rather than establishing a formula to fit all situations and to support one reporting protocol. Reporting, however, should not be viewed as the final stage in managing cases of suspected child abuse. The issues that initially lead to reporting should be a priority for continued treatment, particularly when the issues fit well with presenting problems. Likewise, suspected abuse that arises out of an evaluation or assessment requires referrals that are relevant for addressing the initial issues. Finally, clinicians should try to elicit concern for the child from his or her parents and obtain their consent for reporting. Although professionals should not delay reporting to obtain consent, there is value in accruing as much support as possible for the report in order to maintain trust in the therapeutic relationship, even with breaches in confidentiality.

## CONCLUSIONS

Mandatory reporting laws require that professionals report suspected child abuse in a timely manner. However, the law does not prescribe how professionals should proceed in their reporting. Therapeutic jurisprudence offers a refreshing perspective that mandated reporters can consider when faced with reporting suspected abuse. Reporting requires professionals to focus on the child and the child's safety. Therefore, professionals should ask themselves several questions: Will reporting place the child at greater danger? How can the threat against the child be reduced and eliminated? Will reporting in the presence of the client limit his or her paranoia about what the caseworkers are being told? Should the therapist encourage the client to report him- or herself? How much information should the reporter disclose in his or her report? How can the reporter balance breaching confidentiality with ensuring adequate child protection agency involvement? Can the reporter restate the circumstances that bring him or her to report in such a way that emphasizes his or her concern for the child? Are the potential benefits of child protection and safety clear to the client? Gaining acceptance and consent for reporting can, therefore, mean eliciting mutual concern for the child. Breaking confidentiality by reporting does not automatically mean detrimental effects on treatment. Can reporting occur while maintaining trust? Is it possible to report within the context of a close and caring therapeutic alliance? Careful consideration of these and other questions that originate from a therapeutic stance will likely enhance the therapeutic outcomes of reporting.

# 5

# UNREPORTED CASES OF SUSPECTED CHILD ABUSE

There are many reasons why professionals do not report suspected child abuse. But failure to report abuse places professionals at risk for civil and criminal liability, and may place children and families at risk for continued abuse. The following cases present situations in which professionals suspected child abuse but elected not to report. Each case demonstrates a conflict that a mandated reporter experienced when he or she decided not to report suspected abuse. The commentaries that follow each case highlight the most salient features and summarize the lessons gleaned from each case.

## CASE 5.1. EMILY: WEIGHING THE RISKS AND BENEFITS OF REPORTING

This case concerns a mental health counselor who provided outpatient services at a community mental health center. The client was a 4-year-old girl, Emily, and her family. Emily had been causing a number of behavior management problems at home. The family was referred by a school social worker for services to the mental health center. It was known that her teenage cousin had sexually abused Emily when she was 2 years old. Appropriate interventions had stopped the abuse and he was no longer in contact with Emily.

Emily's family lived in low-income housing, and they had limited social supports and resources. During the course of family therapy, the counselor became aware of several incidents that caused her to suspect that Emily was currently experiencing physical abuse. Both of Emily's parents said that they were living under extreme financial stress and that they became easily frustrated with Emily's behavior. They said that they frequently lost their tempers when Emily misbehaved. Emily's father once spoke of "giving her a good whoop" on the head when she would not keep quiet in the car. On another occasion, he had "accidentally hit" Emily's head with a bathroom door. Although the counselor never saw physical signs of abuse or injuries inflicted on Emily, and Emily did not report any such injuries, the counselor was concerned that even more severe acts of abuse were being committed.

Emily's mother described situations in which Emily had been placed in dangerous situations, each of which could have been prevented had Emily been more closely supervised. There was the time, for example, that Emily was climbing on a kitchen cabinet that fell on top of her. Another time Emily swallowed the contents of a bottle of her mother's makeup. On yet another occasion, Emily stuffed a pencil eraser into her nose, only to be discovered after it had become infected. Emily was injured in each of these incidents and was taken to the hospital emergency room. Because the counselor believed that the physicians and other hospital staff were in a better position to assess Emily's injuries, she felt that they would have surely reported the incidents as suspected abuse if it was warranted.

During the course of family counseling, however, a neighbor reported the family for leaving Emily unattended for extended periods of time. The neighbor's report was followed by a child protective services investigation, the result of which did not substantiate child abuse or neglect. Although the counselor remained concerned about Emily and her family, she still did not report, because the family was actively participating in their treatment and was showing signs of improvement. The parents said that they were feeling less frustrated and more in control, and that Emily's behavior was more manageable. Thus, the counselor feared that reporting the family would interfere with their progress and could damage the therapeutic relationship she had established with the parents. The counselor believed that reporting would eventually drive the family out of treatment. She also believed that not reporting was further justified by her not having seen any physical signs of abuse, by the facts that Emily received medical attention for her injuries, and the parents were seeking help, and by her own uncertainty that the incidents she has heard about would constitute abuse. Also, the family had been investigated and abuse was not substantiated. Thus, because the family had previous involvement with child protective services, the counselor believed that yet another report would probably serve little purpose.

**Commentary**

In Emily's case, her counselor may have reported if she felt there were better reasons. The signs and situations clearly led the counselor to suspect that Emily was in danger, but the risk did not pose a serious enough threat to warrant reporting. Of course, the counselor was not exactly looking for reasons to report. She did not ask Emily's father what he meant by "whooping" Emily on the head or how it was that he "accidentally" hit her in the head with a door. Although these descriptions seem to reveal acts of abuse, the counselor was skeptical of abuse because Emily did not have visible injuries and because Emily herself did not describe abusive situations. The parents also sought medical care for Emily after she was injured, again causing the counselor to refrain from reporting. That the emergency room personnel did not report further justified the counselor's reluctance. The counselor believed that the physicians and nurses would be in a better position to report because they would be more likely to observe Emily's injuries. The counselor was also reassured that not reporting was justified because the report made by the family's neighbor was investigated and not substantiated.

Regardless of everything else, the counselor suspected that Emily may have been abused. This made her required by law to report. The counselor was therefore at risk of being charged with failure to report suspected abuse. It was an error for the counselor to believe that filing another report of suspected child abuse would not mean much to child protective service workers. Repeated reports accumulate and can help child protective service employees to determine the priority and risk associated with a case. However, the counselor weighed the situation and decided that Emily was not in immediate danger and that reporting could throw off the family's therapeutic progress. The counselor's interpretation of the situation was such that she saw little benefit coming from reporting and chose to keep the family in counseling.

The initial clinical goal of Emily's treatment was to address behavior management problems, parenting skills, and parental frustration tolerance. However, the focus of treatment changed when the counselor identified situations that suggested child abuse. Emily's behavior—once the presenting problem—soon became conceptualized as a symptom of abuse that was either a residual symptom of her earlier sexual abuse, current physical abuse and neglect, or both. Given the frequency of potential abuse and neglect experienced by Emily, an immediate report to child protective services may have seemed warranted. The report could have been placed in the context of Emily's prior injuries. The mental health counselor could have acknowledged that the situations described by Emily's parents caused alarm and he or she could capitalize, upon the parents' shared concerns for their daughter's safety. The counselor might have explained that child protection agencies are better equipped to assess Emily's risk for injury and could help make recommendations to keep her safe. Reporting could therefore have raised Emily's parents' concerns and mobilized them to examine their own behavior as it related to placing Emily at risk. In this case, it may have been possible for the counselor to report the situation in the presence of the parents, reducing their anxiety about what was said to the child protection agency. By focusing on Emily's injuries in the report, rather than the parent's behavior, the counselor may have been able to sustain their trust while also initiating a report of suspected abuse.

**Lessons Learned**

- It is not necessary to observe injuries to report.
- Assuming that other professionals have reported or had the opportunity to report does not justify not reporting suspected abuse.
- Previous reports and investigations do not preclude filing a report of suspected abuse.
- Regardless of the bases for suspected child abuse, the law requires reporting.
- Each report of suspected abuse and the investigation it may trigger is an independent event; cumulative reports are factored into child protection services.
- Reporting can occur in a therapeutic context that does not necessarily jeopardize progress in therapy.

## CASE 5.2. ELIZABETH: PUSHING BACK THE LIMITS OF CONFIDENTIALITY

This case involves a psychologist in private practice who was treating a 15-year-old girl named Elizabeth for depression and academic problems. Following the advice of Elizabeth's teacher, her mother brought Elizabeth to a child and family therapist. At the start of her first session, Elizabeth asked the therapist whether he would have to tell her parents all of her secrets. The therapist told Elizabeth that what they talked about would be private, with the only exceptions being if she was thinking of hurting herself or thinking of hurting someone else. If he learned of either of these, he would have to tell her parents for her own safety. Elizabeth proceeded to tell the psychologist that an adult cousin had fondled her when she was 12 years old. The cousin, who was now living out of state, could no longer hurt her, but she kept the experience secret from her parents. Elizabeth said that if the therapist told her parents about this, she would never come back to therapy. The therapist tried to convince Elizabeth to tell her parents herself, but she refused. Concerned that revealing the past abuse would cause an early breach of trust in their relationship, the therapist decided to initiate therapy without disclosing the abuse. After several sessions— some of which addressed Elizabeth's sexual abuse—Elizabeth started getting into trouble both in school and at home. She started smoking marijuana, became increasingly truant from school, and behaved even more belligerently toward her parents. The therapist called for a family conference with Elizabeth's parents in which he hinted about the sexual abuse by asking her mother and father whether they had any knowledge of Elizabeth experiencing abuse or trauma. The therapist hoped that the parents would initiate a discussion of Elizabeth's history that would address the abuse without the therapist actually revealing it. The therapist felt that Elizabeth could benefit from therapy, and believed that by breaking confidentiality she would indeed stop coming. Despite the therapist's efforts, Elizabeth did eventually drop out of therapy. Weeks after her last session, Elizabeth's mother called the therapist stating that Elizabeth had told her about the sexual abuse. In that conversation, the therapist informed the mother that the girl had disclosed the abuse to him and explained how he addressed the situation in therapy and why it was not discussed in their conference. Elizabeth's mother was upset about the entire ordeal, but did not hold anything against the therapist. Therapy with Elizabeth did not resume, and the abuse was not reported.

## Commentary

The specific indicators of abuse in this case surpassed even the strictest criteria for reporting. The decision not to report was influenced by concerns about confidentiality and acting on behalf of the child's immediate welfare. The therapist could have avoided much of his dilemma by accurately stating the limits of confidentiality at the outset of therapy. Although the therapist stated that he would have to inform Elizabeth's parents if she intended to harm herself or someone else, he failed to list harm caused by a third party as a condition of limited confidentiality. The therapist anguished over telling Elizabeth's parents about the abuse, but there is no indication that he ever considered reporting the situation to child protection services. The therapist's decision not to tell Elizabeth's parents about the past abuse abridged their parental rights, regardless of promises made between the therapist and the child.

An additional concern related to this case is the potential for future sexual abuse perpetrated against other children. The unreported incident could have been an isolated event, but it could also have been only one incident in a broader spectrum of abuse. Although Elizabeth was not currently at risk of further harm, it was impossible to know whether she or other children would be at risk in the future.

**Lessons Learned**

- Clients should be informed of the limits of confidentiality at the outset of therapy.
- Providing written informed consent that includes the limits of confidentiality avoids confusion and ensures that all parties are aware of the terms and conditions of care.
- The absence of any current threats of harm should not deter reporting past abuse.
- Therapists should not allow a client to use the threat of withdrawing from therapy as leverage against reporting.
- Parental rights must be considered and observed when treating minors, unless specific actions place the child at risk for abuse.

## CASE 5.3. DANNY: THIRD-PARTY DISCLOSURE OF ABUSE

Lucinda was a 37-year-old woman who was being treated in outpatient psychotherapy for depression. Lucinda and her husband had been divorced for 4 years. She still saw her ex-husband occasionally, particularly when he visited their 11-year-old son Danny in her home. As he had throughout their marriage, Danny's father emotionally abused Lucinda. Although Lucinda protested joint custody, Danny's father saw his son at least once a week since their divorce.

After 3 months of therapy Lucinda was making progress. She was less depressed and feeling more positive about herself. However, during one of her later sessions, Lucinda described the following incident to her therapist: During a parent–teacher conference at Danny's school, Danny's father stood up in the middle of a discussion with the teacher and decided that it was time to go. Danny's father abruptly told Danny that they were leaving. Against his father's protests, Danny stayed and talked with his friends. After about 10 min, Danny's father returned to the classroom. He was obviously angry that Danny was still there. In front of other children, parents, and teachers, the father grabbed Danny by the shoulders and ridiculed him for not listening, and pushed him out the door. Concerned about the incident, Danny's teacher called both Danny's mother and father that evening and scheduled another parent–teacher conference. Not surprisingly, Danny's father refused to attend. Danny's teacher did not report the incident to child protective services because she was not sure that the problem was serious enough to warrant reporting. Hearing about the incident concerned Lucinda's therapist because he thought that Danny may be experiencing emotional abuse. Still, the therapist was not comfortable enough to report the situation because he had not witnessed the acts himself. In fact, he had never met Danny or his father. The therapist continued to work with the mother on setting limits with Danny's father and to foster communication with Danny about his relationship with his father.

**Commentary**

This case demonstrates that suspected abuse may occur without direct contact between the victim and perpetrator. Although some states have required that a child suspected of being abused be seen by the reporting professional, most of these laws have now been amended to remove these requirements. Nevertheless, professionals are always permitted to report suspected child abuse even if the law does not require reporting. On the basis of the mother's description of Danny's humiliation it might have been good to have Danny's mother bring him in for a brief interview. Although such an interview was by no means necessary to report, the therapist could have assessed Danny's well-being. The potential for continued abuse seems quite high in this case because Danny's father had contact with him. If nothing else, the specter of potential abuse might have prompted the therapist to report. Finally, the teacher's actions should not be left without comment. Acknowledging that the definition of emotional abuse is ambiguous, mandated reporters should not make judgments about which forms of abuse are more or less serious and, therefore, more or less worthy of reporting. By not reporting the incident, the teacher in this case may have downplayed the seriousness of the situation.

**Lessons Learned**

- Knowing a child may be experiencing abuse is sufficient grounds for taking action.
- Suspected abuse can arise in nearly any service delivery setting.
- Second-hand accounts of abusive situations are sufficient to warrant reporting.
- The necessity of protecting children should supercede the goals and plans of therapy.

## CASE 5.4. NATHAN: MISINTERPRETING ALLEGATIONS OF ABUSE AS PSYCHIATRIC SYMPTOMS

Nathan was a 16-year-old boy who was admitted to an inpatient psychiatric unit for incorrigible behavior and assaulting a schoolteacher. During an interview with a staff psychologist, Nathan alleged that a female occupational therapist had made sexual advances toward him while conducting a routine assessment of progress on his treatment plan. When the psychologist questioned Nathan about the situation, he said that the occupational therapist had been giving him looks and that she had brushed her breasts against him in the day area. Nathan's most serious allegation was that the occupational therapist had entered the shower room while he was naked and then made some suggestive remarks about his body as she grabbed his crotch. Alarmed by Nathan's allegations, the psychologist reviewed the ward notes for an incident report. The female occupational therapist wrote a report that stated Nathan had lured her into the shower room by asking for help, and then dropped his towel to expose himself. She also wrote that Nathan approached her and she pushed him away, telling him to get dressed. She then left the room and wrote up the incident. Nathan had a history of complaints about similar acts with other female staff, which had been clearly documented in his chart. The psychologist considered reporting the situation as a case of suspected sexual abuse to both internal and external authorities, but decided against reporting because the shift supervisor would review the incident. The incident was included in Nathan's treatment plan.

**Commentary**

Although this case involved a verbal disclosure of sexual abuse, the allegation was interpreted as part of Nathan's emotional–behavioral problems. Institutional abuse, however, is becoming increasingly more recognized, and systems are needed for specific interventions in these settings. Nevertheless, mandatory reporting statutes apply within inpatient facilities. Although investigating child abuse is the role of child protection agencies, the psychologist in this case chose not to report, on the basis of his own conclusions. Reporting the incident would have benefited the client and others if the abuse were substantiated. If not substantiated, an investigation would have served to clear the occupational therapist of Nathan's allegations.

**Lessons Learned**

- Allegations of abuse can be a cry for help regardless of whether abuse has occurred.
- Verbal disclosures of sexual abuse should surpass reporting thresholds.
- Stereotypes concerning age and gender can influence reporting. Cases involving teenage boys may be least likely to be reported. Clinicians should be aware of their own potential biases.

- Institutions and clinical agencies should clearly define the procedures for managing all allegations of abuse.

## CASE 5.5. LEAH: USING THE THREAT OF REPORTING TO FACILITATE CHANGE

Leah was a 13-year-old girl who was seeing a school counselor for unexcused absences, rapidly deteriorating grades, and behavioral problems. During their third counseling session, the school counselor noticed that Leah had several sizable bruises on her left arm. Leah told her counselor that she and her older brother had been fighting and that he was the one who bruised her arm. Leah said that her mother was there at the time but did not do anything to help her or stop her brother from hitting her. After consulting with Leah's teacher, the counselor decided that the incident was not "abuse" because it involved Leah's 16-year-old brother, rather than an adult. The counselor, however, was concerned about Leah because her mother may have neglected the situation, potentially leaving Leah at risk for future injuries. Still, the counselor did not feel that the incident constituted a pattern of neglect. The counselor talked with Leah's mother to help her realize the seriousness of the situation. She also tried to convince Leah's mother to intervene in situations in which Leah could be at risk. The counselor told Leah's mother that by not intervening, problems such as these can get worse and may eventually require reporting to child protection services.

**Commentary**

In this case, the school counselor was aware of her duty to report. However, her interpretation of her duty was flawed. The fact that Leah's injuries were caused by her brother should not have deterred reporting. In addition, Leah's reaction to the situation seemed to indicate that she was at least somewhat traumatized. The facts that she had daily contact with her brother and given that her mother had not intervened to protect her in the past suggests that Leah could be at risk. In this case, the counselor's logic was to report if the situation literally fit the legal definitions of abuse and neglect. The counselor also used reporting as a threat to motivate Leah's mother to protect her daughter. In the long run, this strategy could stifle future disclosures of abuse and frame reporting as a punishment rather than a potential source for help.

**Lessons Learned**

- There may be much more to a situation than what a child discloses.

- Injuries should be reported regardless of the age of the person causing them.
- Judgments of the severity of injuries should not delay reporting.
- Threats of reporting should not be used as a tool to manipulate parental practices.

## CASE 5.6. MALLORY: REVELATION OF ABUSE IN A RESEARCH SETTING

This case involves an experimental psychologist who was conducting research on stressful life events and coping in grade school children. The research used a standard scale for assessing self-reported stressful life events, and included items such as "I was touched in a way that I did not like" and "My parents have been mean to me." The researchers saw these items as important indicators of childhood stress, and were well aware that they could be indicators of child abuse. The researchers followed standard ethical guidelines for conducting studies with children, and assured parents that the study was approved by the University Institutional Review Board as well as the school administration where the study activities occurred. Parents provided informed consent on the basis of a detailed description of the study, which emphasized that the research concerned stressful events experienced by children. The research instruments were available to parents, although no parents requested to see them.

The researchers were aware of their requirement to report suspected child abuse if it should occur during the course of their study. To avoid such conflicts the investigators decided to collect the children's data anonymously—a procedure that they believed would encourage honest and forthcoming responses. The researchers thought it would be of questionable ethical practice to assure the children that their responses were anonymous and confidential, and then ask children who indicate abuse to come forward. The researchers tried to balance confidentiality and compliance with mandatory reporting laws. The researchers discussed their methods with colleagues, reviewed the APA *Ethical Principles for Research With Human Participants*, and consulted the university legal department in an effort to develop procedures for handling situations of suspected abuse. A system was also established to make counselors available for children who seemed troubled by responding to the questionnaires. The children were told that they should talk with their parents, teacher, or school social worker about anything that might be troubling them. Finally, the researchers informed the children that if they told them about anything in person that was seriously bothering them, the researchers would have to tell the school administration. Thus, this research team took multiple steps toward managing any trauma that children might reveal during the study.

After several days of data collection, Mallory, a 10-year-old girl who completed the measures for the study, told a research assistant that the question about having been touched in a way that she did not like made her think about something bad that happened to her. The research assistant was concerned and questioned Mallory further about what happened to her. Mallory said "never mind" and walked away. The research assistant discussed the situation with her project supervisor, and they decided to inform the school principal about the incident. After telling the principal, the researchers took no further action and were not aware of any action taken by the school.

**Commentary**

Suspicions of child abuse are probably common in developmental, experimental–child, educational, and school-based research. The researchers in this case were sensitive to the measures they used and the emotional response they may have evoked. The researchers considered the possibility that items on their measures could prompt a disclosure of abuse and so took several preventive steps. Although their data collection was anonymous, the researchers made an effort to communicate the need to discuss difficulties related to stressful events with parents or teachers. The investigators also included the necessity of telling school personnel about identifiable information regarding things that might be seriously bothering a child in the informed-consent procedure. Despite their caution, the researchers failed to report suspected abuse. Informing school personnel of suspected abuse is not the same as filing a report. Although some states include a clause that allows mandated reporters to "cause a report to be filed" as an option, the researchers in this case did not follow up on actions taken by the school and did not verify that a report had been filed. Because the researchers themselves were mandated reporters, a more general statement as to who would have to be notified in cases of suspected abuse should have been included in the informed consent. For example, the researchers should have told children that they would be required to tell "people whose job it is to protect children from harm." Such a statement would accurately describe informing child protective services. A similar statement should also be included in parental consent. Finally, the system that the researchers carefully crafted at the outset of the study should have included procedures for reporting suspected child abuse.

**Lessons Learned**

- Suspected child abuse can arise in any professional setting, including research settings.

- Researchers are usually considered mandated reporters.
- Establishing systems for managing disclosures of abuse within a research protocol must include detailed instructions for reporting.
- Informing school authorities does not substitute for filing a report of suspected abuse unless it is known that the school authorities reported.

## CASE 5.7. STEPHANIE: THERAPIST ACTING AS INVESTIGATOR

This case concerns a marital therapist who was treating Sharon and Mike, a couple who were experiencing conflicts over finances and a lack of emotional intimacy. During their fifth therapy session, Sharon told her therapist that their 3-year-old daughter, Stephanie, as well as a 3-year-old friend had been fondled and coerced into sexual play by a 14-year-old boy in the neighborhood. The couple told the therapist that they had informed the boy's parents of the situation and took several steps to ensure that he would not go anywhere near Stephanie again. The therapist asked very specific questions regarding the action the parents took to protect their daughter from further abuse and felt that Stephanie was not in present danger. Still, the therapist was concerned about Stephanie and asked if she could meet her during their next visit. Complying with the therapist's request, Stephanie came to the next session. After a brief interview with Stephanie, the therapist saw that she was not presenting signs of trauma, and felt confident that both Stephanie and her friend were not in danger. The therapist was diligent about asking how Stephanie was doing during later sessions. The therapist did not report to the child protection system because she did not know who the boy was and the parents did not want to report. The therapist was therefore persuaded not to report, because the parents had done an adequate job protecting their daughter.

**Commentary**

A verbal account of two children who were sexually abused was not reported in this case because the therapist wanted to honor the parent's wishes and because the children appeared protected. The therapist interviewed one of the 3-year-olds and believed that steps had been taken to protect the children. However, the safety of other children might have been considered in the reporting decision. In addition, there would be no opportunity to intervene with the suspected perpetrator because the therapist did not report. Given that the therapist was concerned enough to bring Stephanie in for an interview, and given the potential danger posed to two known young victims, reporting in this case was warranted.

## Lessons Learned

- The ability of the mandated reporter to identify the suspected perpetrator is not necessary for reporting suspected abuse.
- When deciding whether to report, therapists should avoid acting as investigators and restrict their actions to interviewing, evaluating, or studying situations.
- The safety of children cannot be adequately judged by a single interview with a child or even multiple interviews with the child's parents.
- Other victims should be considered in reporting decisions.


## CASE 5.8. NICOLE: REPORTING TO PROTECT ALL CHILDREN

A school psychologist was treating an 11-year-old girl, Nicole, for aggressive behavior in school. She was also showing signs of depression and using foul language at home and school. During their third session, Nicole told her psychologist that her father, now divorced from her mother, had touched her "down below." Nicole said that the first time he had done this was before her parents were separated and that the touching continued almost every time she visited her father. The therapist called Nicole's mother about the revelation and her mother said that she was aware of the abuse. Nicole's mother said that her ex-husband was an alcoholic and was unemployed. He had failed to make several child support payments and she was successful at removing his visitation rights. She also said that she had told a social worker about the sexual abuse, but that there was no way they could prove the abuse. The psychologist decided not to report Nicole's disclosure because of concerns that she and her mother could not manage any additional stress, particularly the stress that would likely result from a prolonged investigation. The school psychologist addressed the abuse in later sessions with Nicole. The therapist also involved the mother in therapy to further address these issues.


## Commentary

The school psychologist in this case did not report out of concern for the mother and daughter. He also refrained because Nicole was no longer permitted to have contact with her father, and, therefore, felt her safety was secured. Nevertheless, the father was at continued risk for sexually abusing Nicole in the future and perhaps other children as well. Without intervention, it would not be possible to bring external pressure on the father to receive treatment and to keep him from harming other children.

## Lessons Learned

- A child's apparent current safety should not preclude reporting.
- Being aware that another person may have filed a previous report does not mean that reporting is no longer required.
- Reporting is justified by the need to protect all children who may be at risk of abuse.
- Recognizing the potential stress that may result from a child abuse investigation should lead to support and care for victims and families, but such concerns should not deter reporting.

## CASE 5.9. DILLON: WAITING UNTIL THE NEXT TIME TO REPORT

This case involves Dillon, a 10-year-old boy who was placed in an alternative school for emotionally disturbed children. Dillon lived at home with his mother and three younger sisters. He was unable to concentrate in school and was often nonresponsive to teachers or anything else in his environment. After several weeks of regular appointments with his lead counselor, Dillon stated that he was sad and that he was thinking about killing himself. The counselor explored Dillon's feelings and his thoughts of suicide. They talked about Dillon's progress as well as his remaining challenges. During their discussion, Dillon revealed that his father had hit him across the back with a dog leash during a visit the previous week. The counselor asked Dillon if she could see his back, but upon doing so she did not find any marks, welts, or other signs of trauma. Dillon cried and told the counselor that his father hit him almost every time he saw him. Dillon's mother and father had been divorced since he was 6 years old. Dillon said that his mother was never there when his father hit him, but that he had told her about it. The counselor contracted with Dillon not to hurt himself and told Dillon that she was going to call his mother to discuss the beatings and his safety.

The counselor had regular contact with Dillon's mother and spoke with her regarding Dillon's desire to hurt himself and the abuse that he had described. Dillon's mother told the counselor that she knew that her husband hit their son, but that it was just his way of punishing the boy; she never knew it to get out of hand. The mother said that she was not aware of anything that she would call a "beating" and never saw any marks or bruises on Dillon. His mother was surprised and concerned, however, about Dillon's thoughts of suicide. The counselor told Dillon's mother that if her son ever reported any beatings in the future or if there were ever any marks found on Dillon, the school would have to immediately report the incident.

## Commentary

The counselor in this case elected not to report the abuse despite Dillon's disclosure of abuse. The counselor was, however, compelled to examine Dillon's back for injuries and to discuss the abuse with his mother. The counselor trusted Dillon's mother to judge the limits of her ex-husband's use of punishment and the mother's ability to monitor situations in which she had little control. The counselor therefore treated reporting as if it were a last resort without taking any intermediate steps to protect the child. Dillon expressing thoughts of harming himself further complicates the case. By not reporting, the counselor may have risked Dillon being pushed over the edge and resorting to self-inflicted harm as a desperate cry for help.

With respect to report decision making, this case illustrates the difficulties in distinguishing abuse from corporal punishment. For mandated reporters, the distinction between abuse and corporal punishment may boil down to whether or not there are visible physical injuries. The philosophical debate between parental rights and child protection notwithstanding, professionals are charged with reporting suspected abuse on the basis of their own observations. This is particularly problematic when nonmedical professionals suspect physical and sexual abuse but are not qualified to physically examine children. Thus, the proper differential determination between abuse and corporal punishment must be left to an appropriate investigation that may include physical examinations by health care professionals, home visits, and interviews.

## Lessons Learned

- Differentiating child abuse from corporal punishment requires the type of information that is gained in a child abuse investigation.
- Evidence of physical abuse is not a prerequisite for reporting.
- Mental health professionals dilute their roles and overstep their areas of competence by conducting physical examinations.
- Delaying reporting until the next incident of abuse may unnecessarily place children at risk.

# CASE 5.10. PAIGE: WALKING THE LINE ON PUNISHMENT AND ABUSE

Researchers who were studying children's memory for recent and distant past life events in an elementary school found themselves involved in this case of abuse. The parent's informed-consent policy included a clear statement of the limits of confidentiality. Specifically, the informed-consent form stated that "any information identified during the course of the study that revealed harm or possible harm to your child will be reported to school officials and to local child protection authorities." It was within this context that an 8-year-old girl named Paige described her memory of an incident that involved being hit by her mother. She said that when she did not follow her mother's directions, her mother hit her "very hard and that it hurt bad for a long time." The researcher who interviewed the girl discussed the situation with the research team. These discussions led the researcher to call Paige's parents to ask them about the situation. Her parents came to the school to talk with the researchers and acknowledged the incident that Paige had described. They openly discussed their use of corporal punishment without any defensiveness. The parents said that they had established limits for their use of punishment and punished Paige only under certain circumstances. Both parents said that they did not feel that they were extreme in their use of punishment. The researchers discussed their conversation with the parents in their next team meeting and decided that the situation did not constitute child abuse and therefore did not report the case. However, the researchers did call Paige back to tell her that if she ever felt that someone, including her parents, were hurting her, she should tell her teacher, principal, and other adults about what was happening.

## Commentary

This case illustrates how professionals can blur their professional roles when they evaluate suspected child abuse before reporting. The researchers in this case sought information from Paige's parents to find out more about the situation in which Paige described herself as being hurt. The researchers explored their suspicions before reporting, despite their provisions in the informed consent process that clearly stated the necessity of reporting suspected child abuse. The researchers also acted outside of their professional roles to discuss what Paige should do if she felt she was being hurt again. The message that Paige was given, therefore, was a mixed one. She was told that she should tell an adult if her parents hurt her, even though she already did tell the researchers, who chose not to intervene.

**Lessons Learned**

- Researchers, like clinicians, should not take it upon themselves to investigate their suspicions of abuse before reporting.
- Researchers who assess a family for child abuse potential before reaching a decision to report are acting outside of their professional roles.

## CASE 5.11. RITA: RESPONSIBILITIES FOR ENSURING THE REPORT

This case concerns a psychologist who was working as a consultant to a child abuse prevention program. Her primary role with this agency was to conduct public information and education presentations to children in schools. After completing a presentation, an 8-year-old girl named Rita approached the psychologist and told her, "My aunt hits me in ways like you said." The psychologist took Rita aside and gently asked her what she meant. Rita said that she lives with her aunt and that her aunt "beat" her with a belt. As a consultant to the program, the psychologist believed that it would be most appropriate to discuss the situation with her project supervisor, who was also the director of the agency. The director was quite concerned about Rita and told the psychologist that the situation would be reported. Nevertheless, the psychologist told the agency director that, as a mandated reporter, she should report the situation herself. The director said that consulting psychologists did not have any need or authority to report suspected abuse because the staff social workers managed these responsibilities. The psychologist honored the director's policy and did not file a report with the child protection system. However, the psychologist was not informed as to whether a report was actually filed and what its outcome was.

**Commentary**

Professionals who work within an agency or service organization must attend to the agency's requirements, policies, and procedures for reporting suspected child abuse. Consultants to such agencies will also have to work within these same constraints. However, a consultant as well as a part-time staff person may find himself or herself with poorly defined roles. As a mandated reporter, the psychologist recognized that it was necessary to report the case as suspected abuse. However, the agency's policies for reporting required that the report be filed by a staff social worker. Although the psychologist did inform the program director of the suspected abuse, she was not informed that an official report was filed. In many states, mandated reporters can *cause* a report in response to suspected abuse, but the professional who suspects abuse must ultimately be responsible for following up to ensure that a report was, in fact, filed. In this case, the psychologist was under the impression that the agency would report, but the psychologist did not know that they did report.

**Lessons Learned**

- States that allow professionals who suspect abuse to cause a report in place of making the report place a burden on the professional who suspects abuse to ensure that a report is indeed filed.
- State reporting laws supercede agency policies on mandated reporting.
- Duplicate reports for the same suspicion of abuse should be avoided, but a duplicate report is probably better than no report at all.

## CASE 5.12. MEGAN: SUSPECTED ABUSE DEFINED BY VISIBLE INJURIES

This case involves an outpatient therapist who was working at a community mental health center. The therapist was referred a 14-year-old girl, Megan, whose academic performance had quickly deteriorated. Megan's school counselor made the referral and stated that Megan was acting disrespectfully toward her mother. Megan lived with her twin brother and their mother. Megan's mother had been divorced since the children were 5 years old. During their first session, the therapist interviewed Megan and her mother, both separately and together. The therapist found that Megan's and her mother's accounts of Megan's behavior were similar. They both said that Megan was unmotivated in school and that she had started smoking cigarettes, skipping classes, and staying out past the time her mother set for her to be home. Megan's mother felt out of control and unable to manage Megan's behavior. During the session she cried and said that she needed help.

The therapist asked Megan and her mother to describe the way in which the mother disciplined Megan and her brother. The mother stated that curfews and grounding had failed with Megan because she disregarded her mother's rules. It was such blatant disregard that led Megan's mother to use other forms of punishment. Megan's mother said that she punished her daughter by "hitting her on the backside with a heavy cloth belt." The therapist directly asked Megan's mother if the hitting ever left marks on her daughter, to which the mother said absolutely not. The mother did, however, admit that hitting Megan did not help matters, but that she felt better because hitting helped her release her frustration and anger.

Wanting to verify the mother's account of what was happening, the therapist asked Megan about the discipline. Her description was strikingly similar to her mother's. Although she hesitated at first, Megan also said that her mother hit her with a cloth belt. The therapist, whose entire practice involved child and family therapy, had established a working threshold for reporting physical child abuse: She reported only when there were bruises, welts, or other physical symptoms and injuries caused by abuse.

**Commentary**

This case illustrates a working definition of *reasonable suspicion* and how it is used as a trigger for reporting suspected child abuse. The therapist in this case set a standard for reporting physical abuse that was based on visible marks on the child, a criterion consistent with many legal definitions of abuse. On the basis of the verbal reports of Megan and her mother, the therapist believed that the mother's punishment was harsh but that it did not constitute child abuse. If this case were more broadly interpreted by a law that focuses on potential harm, it would surpass legal standards for reporting. This case therefore illustrates the role of professional judgment and professional discretion in interpreting legal standards and in deciding when to report suspected abuse.

**Lessons Learned**

- Setting a working threshold for reporting suspected child abuse could cause professionals to ignore the unique aspects of an individual case.
- Mental health professionals are not qualified to perform physical examinations, so relying on physical symptoms to report will lead to low rates of reporting.
- Deciding not to report suspected child abuse places an added service burden on therapists, counselors, and other mandated reporters who must then work on their own to protect children.

## CONCLUSIONS

These cases demonstrate complex interactions among factors that raise suspicions of child abuse, and how these factors complicate reporting decisions. Although some cases of suspected child abuse involve salient and apparent signs of abuse, suspected abuse can also arise from vague circumstances. Even when salient signs of abuse are present, reporting is tempered by a number of factors. For example, cases of abuse are often left unreported because they occurred in the past, and because the abuser no longer has access to the child and therefore seems to pose no further threat of abuse. Concerns about confidentiality, shielding children and families from involvement with the child protection system, and beliefs about child protection services also influence decisions not to report suspected child abuse.

Suspected abuse that occurs in educational and mental health service settings will almost invariably involve an inability to detect the battered child syndrome. Thus, unlike medical professionals, mental health professionals must rely on disclosures of abuse, descriptions of abusive situations, and inferences about the emotional and physical well-being of a child. Suspicions of abuse based on subtleties often occur within the context of ongoing therapeutic relationships, when concerns about privacy, trust, and respect play crucial roles in providing services. Applying a standard to diverse professions has led to many mental health professionals' dissatisfaction with mandatory reporting laws. Nevertheless, mental health professionals commonly endorse the need for required reporting and the need to obey state reporting laws. Chapter 6 presents cases of suspected abuse in which reports were filed.

# 6

# REPORTED CASES OF SUSPECTED CHILD ABUSE

The cases described in this chapter concern suspected child abuse that was reported to the child protection system. As in the previous chapter, these situations are neither exhaustive nor representative. They were edited to disguise the identity of participants.

## CASE 6.1. JAKE: SUSPECTED SEXUAL ABUSE REPORTED BY A STUDENT INTERN

A predoctoral psychology intern working at a medical center was rotating on a substance abuse treatment ward. During a routine screening of Jake, a 35-year-old patient being admitted for detoxification, the intern completed a standard assessment protocol. While being interviewed, the patient complained of depression and family problems. Jake believed that many of his problems, including his drinking, stemmed from his relationship with his wife and stepchildren. Jake's wife was waiting for him in the lobby, so the intern requested to speak with her to obtain her perspective. It was common practice on this ward to include family members as part of the comprehensive assessment. Although reluctant, Jake eventually agreed to allow his wife, Veronica, to join the interview.

At the start of the couple's interview, Veronica began to cry and said to the intern, "Did he tell you what he did to my baby?" In front of Jake, Veronica proceeded to tell the intern that Jake had fondled her 10-year-old daughter from her previous marriage. Jake admitted to fondling the girl and began to cry, saying that he was sorry for what he had done. Jake said that he wanted help for all of his problems, including what he had done to his stepdaughter.

Exposed to mandated reporting laws in graduate school, the intern was certain that he was required to report the case and informed Jake and Veronica that a report would be filed. Before reporting, however, the intern discussed the case with his rotation supervisor. Much to the intern's surprise, his supervisor stated that hospital policy was to never disclose any information about adult patients without a signed release. In addition, the intern was told that the state reporting statute, unlike the law in his home state, specified that a child needed to be seen directly by a mandated reporter before a report became required. The hospital policy was therefore consistent with the state reporting law. The intern was ultimately instructed by the rotation supervisor not to report.

Troubled by the situation, the intern went to the internship clinical training director. After relating the incident and the supervisor's response, the director informed the intern that the supervisor understood the law correctly and the intern was not required to report. However, the director believed that there was an ethical and moral obligation to report the case, including protecting children and getting the patient into treatment. The director overruled the intern's supervisor and instructed the intern to report and to inform the family that a report had been filed.

### Commentary

This case represents an instance when abuse was reported but the law did not technically mandate reporting. The case represents two different perspectives displayed by two supervisors: the first, who responded in accord with the law; and the second, who believed that reporting was the ethical course of action. The rotation supervisor may have been concerned with hospital policy, patient rights, and the fact that the man was seeking treatment for substance abuse. On the other hand, the clinical training director expressed concern for protecting the alleged victim as well as other children from abuse. The law did not require reporting in this case, but reporting was viewed as the ethically correct thing to do.

### Lessons Learned

- Including the limits of confidentiality in informed consent reduces potential confidentiality conflicts in reporting.
- Subordinates and trainees can find themselves caught among

agency policies, supervisor's orders, the law, and their own conscience. Sources for resolving such conflicts in training settings are essential.

- Ethical and moral obligations to protect children should supercede the letter of the law.

## CASE 6.2. CLAUDIA: PHYSICAL ABUSE OF AN ADOLESCENT GIRL

A therapist started seeing a 14-year-old girl, Claudia, in individual counseling. Claudia was brought in for treatment after her mother learned that a 17-year-old boy in their neighborhood had sexually assaulted her daughter. Claudia discussed the incident with her parents, who then called the police. Claudia exhibited many symptoms common to adolescents with a history of sexual abuse, including thoughts of harming herself, depression, and erratic changes in mood. She attended only two sessions with the therapist before refusing to come back to therapy. Although they wanted her to continue therapy, Claudia's parents did not force her to attend.

Three weeks after Claudia's last session, the therapist received a phone call from her father, who said that an argument he was having with his daughter had gotten out of control and that he ended up "smacking her." The family came in for a session the next day, and the therapist noticed a sizable bruise on the side of Claudia's face. When the therapist questioned Claudia about the bruise, she said that her father had slapped her the previous day during an argument. Although it seemed that such acts of violence were rare, the therapist believed striking Claudia that hard on the face warranted the attention of child protective services. The therapist proceeded to inform the family that she would file a report with the authorities. The therapist was motivated to report because it seemed that the external pressures on the family would get them back into therapy.

**Commentary**

In addition to following legal requirements to report, the therapist in this case was motivated to report to help structure consistent interventions for the family. The message the therapist sent to the family was that the situation was serious and deserving of attention. The professional did, however, delay reporting the situation in order to schedule an appointment the next day to see the child and further discuss the situation. Although a report may have been filed immediately, the professional exercised discretion based on previous experiences and her therapeutic relationship with the family. The therapist in this case, therefore, acted in the best interests of the child and family as well as adhering to the mandatory reporting law.

### Lessons Learned

- Reporting should be constructed within the context of therapeutic relationships.
- Failure to support parents of abused children will increase family stress and potentially lead to further abuse.

## CASE 6.3. MARIA: SEXUAL ABUSE INFLICTED BY A FELLOW PROFESSIONAL

Janice was a 45-year-old woman being seen in therapy to help her adjust to her recent divorce. Janice had a 14-year-old daughter, Maria, who lived with her. Janice told her therapist that Maria was in mandated treatment at a local sex therapy clinic because her father had sexually abused her and the abuse had been substantiated through a child protective agency investigation. Although Maria no longer had contact with her father, Janice was still concerned about her daughter and continued to discuss her with the therapist. Janice told the therapist that Maria had revealed that when she was about 7 years old, she and her younger brother, who was 3 years old at the time, engaged in "sexual exploration." Maria's child therapist told Janice that she believed Maria was a perpetrator as well as a victim and wanted to do some testing on her that would include a vaginal plethysmograph—a vaginally inserted instrument that measures changes in pelvic blood flow. Maria would be shown sexually explicit pictures to which her responses would be monitored and interpreted. Janice said that she was hesitant to allow this procedure but was being pressured by the treatment center. Janice told her therapist about these events and her concerns, seeking her advice. The therapist stated that, in her opinion, this examination could be sexually traumatic to Maria, especially given Maria's history of sexual assault. Concerned about the potential for further harm to the child, Janice's therapist felt responsible to report this information to the local child protection agency.

### Commentary

The therapist in this case was concerned about the potential trauma that could result from another professional's use of invasive assessment procedures. Reporting was therefore consistent with protecting the child and within the scope of mandatory reporting laws. This case helps demonstrate the breadth of circumstances that could be reasonably considered suspected child abuse. The therapist, however, may have first notified Maria's therapist as a professional courtesy and to clarify intent. Contacting professionals directly before reporting their actions to a regulating agency or other authority is itself the ethical course of action. Making contact, however, would not have replaced the report to the child protection system. Directly informing the therapist of the concerns may have opened a channel for discussion, which could have been beneficial to all involved.

### Lessons Learned

- In concert with professional ethics, professionals should contact colleagues before reporting their conduct to authorities.
- Cycles of abuse can be perpetuated by questionable therapeutic and evaluation practices.

## CASE 6.4. BILLY: REPORTING PSYCHOLOGICAL–EMOTIONAL ABUSE

During a psychoeducational evaluation, a school psychologist interviewed a 10-year-old boy named Billy, who appeared depressed and withdrawn. Although Billy denied serious problems at home, his affect was sad when he talked about his family. To help build rapport with Billy at the start of the evaluation the psychologist asked him to answer the following question: If you could be any animal, what kind of animal would you like to be? Billy responded, "A horse." When the psychologist asked him to explain his response, Billy said, "Well, they mostly work and people ride on them." The psychologist then said, "That does not sound like fun, what wouldn't you want to be?" Billy replied, "A cow ... because you'd be butchered and eaten." The psychologist placed importance in these responses because they occurred in the context of Billy's negative affect. The psychologist therefore proceeded to talk with Billy at greater length, asking him many abuse-related questions. In doing so, the psychologist learned that Billy's parents left him alone for long periods of time and criticized his behavior and appearance, often leaving him feeling verbally attacked. Billy said that his parents did not hit him, and yet his entire demeanor clearly showed his fear of adults. As a part of the evaluation, the psychologist interviewed Billy's parents, who confirmed what their son had said about his home situation. Although they viewed themselves as strict and saw Billy as needing a great deal of discipline, it became clear that Billy's parents were verbally abusive and had been leaving him alone for extended periods of time, often as long as 6 hr. The psychologist informed the parents about her concerns for Billy and told them that it was necessary to report the situation to the child protection system.

**Commentary**

Emotional abuse poses many challenges to mandated reporting. Unlike sexual abuse, interpreting situations and actions as emotional abuse relies on judgments and definitions that everyone may not agree on. And unlike physical abuse, emotional maltreatment does not leave visible scars to confirm one's judgments. However, when one sees an act of emotional abuse as well as its effects, there is little doubt that abuse has occurred. In this case, the school psychologist acted consistently with how one might handle any type of abuse. The psychologist informed the parents of the report beforehand and framed the report within a therapeutic context. The case also illustrates how different types of professional relationships bring different issues to the reporting situation. Professionals who report within an evaluation or assessment relationship do not break the same level of trust as those within a therapeutic relationship. Indeed, detecting emotional abuse could be viewed as a natural occurrence in evaluating a case such as this one. Provisions for reporting and its implications for evaluation, referral, and subsequent treatment should therefore be established in practice.

**Lessons Learned**

- Emotional abuse requires the same consideration given to other types of abuse.
- Confirmation of abuse by a parent or other adult is not necessary when reporting suspected child abuse.
- Professional relationships, such as those of an evaluator, assessor, or therapist, differ and have different implications for reporting suspected abuse.

## CASE 6.5. AMY: SUSPECTED NEGLECT IN A SCHOOL SETTING

This case involves a counselor employed in an inner-city therapeutic school who managed the treatment program of a 13-year-old girl, Amy, for more than 2 years. The counselor, who had frequent contact with Amy and her family, was familiar with her living situation. Amy's mother was an unemployed single parent. The family's two-bedroom apartment was often home to as many as 10 people at a given time. Thus, Amy's environment was often chaotic.

Aware of Amy's living conditions, the counselor recognized how disadvantage can affect a family and was careful not to confuse poverty with neglect. However, during the school year, Amy's family began to present a number of problems the counselor had never seen before. Amy began to be frequently absent from school, and her mother did not respond to calls from the school. In addition, Amy often complained of being ill, but was not receiving medical attention. She was also acting out when she was in school. She was caught showing pictures of herself in her underwear, openly discussing drinking alcohol, and bragging about stealing from local convenience stores. Despite numerous attempts, the counselor was unable to reach Amy's mother. The counselor subsequently reported her concerns to child protective services at two different times; first, when Amy was repeatedly truant and second when she was caught drinking alcohol. The counselor became increasingly concerned and recontacted the intake worker who handled Amy's case. The child protection worker assigned to Amy stated that neglect was difficult to substantiate in poverty-stricken families and that they were doing all that they could to help Amy and her family.

### Commentary

The distinction between impoverished living conditions and child neglect is well illustrated by this case. The counselor defined neglect on the basis of the mother's actions and absence of actions. As signs of child neglect accumulated, it became apparent that Amy's welfare was not being considered. The counselor thus became increasingly inclined to report. The counselor also suspected neglect when Amy exhibited behaviors that could put her at risk for injury and long-term harm. Finally, the counselor was not able to get a response from direct attempts to contact Amy's mother. It was obvious that a pattern of neglect had emerged that warranted reporting.

The counselor also took initiative to directly contact the child protection worker to follow up on the report. Forming a direct relationship with a caseworker can benefit the outcome of the case at hand, and work toward improving relationships between mandated reporters and child protection workers. When there is consistency and continuity in reporting, the process can become part of an overall effort to care for children and families rather than contribute to isolated events or legal duties.

### Lessons Learned

- Poverty can mask neglect, but the two are not the same.
- Mandated reporters should establish direct contact with child protection workers to follow up on cases and improve consistency of care.

## CASE 6.6. SARINA: SUSPECTED SEXUAL ABUSE IN FOSTER CARE

A foster care agency consulted a psychologist to conduct evaluations and provide crisis intervention one day a week. The psychologist was working with a biological mother whose 6-year-old daughter, Sarina, had been placed in foster care. Sarina was removed from her mother's care following her mother's arrest for possession of cocaine. The psychologist had previously evaluated Sarina for foster placement, and was familiar with the family. Sarina's mother told the psychologist that she had visited Sarina the previous weekend only to discover that she was left alone with two teenage boys living in the foster home. The mother was surprised and upset that Sarina was alone with the boys. One of the boys told Sarina's mother that he was "in charge" of Sarina's care. He also said that he cared for her at night and that they slept in the same bed. The mother took her daughter aside and asked her if anyone had been touching her "down there" (pointing to her pelvic area). The mother told the psychologist that Sarina answered yes, but that she did not elaborate on any incidents of abuse. The psychologist told the mother that she believed the situation should be reported to child protection services. Subsequently, the child was placed in a new foster home because she was being left unattended for extended periods of time. Sexual abuse was never substantiated.

**Commentary**

The psychologist in this case reported a disclosure of suspected sexual abuse without acting to verify the allegations, interviewing the child, or taking any other steps to support her suspicion of abuse. Although almost all states require reporting suspicions of abuse regardless of whether the child is seen by the professional, some states do not require reporting unless the child was directly observed by the mandated reporter. Although professionals may report any suspicion in any state, specific requirements for reporting vary from state to state. Still, the action taken by the professional in this case provides an example of directly responding without hesitation by reporting.

**Lessons Learned**

- Professionals who do not have direct observation of the child suspected of being abused should report their suspicions of abuse.
- Context and circumstances are important considerations when interpreting vague conditions that suggest abuse.

## CASE 6.7. NANCY: FROM ANGER TO PHYSICAL ABUSE

A therapist working in an outpatient alcohol and drug treatment center had been counseling a woman for alcohol abuse. Their 3-month therapeutic relationship began after the woman completed her inpatient treatment. The woman, Nancy, was the mother of a 14-year-old boy and a 10-year-old girl. She was divorced from her children's father for 7 years and was currently separated from her second husband. Nancy had developed a trusted alliance with her therapist, and she made great progress, remaining drug free since initiating treatment. However, during a session, Nancy told her therapist that she had been having a difficult time coping with the stress of raising her two children. Nancy said that she was becoming increasingly frustrated and felt that she could not manage her children's behavior, particularly her son's. Nancy's ability to tolerate the stress seemed to be growing weaker the longer that she remained drug free.

The therapist questioned Nancy about what she was doing to cope with the stress she experienced from parenting. Nancy said that when she found herself unable to effectively parent her son, she ended up getting very angry with him several times a day. When asked how she vented her anger, Nancy said that she sometimes hit him. Although Nancy did not believe that hitting her son would help with his behavior, she said that it relieved her anger and made her feel more in control. The therapist asked her to describe how she hit her son. Nancy was very forthcoming and told the therapist that she hit him on the lower back with the rubber end of a toilet plunger. Nancy said that she used the plunger because it was the most readily available object. She said that she felt ashamed of herself, but could not help it.

The therapist believed that Nancy's behavior constituted child abuse and thus required reporting. Her decision was based solely on the fact that an object had been used to hit the child in the midst of anger. During that same session, the therapist discussed the potential harm that Nancy could cause when her anger was out of control. The therapist told Nancy that she seemed to be experiencing some really tough times and that the problems she was having should become the immediate focus of their therapy. The therapist also told her that it was necessary to report the incident to social services, and that they could provide additional assistance to help keep her children safe.

### Commentary

This case illustrates two important factors that come to play in decisions to report suspected child abuse. First, the act described by Nancy—hitting her adolescent son with a rubber plunger—surpassed the professional's reporting threshold, even without knowledge of injury, visible marks, or other trauma. Second, the decision to report was influenced by the potential for future harm because the mother's anger was escalating. Thus, the therapist may have reported in response to the law, but also did so to protect Nancy and her children.

The therapist's manner of reporting is also worth noting. The context of the report was within an established therapeutic relationship that had helped Nancy to make substantial gains. The therapist was up front with Nancy about reporting and the need to break confidentiality. Reporting was placed in the context of their ongoing therapy and framed as a necessary step in dealing with Nancy's problems. Filing the report in the spirit of a therapeutic alliance kept the focus on Nancy, her treatment, and her therapist's commitment to help her.

**Lessons Learned**

- Disclosure of abuse can occur in trusting relationships where there is an obligation to help.
- Reporting abuse necessarily breaks confidentiality but does not necessarily break trust.

## CONCLUSIONS

Mandatory child abuse reporting laws were enacted to require physicians to report injuries that might otherwise go unrecognized as possible child abuse. Reporting laws were broadened with the intent of making all human service professionals responsible for identifying cases of child abuse. In this respect, mandated reporting has been successful at increasing the number of reports filed by professionals.

Despite the difficulties that reporting requirements pose, few commentators have suggested a complete reversal of mandatory reporting laws. Rarely are policies proposed to allow professionals full discretion in reporting suspected child abuse. Rather, many observers have called for legislative reform, such as clarifying definitions of abuse and neglect (J. Jones & Welch, 1989; Melton & Davidson, 1987), or allowing for delayed reporting by professionals addressing the abusive situation in therapy (Berlin et al., 1991). Others have suggested that there are no problems with reporting laws per se, but rather that the child protection system is underresourced, and so cannot deal with the magnitude of the child maltreatment crisis.

Mandated reporters are most concerned with the welfare of children and families, and therefore share common goals with the child protection system. As seen in the cases reviewed in this chapter, reporting decisions take into consideration the constraints of a situation, past reporting experiences, and the circumstances of the family. However, the outcomes of reporting for the child, family, and professional relationship are partially determined by the process by which the report occurs. Unfortunately, mandated reporters receive little guidance for reporting and must often establish reporting procedures through trial and error. Part III attempts to fill this void by offering guidelines for improving reporting, practice, and policy.

# III

# MANDATORY REPORTING PRACTICE AND POLICY

# INTRODUCTION

# MANDATORY REPORTING PRACTICE AND POLICY

Few people proclaim that mandatory reporting laws are the sole solution to the child abuse crisis. However, when they function at their best, mandatory reporting laws can act as a link between families and child welfare services. In Parts I and II I discussed the complex professional dilemmas associated with mandated child abuse reporting. These final three chapters in Part III explore promising avenues for responding to mandated reporting policies and practices. In chapter 7, I offer a framework for managing reports of suspected child abuse. In chapter 8, training and practice initiatives for improving mandated reporting are outlined. Finally, in chapter 9, I discuss policy initiatives to reform mandatory reporting laws.

# 7

# GUIDELINES FOR REPORTING SUSPECTED CHILD ABUSE

The enactment of a reporting statute is a foolish business unless reported children are, in fact, protected from further injury and offered a brighter life either within the family or with others, should remaining at home prove impossible (Paulsen, 1967, p. 3).

I have difficulty reporting suspected abuse to over-staffed, under-paid [sic], and often inexperienced social service workers. Too often reports are made, social services come into a family, make charges, write a report and proceed to do nothing for children. The therapy process is disrupted due to reporting and can be damaging to families. Reporting abuse does not seem to always be the best solution to abuse—but it is the law in my state. (Survey participant, Kalichman & Brosig, 1992)

Mandated reporters tend to lack formal training in reporting procedures, and there are no standards for managing reports of suspected child abuse. Indeed, graduate education rarely offers specific training for managing cases of child abuse (Howe, Bonner, Parker, & Sausen, 1992; Kalichman & Brosig, 1993; Pope & Feldman-Summers, 1992). Professionals are often left alone to decide when and how to report suspected abuse. Practical experiences are what shape professional attitudes toward reporting and practices for handling abuse cases. Experience can also increase one's accuracy and efficiency of reporting, and build skills that transfer to future reporting decisions. Despite the virtues of experience, research shows that clinical experience is often unrelated to clinical judgment (Dawes, 1989; Garb, 1989). Accumulated experiences in reporting suspected child abuse do not, therefore, necessarily improve clinical decision making. Because each case of child abuse is unique, and because child protection policies vary across local agencies, it is difficult to conceive of general guidelines that are applicable to all settings and professions. For example, factors that influence emergency-room physicians to report usually vary from those that influence primary-care physicians (Warner & Hansen, 1994). There are, however, rules of thumb to assist professionals in reporting and to improve reporting practices. Offering a source of guidance seems particularly important because mandated reporters play important roles in the child protection system.

Reports of suspected abuse set into motion a series of events within the child protection system. Like in a game of dominos, once a report is filed, and a case enters a screening process, an investigation is triggered that includes risk assessments and various forms of interventions. To facilitate the reporting process and track the progress of a report, mandated reporters need to maintain communications with caseworkers. Compaan, Doueck, and Levine (1997) found that mandated reporters' satisfaction with the child protection system was influenced by the quality of contact among reporters and caseworkers. In this case, quality was determined by such factors as the exchange of information and the perceived sensitivity of workers. Involvement with the system also makes it possible to follow up on a report, and to provide information that may be important to an ongoing professional relationship with the family. Thus, although reporting starts with a simple phone call, professionals can expand their roles within the child protection process to include multiple forms of intervention (Besharov, 1988). Unfortunately, many mandated reporters have not yet acquired a working knowledge of the child protection system that affords effective and efficient reporting. Figure 7.1 represents the common flow of events that follow the reporting of suspected child abuse to child protection agencies.

Once a professional has decided to report suspected child abuse, he or she must make a series of additional decisions, including the following: how to inform parents or guardians and children of the report, what appropriate information to release in the report, and what strategies to use to follow up on the report. To aid mandated reporters with these issues, several states have prepared brochures that provide information on reporting. For example, the Michigan-based Child Abuse Prevention Services distributes a brief guide to responding to abuse. Among its suggestions for responding are the following: Believe the child who discloses abuse, be a good listener, reassure the child that he or she will be protected, help the child process guilty feelings and combat self-blame for the abuse, be available to the child for

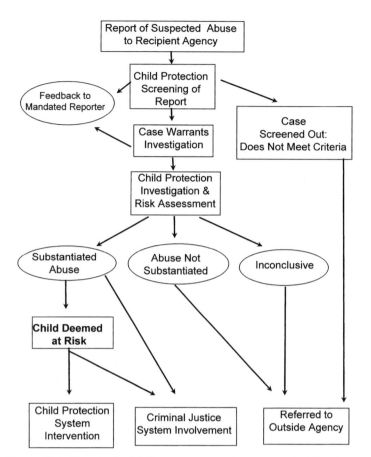

*Figure 7.1.* Events that follow a report of suspected child abuse.

support and understanding, protect the child's rights to privacy, and follow up on the report. However, there are few guidelines for reporting suspected child abuse that address these issues in greater detail. This chapter aims to provide practical suggestions for reporting suspected abuse in mental health services, as well as in other human service arenas.

## INTERVIEWING CHILDREN

Suspected child abuse arises primarily in two clinical contexts: treatment or evaluation of adults who reveal abuse or describe abusive situations, and treatment and evaluation of children. Although there are frustrating problems associated with trying to assess the presence abuse from the words of adults receiving clinical services (Kalichman, Brosig, & Kalichman, 1994), these pale in comparison to the difficulty of detecting abuse through clinical interventions with children. A complete discussion of interviewing those children suspected of being abused is well beyond the scope of this book (see Ceci & Bruck, 1995; Poole & Lamb, 1998), but this section will briefly review key issues in interviewing children who may have experienced abuse.

Few areas of clinical service are as controversial as the accuracy and reliability of children's recall of past events. Particularly controversial are questions regarding the influence of adults on children's memories, especially on those of abuse. Research shows that detailed clinical interviews and investigative questioning can alter the perceptions and reported memories of young children. Child suggestibility research also shows that young children's memories can be manipulated by subtle suggestions (Ceci & Bruck, 1995; Ceci, Loftus, Leichtman, & Bruck, 1994). Even slight changes in wording or alterations in the environment create social pressures that bias children's memories and descriptions of events (Goodman, Bottoms, Schwartz-Kenny, & Rudy, 1991). Thus, clinicians who lack specialized training in interviewing abused children are cautioned against conducting these interviews. A poorly conducted interview not only yields misinformation, but it can also bias responses in later interviews.

Another significant issue in interviewing children is a child's developmental level and its implications for his or her ability to interpret questions and provide reliable answers. The quality of information collected from children is dependent on a child's cognitive skills, including attention, memory, conversational descriptions of memories, understanding the distinction between truth and lies, and distinguishing fantasy from reality (Melton et al., 1995; Poole & Lamb, 1998). Of particular importance is memory source monitoring, or the process of identifying the origin of a memory. Children under age 10 experience difficulty remembering how they acquired a particular memory. Remembering that the source of a memory is even more complicated when there are similar potential people or settings that are easily confused (Parker, 1995). Young children may therefore provide an honest account of an experience, but they are vulnerable to confusing details of a memory, including its origin.

Finally, the quality of an interview with a child is affected by the skills of the interviewer. Clinically interviewing children requires specialized training, and interviewing abused children requires even further specialization. Mental health professionals who primarily serve adults should exercise caution when interviewing children suspected of being abused. One reason why some professionals have been held liable for failing to report suspected abuse is the fact that they conducted child clinical interviews without proper training. Thus, they may have been practicing outside of their competence.

N. E. Walker and Nguyen (1996) discussed guidelines for interviewing child witnesses that may be applied to interviewing victims of child abuse. Interviewers, they suggested, should prepare for the interview, create an appropriate environment and climate for the interview, and frame all questions and interview content in developmentally appropriate language and concepts. More specifically, they encouraged interviewers to use an active voice to keep the child's attention; to avoid negatives, such as "is it not true ..."; to use simple words; and to include only one query within a question. N. E. Walker and Nguyen also emphasized the importance of establishing rapport, of explaining what can be expected in the interview, and of engaging the child in the interview process. Without careful attention to the needs and characteristics of children, child interviews may do more harm than good in detecting abuse and protecting children.

## INFORMING PARENTS, GUARDIANS, AND CHILDREN

Professionals who report suspected child abuse must decide the extent to which parents, guardians, and children will be involved in the reporting process. In many cases, parents or guardians are informed about the necessity to report and are provided with a sense for what to expect following the report (Racusin & Felsman, 1986). The potential exists for angry parents to react to the report by lashing out at the professional, or by abusing the child again. Professionals who inform parents of the report before contacting the child protection system can assess the situation and take appropriate action to reduce parental anger. However, there are instances when parents should not be informed, such as when doing so could increase a child's risk for further abuse (Besharov, 1990). The danger of not informing parents and children about the need to report is that it can create a secrecy around reporting and give the impression that reporting is the wrong thing to do.

There is also an ethical obligation to inform parents of breached confidentiality. According to the *Ethical Principles of Psychologists and Code of Conduct* (APA, 1992), discussions of confidentiality should be renewed with clients "as new circumstances may warrant" (Principle 5.1). Telling parents and children that a breach of confidentiality is necessary is easiest when an informed consent policy has already fully explained the limits to confidentiality. Individuals who have been informed of the limits to confidentiality may actually come to expect a report to be filed when questions of child abuse surface. When reporting is understood at the outset, parents can be encouraged to openly discuss their feelings about the report, and it may be possible to resolve their anger in a clinical setting.

When a suspected perpetrator of abuse is informed of the need to report, it may be possible to encourage them to self-report to child protection services (Stadler, 1989). Although self-reports do not replace a professional's mandate to report, self-reported abuse can demonstrate the perpetrator's recognition of the problem and the seriousness of the situation.

It can also serve as a call for help. Self-reporting also affords opportunities to assume responsibility for one's own actions and allows for at least some control in what might otherwise be a powerless situation. Perpetrators can report abuse directly from the professional's office, so that the professional can support him or her before, during, and after the report. Again, the benefits of self-reporting, including admitting a need for help, may be explained to suspected perpetrators, and they should be encouraged to report themselves if possible. Professionals should follow up on self-reports and work with child protection workers to monitor the progress and disposition of the report.

Reactions of parents and children who are informed of an impending report of suspected child abuse are primarily determined by the context within which the information is delivered. Professionals might communicate that the report is being made out of care and concern for the child and family, as well as the professional's ethical responsibilities and legal mandate. Expressing concern and a willingness to get involved by reporting focuses attention on protecting the child and can even increase trust in professional relationships (M. Levine, Anderson, Terretti, Sharma, et al., 1991; M. Levine, Anderson, Terretti, Steinberg, et al., 1991; Watson & Levine, 1989). In a treatment setting, reporting should also be related to ongoing efforts to resolve family conflicts and child emotional well-being.

## PREPARING FOR THE REPORT

Reporting suspected child abuse involves more than a simple call to a child abuse hotline. Before reporting, professionals should first collect and organize information that will be needed to make the report (Finlayson & Koocher, 1991). Local child protection agencies differ with respect to the details they require to take a report of suspected child abuse, but there are certain elements of information that are almost universally included in a report that will optimally assist child protection workers. For example, the name of the child, the child's age, sex, address, and current whereabouts are necessary for a report to be accepted. In addition, information about other children in the home, the names and addresses of the child's parents, information regarding the circumstances of abuse, and the identity of the suspected perpetrator are almost invariably required for reporting. In addition, intake workers should know who else has been informed about the report. Information about the child's safety and the child's risk for future abuse are also important elements. One state has delineated the following seven areas that should be included in a report of abuse: (a) the name, address, telephone number, and occupation of the person reporting; (b) the name and address of the victim; (c) the date, time, and place of the incident; (d) details of the reporters observations and beliefs concerning the incident; (e) statements relating to the incident made by the victim; (f) the names of persons believed to have knowledge of the incident; and (g) the name of individuals believed to be responsible for the incident and their connection to the victim (Caudill & Pope, 1995). Exhibit 7.1 shows a sample form for organizing and documenting information that should be collected prior to reporting. Although much of the desirable information may be missing, a report should be filed with as much information as possible. Aggregated reports of abuse are often necessary for launching an investigation, so even reports with incomplete information can make a difference.

Mandated reporters must provide their name to intake workers when they file a report. Although in most cases the reporter's identity remains confidential, the limits of this confidentiality should be discussed with the intake worker, because states vary in the terms and degree of confidentiality granted to mandated reports (Meriwether, 1986). Under most conditions, however, maintaining confidentiality of the report is of minimal concern to mandated reporters because of their duty to report and potential liability for failing to report. Obviously, filing an anonymous report will not serve

EXHIBIT 7.1
Sample Form Used to Document the Information Collected
During Report

---

Prereporting Checklist for
Organizing Information Needed for the Report

---

Identifying information about the child

| | |
|---|---|
| Name | Address |
| Age | Sex |
| Current whereabouts | Additional information |

Circumstances of abuse
Date and time information about
abuse was obtained
Date and time of most recent
abuse
Type of abuse
Signs of abuse recorded
Perceived severity of abuse

Information about suspected perpetrator

| | |
|---|---|
| Name | Address |
| Age | Sex |
| Current whereabouts | |

Additional information, such as information about siblings, parents, and home environment

Current circumstance and potential risks

---

to protect mandated reporters from liability, because there will be no record of the report.

Mandated reporters should also collect information from the worker who receives the report, including his or her name, position, and contact information. The reporter may also try to determine whether the report will be investigated and what the expected time frame is for screening and investigation. Documenting the information contained in a report provides a record for the mandated reporter and makes it unnecessary to remember exactly what he or she said in their report (Finlayson & Koocher, 1991).

## REPORTING SUSPECTED CHILD ABUSE

Once the information that is needed to report is collected and organized, the next step is to contact the social service agency responsible for taking reports (see Appendix C for a listing of state reporting agencies). There are, however, additional ethical considerations to make when determining what to include in a report. The level of detail released in a report should be limited to an amount that minimizes breaches in confidentiality while maximizing child protection (Melton & Limber, 1989). It is not necessary to release information in a report unless it will assist the social service agency in making determinations of abuse or will help the agency to take action on behalf of the child and family. As stated in the *Ethical Principles of Psychologists and Code of Conduct* (APA, 1992), "In order to minimize intrusions on privacy, psychologists include in written and oral reports, consultations, and the like, only information germane to the purpose for which the communication is made" (Standard 5.03a). In reporting suspected child abuse, the purpose of the information released is to protect children. Information should therefore be limited to the degree to which child protection will be achieved.

State statutes have detailed the minimum amount of information required in a report. For example, in Minnesota,

> Any report should be of sufficient length to identify the child, any person believed to be responsible for the abuse or neglect of the child if the person is known, the nature of the child's injuries, and the name and address of the reporter. (NCCAN, 1989, p. MN-6)

Likewise, in Oregon,

> If known, such reports shall contain the names and addresses of the child and his parents or other persons responsible for his care, the child's age, the nature and extent of the abuse (including any evidence of previous abuse), the explanation given for the abuse and any other information the person making the report believes will be helpful in establishing the cause of the abuse and the identity of the perpetrator. (NCCAN, 1989, p. OR-3)

Professionals should be aware that including more information than is necessary in a mandated report, and providing additional information after a report is filed, can violate privacy rights and can raise issues of liability (Pope & Vasquez, 1991). Circumstances unrelated to the suspicion of abuse, such as details of family life and family relationships that are peripheral to the abuse, need not be included in a report. For example, information about marital relationships or a parent's history of being abused as a child may be of clinical importance, but are not necessarily relevant for the purposes of reporting. The narrative section of a report describes the circumstances of suspected abuse and should be limited to the signs, symptoms, acts, omissions, and verbal disclosures that support the suspicion of abuse that subsequently led to the reporting decision. Law requires that information be included in the report, but participating in an investigation is not required. Releasing information following a report may be an unethical breach of confidentiality. Mandated reporters are encouraged to cooperate with the child protection system, but should also carefully consider information that is later divulged after the initial report (Pope & Vasquez, 1991).

Intake workers may request information from mandated reporters that they believe is necessary to conduct assessments and to investigate the report. For example, workers may want to know whether or not the child requires medical attention or if medical services have already been requested. Workers may also want to know about the lapses of time between the reporter's awareness of the situation and the initial report, as well as the names of potential witnesses to the abuse, involvement of substance abuse, and information regarding current risks or danger to the child (Wisconsin Department of Health and Social Services, 1985). When unsure about the ethics of divulging certain details in their reports, professionals should communicate their concerns to the worker and take steps toward providing sufficient information for child protection that also maintains the greatest possible confidentiality (Melton & Limber, 1989).

Telephoning a state or local child protection agency almost always initiates reports of suspected child abuse. In many states, a written report is required to follow a verbal report. This is another reason why a written record of the information included in the verbal report is useful. Many states provide forms for written reports. This limits the amount of detail required. Figure 7.2 presents an example of a written report form used by Connecticut. State agencies often make these forms available to reporters, and they can be useful for organizing information for both verbal and written reports. Connecticut, for example, has made its forms available through the Internet (http://www.smith-lawfirm.com/mandatory_reporting.htm). After receiving a report of suspected child abuse, the child protection agency first screens the report and conducts an assessment of the child's potential risk for abuse.

**REPORT OF SUSPECTED CHILD ABUSE/NEGLECT**
DCF-136  08/97 (Rev)

HOTLINE
1-800-842-2288

See the reverse side of this form for a summary of Connecticut law concerning the protection of children.

Within forty-eight hours of making an oral report, a mandated reporter shall submit a written report (DCF-136) to the Hotline.

*Please print or type*

| CHILD'S NAME | ☐ Male ☐ Female | AGE OR BIRTH DATE |
|---|---|---|

CHILD'S ADDRESS

| NAME OF PARENTS OR OTHER PERSON RESPONSIBLE FOR CHILD'S CARE | ADDRESS |
|---|---|

| WHERE IS THE CHILD STAYING PRESENTLY IF NOT AT HOME? | DATE PROBLEM(S) NOTED |
|---|---|

| NAME OF HOTLINE WORKER TO WHOM ORAL REPORT WAS MADE | DATE OF ORAL REPORT | DATE AND TIME OF SUSPECTED ABUSE/NEGLECT |
|---|---|---|

| NAME OF SUSPECTED PERPETRATOR, IF KNOWN | ADDRESS | RELATIONSHIP TO CHILD |
|---|---|---|

NATURE AND EXTENT OF THE CHILD'S INJURY(IES), MALTREATMENT OR NEGLECT:

INFORMATION CONCERNING ANY PREVIOUS INJURY(IES), MALTREATMENT OR NEGLECT OF THE CHILD OR HIS/HER SIBLINGS.

LIST NAMES AND AGES OF SIBLINGS, IF KNOWN.

DESCRIBE THE CIRCUMSTANCES IN WHICH THE INJURY(IES), MALTREATMENT OR NEGLECT CAME TO BE KNOWN TO THE REPORTER.

WHAT ACTION, IF ANY, HAS BEEN TAKEN TO TREAT, PROVIDE SHELTER OR OTHERWISE ASSIST THE CHILD?

| REPORTER'S NAME AND AGENCY | ADDRESS | TELEPHONE NUMBER |
|---|---|---|
| REPORTER'S SIGNATURE | POSITION | DATE |

WHITE COPY: TO HOTLINE  PO BOX 882  MIDDLETOWN, CONNECTICUT 06457    YELLOW COPY: REPORTER COPY

*Figure 7.2.* Child abuse report form used by child protection intake workers in Connecticut.

## SCREENING AND INITIAL RISK ASSESSMENTS

The growing number of child abuse reports has created a series of gates through which reports of suspected abuse are channeled. Managing reports of suspected child abuse includes an initial screening process, prioritizing reports that are screened into the system, and preliminary assessments of child risk (Besharov, 1987a, 1990; Wells et al., 1989). In screening reports, child protection workers evaluate information obtained in the report by using a number of parameters to determine the status of the report in the child protection system. Table 7.1 summarizes the activities that commonly occur after a report is received, particularly screening and initial risk assessments. Reports can only move past the initial screening if they surpass a second decision threshold set by the child protection system. Screening cases includes an initial risk assessment, which allows the intake agency to use discretion in determining whether to accept a report for investigation (Wells et al., 1989).

Screening criteria vary considerably across local child protection agencies (Wells et al., 1989). Criteria for screening can simply include that enough information be provided to enable the location of the child and the parents who are the subjects of the report. Or screening may also include a determination of whether or not the indicators of abuse included in the report fit the state's definitions of child abuse or neglect. For example, a child protection agency may retain reports under the condition that "if the allegation presented were true, the situation would constitute abuse or neglect as defined . . ." (Illinois Department of Child and Family Services, 1992, pp. 300–306). Thus, reports must usually meet with state definitions of abuse or neglect to proceed further into the child protection system.

Intake workers receiving the report may immediately conduct an initial screening and formulate a decision as to whether the report proceeds. The reporter can therefore request information regarding the status of the report during this first contact. The caseworker may tell the reporter whether the information provided warrants an investigation. Reports that

## TABLE 7.1
### Child Protective Service Actions Following Reported Suspected Abuse

| I<br>Intake | II<br>Meets Screening Criteria:<br>Initial Assessment | III<br>Substantiated Case:<br>Provision of Services |
|---|---|---|
| Report received | Investigative contacts and visits conducted | Risk assessment continued |
| Family is checked for current and previous recorded reports | Child risk assessment continued | Thorough family assessment conducted |
| Report is screened | Emergency services provided | Intervention strategy developed and executed |
| Apropriate referrals are considered | Court involvement determined | Appropriate services provided and progress evaluated |
| Investigation status is determined | Case management assigned | |

are weeded out of the system may be terminated from further action, or may be referred to another agency outside of the child protection system for intervention. Reports deemed inappropriate for action because they do not meet the minimum criteria for investigation may still warrant services. If the report is not investigated, professionals can request that the report remain on file in case the same family is reported again in the future. Reports kept on file also provide an official record of the mandated report. Reports that are found appropriate for child protective system involvement are investigated and undergo a more thorough and comprehensive process of risk assessment.

Once screened for investigation, reports are prioritized using criteria that may include the severity of abuse, type of abuse, child's age, and the apparent risk of injury or harm to the child. Reports can also be prioritized according to the caseload demands of the agency and available agency resources. Some states terminate the investigation of a report when it does not meet a minimum level of risk or when it contains insufficient information to identify or locate the child and parents (Wells et al., 1989). On the other hand, some states prioritize reports and eventually investigate all reports received.

Certain reports of abuse may be classified by the receiving agency as emergencies that require immediate action, perhaps as quickly as within 1 hr. Emergencies are usually defined by a child being in imminent danger, and may involve notifying law-enforcement officers. Reports that are not determined to be emergencies are assigned to a caseworker, who is required to contact the child or family within 24, 48, or 72 hr, depending on the state. Reports can also be prioritized according to the type of abuse described. For example, an agency may prioritize reports into three levels: Highest priority is given to those reports that involve death, brain damage, subdural hematoma, internal injuries, wounds, torture, sexually transmitted diseases, sexual molestation, failure to thrive, and malnutrition; moderate priority is assigned to those reports that include none of the characteristics of the first level, but do involve burns, scalds, poisoning, bone fractures, cuts, bruises, welts, human bites, tying or closed confinement, substantial risk of physical injury, or abandonment; and lowest priority is assigned to reports of inadequate food, shelter, clothing, and other forms of environmental neglect (Illinois Department of Child and Family Services, 1992). Reports may therefore be responded to according to their designated priority level, with the most severe reports slated for immediate investigation.

## CHILD PROTECTION INVESTIGATIONS

When reports are accepted by a child protection agency and proceed through the system, they usually involve a series of actions required by state law. Specific interventions vary with local agencies. For example, in North Carolina,

> The Department of Social Services shall make a prompt and thorough investigation in order to ascertain the facts of the case, the extent of the abuse or neglect and risk of harm to the juvenile, in order to determine whether protective services should be provided or the complaint filed as a petition. When the report alleges abuse, the Director shall immediately, but no later than 24 hours after receipt of the report, initiate the investigation. (NCCAN, 1989, NC-7)

In contrast, Arizona law requires the following:

> After receipt and initial screening ... of any report or information ... immediately: (a) notify the municipal or county law enforcement agency; and (b) make a prompt and thorough investigation of the nature, extent, and cause of any condition which would tend to support or refute the allegation that the child should be adjudicated dependant [sic]. (NCCAN, 1989, p. AZ-8)

As reflected in these two examples, the role of law enforcement agencies in child abuse investigations also varies across community standards. Some states require that law-enforcement officers be notified upon receipt of a report, whereas others require that law-enforcement involvement occur only when reported abuse is substantiated. Still other states immediately involve police, but only in certain types or conditions of abuse. For example, states can require immediate law enforcement notification and a joint investigation with child protection workers only for reports of sexual abuse. When law enforcement officers are involved, it is the child protection agency's responsibility to make these contacts.

Child protection investigations typically involve home visits by caseworkers, who interview the parents, child, and alleged perpetrator. Individuals included in the report as well as those not in the report, such as children, parents, and siblings, are also usually interviewed. Failing to interview persons included in the report is often officially acceptable if a caseworker has made repeated attempts to contact these persons but was unable to do so. In addition, teachers, school administrators, family members, neighbors, and others may be interviewed as a part of the investigation. Child abuse investigative interviews usually solicit information to answer specific questions regarding the alleged abuse. Investigation procedures are typically idiosyncratic—based on the circumstances of the report, the local agency procedures, and the individual style of the assigned worker. Investigations are conducted to determine the child's condition and the potential risk for injury or harm. The purpose of the investigation is therefore one of fact-finding and a search for evidence of maltreatment to determine a child's risk for abuse.

Child abuse investigations serve two purposes: (a) a criminal investigative function—to evaluate the extent of harm and danger posed to a child, and (b) a social service function—to predict whether or not a child will be maltreated in the future. Risk assessments involve comprehensive examinations of the child's well-being, family resources, and living conditions (Pecora, 1991). Although a brief assessment of risk for abuse is conducted during the initial intake, risk assessments are considered an ongoing process and involve more elaborate methods that are introduced during the course of the investigation. One common method used by investigation agencies involves the rating of child and family characteristics along several dimensions of potential risk. Factors that can be assessed in a risk assessment include parenting skills, frequency and severity of abuse, the perpetrator's accessibility to the child, the child's ability for self-protection, and the recency of abuse. Each factor may be rated as having a low, moderate, or high level of risk (Pecora, 1991; Wisconsin Department of Health and Social Services, 1985). A matrix is then constructed to comprehensively represent levels of risk for each assessed factor. Figure 7.3 presents an example of some typical components included in some risk assessment matrices. Risk factors included in the risk assessment may consist of constellations of associated factors or may emphasize empirically defined predictors of child abuse (Pecora, 1991).

In addition to assessments that tabulate risk factors, matrices have been developed to assess family strengths and resources. Family assets and strengths provide valuable information for long-term predictions of abuse that may not be readily apparent to field-workers who are otherwise focused on identifying problems. In addition, family resiliency can be overlooked when working with families from unfamiliar cultural backgrounds (Caldwell et al., 1992). Family strengths and resiliency can form a context within which risk factors are embedded, allowing for more comprehensive deter-

| Risk Factor | Positive Indicator | Low Risk | Moderate Risk | High Risk |
|---|---|---|---|---|
| Protection of Child | Caretaker willing and able to protect child, using good judgment | Caretaker willing but occasionally unable to protect child | Caretaker vacillates or inconsistently protects child | Caretaker refuses or is unable to protect child |
| Extent of Emotional Harm | No emotional harm or behavioral disturbance | Minor distress or impairment in role functioning | Behavioral problems that impair social relationships or role functioning | Extensive emotional or behavioral impairment |
| Extent of Physical Injury or Harm | No injury, no medical treatment required | Superficial injury, no medical attention required | Significant injury, Unlikely to require medical attention | Major injury, substantial effect on development requiring medical treatment |

*Figure 7.3.* Example of a risk-assessment matrix. Adapted with permission from Caldwell et al. (1992).

minations of abuse and service needs. The majority of state child protection agencies have adopted an instrument to facilitate systematic evaluations of children and families (Berkowitz, 1991).

An example of an objective and standardized risk-assessment instrument used by child protection agencies is the *Child at Risk Field* (CARF; Holder & Corey, 1986). The CARF system allows workers to define risk on the basis of a comprehensive evaluation of five factors: (a) the child, (b) parents, (c) family and home, (d) maltreatment, and (e) intervention (Pecora, 1991). Workers identify the potential threats within each factor for each situation by using a set of standard definitions for potential risk. For example, parenting behavior is scored along a continuum from appropriate parenting to destructive parenting. Appropriate parenting is defined by CARF as when

> (the parent) generally exhibits parenting behavior which takes into account the child's age capacity; possesses reasonable expectations for the child; understands and acts on the child's strengths/limitations/ needs; uses varied and acceptable disciplinary approaches; provides basic care, nurturing and support; demonstrates self-control. (Depanfilis, Holder, Corey, & Oelson, 1986, p. 273)

In contrast, destructive parenting is defined as when

> (the parent) exhibits parenting behavior which is based on the parent's needs; demonstrates expectations which are impossible for the child to meet; ignores the child's strengths/limitations/needs; aversion to parenting; employs extreme/harsh disciplinary approaches, including violence, threats and verbal assaults; generally does not provide basic care and/or support; deliberately takes frustrations out on the child; self-righteous. (Depanfilis et al., 1986, p. 273)

CARF therefore provides a framework for the worker's observations, impressions, and judgments to formulate comprehensive estimates of child risk. When correctly implemented, CARF also provides information over the life of a case—from intake to termination. The system also assesses the urgency of maltreatment by using factors related to the child, family, and home. Strengths and weaknesses are aggregated and summarized to determine relative levels of risk. For example, a child under the age of 6 who requires medical attention, with a parent who is impaired or excessively agitated, would constitute an urgent case of maltreatment (Depanfilis et al., 1986). Doueck, Levine, and Bronson (1993) formally evaluated CARF and found that, when implemented correctly, it provides caseworkers with a systematic guide for decision making. In addition, when information obtained from CARF was integrated with other sources of information, Doueck et al. found that specific clinical decisions were enhanced, such as deciding to keep a case open or to obtain additional services. These findings lend support to CARF's usefulness in field applications.

Risk-assessment instruments that utilize matrices and comprehensive rating systems for structuring information gained in abuse evaluations have, unfortunately, limited data to support their reliability and validity (Pecora, 1991). Studies investigating the accuracy of risk-assessment instruments for detecting risk levels have varied. Correct classification rates as low as 15% have been found, and false-negative rates as high as 50% (Pecora, 1991). In addition, studies have been conducted only to determine the association between risk assessments and substantiated abuse. There have been few prospective studies of the predictive validity of risk-assessment instruments (Pecora, 1991).

## WORKING WITH CHILD ABUSE INVESTIGATORS

Mandated reporters may have no further contact with child protection workers after they have filed their report of suspected abuse. However, child protection workers may contact reporters to gather additional information as investigations unfold. Child protection workers may seek details of suspected abuse to supplement information contained in the report, or they may need more information to help clarify discrepancies between the report and investigation findings. Because providing additional information after a report is made could violate confidentiality, interactions with case-workers should be limited to the information contained in the report. Child protection workers, however, may view professionals who have reported the abuse as important sources of information that can help in their investigation. Thus, any opportunity to expedite an investigation will likely be seized by workers given their demanding workloads.

Reporting suspected child abuse could also involve contact with the police. In some states law-enforcement officers are involved in child abuse investigations from the start, whereas in others, the police are involved only in making an arrest. Police officers will usually be less sympathetic about issues of client confidentiality than child protection workers. Still, mandated reporters are no longer under obligation to break confidentiality to assist in an investigation of child abuse, including assisting the police. Mental health professionals are again cautioned against revealing additional information to any investigators seeking evidence in a criminal case. Police officers will, however, likely press for information, because the standards for proving a case of child abuse far exceed the standards for reporting. In other words, more information will be required to prosecute a case of abuse than was necessary to require the initial report (Brahams, 1988). Mandated reporters can cooperate with investigators by focusing on the child's safety, without disclosing new information about the child or family. Keeping written documentation of the report as well as all subsequent communications with investigators is essential.

## CHILD ABUSE INVESTIGATION FINDINGS

The goals of child protection investigations are to assess children's risks and to determine the occurrence or absence of child abuse. Local child protection agencies vary in their definitions and criteria for substantiating child abuse. In almost all systems, however, there are three potential outcomes of a child abuse investigation: (a) *Not able to substantiate/inconclusive*: Maltreatment is left undetermined because of a lack of facts, such as when the child or parents cannot be located for investigative interviews. (b) *Unsubstantiated*: Insufficient information exists to pursue charges of child abuse (Weissman, 1991). Here, abuse and neglect are not found and the family is determined to have no need for protective services. However, the investigation may have uncovered problems that required them to be referred to outside service agencies. (c) *Substantiation*: Abuse or neglect is confirmed and activating child protective services is considered to be appropriate. In this case, the investigation may also have found that individuals or families require intervention. Assuming there are adequate resources available, substantiated abuse triggers some form of intervention. This can range from a referral for services to placing the child in protective care.

Almost half of all reports of child abuse are substantiated upon investigation. However, substantiation rates for reports filed by mandated reporters can be as much as 23% higher for physical abuse and 13% higher for sexual abuse when compared with reports filed by nonmandated reporters (Eckenrode, Munsch, Powers, & Doris, 1988; Eckenrode, Powers, et al., 1988). Not all families in which substantiated abuse is determined, however, receive services. In fact, resources for social services have decreased at the same time that reports have increased. Some studies show that nearly half of confirmed cases of child abuse receive social service intervention (Meddin & Hansen, 1985; Salovitz & Keys, 1988). Nationally, approximately 30% of confirmed cases of child abuse are receiving some type of services (Wang & Daro, 1998). Although over 1 million children were being served in 1994, this number shrank from 1.8 million in 1977. Similar reductions in services are observed for children receiving in-home services, foster care, and other types of child welfare. For families that do receive services, the most common assistance involves preventive, protective, and support services (Wang & Daro, 1998).

Unsubstantiated reports filed by professionals may reflect the narrowing of standards among criteria for reporting suspected child abuse and criteria for substantiating abuse. For example, definitions of abuse are far more narrow for substantiating abuse than the reasonable suspicion of abuse required for reporting (Giovannoni, 1989b). The intent of mandatory reporting laws is to detect a maximum number of cases of child abuse. Therefore, greater sensitivity to detect abuse is invoked in reporting (e.g., reasonable suspicion), compared with the increased burden of proof for substantiation (e.g., preponderance of evidence), which is less restrictive than the standard for convicting in a criminal case (e.g., beyond reasonable doubt). Figure 7.4 shows the different operating standards—reasonable suspicion and preponderance of evidence—in relation to the steps in the child abuse reporting process.

Incomplete information and ambiguity often characterize unsubstantiated reports of abuse. Reports with less detailed information are less likely to proceed through each step of the child protection system (Wells et al., 1989). Unsubstantiated cases do not necessarily mean that abuse has not occurred, but rather that the preponderance of evidence resulting from the investigation does not meet the standards required for substantiation. Criteria set by the child protection system, therefore, result in a higher threshold for intervention. It is accepted that some cases of abuse will go undetected. The logic behind the system as a whole follows that the reporting system accepts higher rates of false positives—cases where abuse may not be occurring, in balance against higher rates of false negatives—cases where abuse is occurring but not substantiated. The result is that there will invariably be more reports made by professionals than there are investigations and more investigations of abuse than there are substantiated cases.

*Figure 7.4.* Reasonable suspicion and preponderance of evidence in relation to child abuse reporting.

One reason for higher substantiation rates among reports filed by mandated reporters is that human service professionals obtain detailed and specific information regarding child abuse. Medical professionals, for example, are likely to observe symptoms consistent with nonaccidental injuries, and these observations are expected to raise suspicions of child abuse. Likewise, mental health professionals frequently observe emotional and behavioral changes in children that raise suspicions of child abuse. Mental health practitioners, guidance counselors, schoolteachers, and other professionals who develop trusting relationships with children are also likely to learn about the lives of children, and thus hear about abuse. However, every instance of suspected child abuse does not constitute a reasonable suspicion, and may not warrant reporting. To help resolve ambiguous cases, mandated reporters should consult their colleagues for an outside perspective. Professionals may also contact child protection workers to informally ask about cases. Child protection workers will often share their impressions about whether the circumstances warrant reporting. Taking such steps can help professionals report cases with greater confidence and to avoid reporting cases that child protective services will consider inappropriate. Ultimately, they will avoid cluttering an already overburdened system.

## REPORTING OTHER VULNERABLE POPULATIONS

Laws that mandate the reporting of suspected abuse have been extended to include victims other than children. Most states, for example, require professionals to report any known or suspected abuse of the elderly (Macolini, 1995). One state defines adult abuse as "the willful infliction of physical pain, injury, or mental anguish; unreasonable confinement, or the willful deprivation of services which are necessary to maintain a person's physical and mental health" (Wulach, 1998, p. 192). In addition, exploitation, defined here as "the act or process of using a person or his resources for another person's profit or advantage," is also required to be reported (Wulach, 1998, p. 192). In addition to abuse of the elderly, abuse and neglect of adults receiving care in a nursing home or other residential setting or institution must be reported. States also consider physical or fiduciary abuse, abandonment, and isolation of dependent adults to be reportable offenses (Caudill & Pope, 1995). Laws pertaining to the required reporting of adult abuse generally include similar definitions of who must report, when a report must be filed, how reports are made, and provisions for immunity from liability. In addition, the penalties for failure to report are similar to those applied to the failure to report suspected child abuse. Another emerging area of mandated reporting is in cases of spousal abuse. Research has shown that women who have experienced domestic violence strongly support mandated reporting requirements (Coulter & Chez, 1997). However, physicians and other mandated reporters may not comply with domestic violence reporting laws. Rodriguez, McLoughlin, Bauer, Paredes, and Grumbach (1999) found that a majority of California physicians believed that laws concerning intimate violence reporting bring potential risks to parties involved and raises ethical concerns. This suggests that physicians are unlikely to comply with the law. Therefore, most of the suggestions offered in this chapter for guiding reports of suspected child abuse can be extended to reporting adult abuse.

## CONCLUSIONS

Child protection workers are overburdened and have poor resources. Agency standards may prohibit assigning more than 25 to 30 new cases a month to workers, but even these limits are often exceeded due to the crisis in child protection. Because they are responsible for heavy workloads, child protection workers are likely to try to manage cases as rapidly and efficiently as possible. Professionals who include well-organized and complete information in a report can assist child protection workers in the process of screening and investigating reports. Mandated reporters should also request information from workers regarding the status of their report, such as the outcome of screening and prioritizing, and try to find out the estimated time line for an investigation of suspected abuse. Reporting laws usually specify that mandated reporters be informed of the final status of their report, but more information throughout the process may be useful to mandated reporters and their clients.

Assuming that a cooperative relationship between mandated reporters and the child protection system will result in greater child protection, professionals can take steps toward building such relationships. For example, contacting workers assigned to a case can facilitate ongoing relationships among reporters and child protection workers. Another mechanism for building relationships with a child protection worker is to request a discussion group or presentation from the child protection agency. Small groups of mandated reporters may interact with workers and ask questions about the child protection system and procedures related to reporting. Direct contact with child protection agencies can open channels for asking questions about future cases. Open communication and cooperation between mandated reporters and child protection workers throughout the reporting and investigation processes will benefit all concerned parties, especially children and their families.

# 8

# PROFESSIONAL PRACTICE
# AND RESEARCH

It is critical that psychologists know what constitutes an appropriate psychological assessment of suspected child abuse so that they know how and when to respond to the legal requirements of mandatory reporting laws. This includes knowing how to recognize reportable situations and what steps to take in specific jurisdictions where they practice. (L. E. Walker et al., 1989, p. 8)

Scientific societies and professional organizations are especially influential in the formation and review of child and family policy. As such, they are able to lead the development and diffusion of relevant knowledge. (U.S. Advisory Board on Child Abuse and Neglect, 1990, p. 52)

Mental health professionals, teachers, school counselors, nurses, and pediatricians stand on the front line in the war against child abuse. Most of the professionals in these fields, however, receive little graduate training in dealing with child abuse. It is therefore not surprising that mandated reporters are often unsure of what to do when faced with suspected child abuse. With millions of children abused in the United States each year and many of these children coming in contact with mental health professionals, there is an obvious need for practical guidance in how to manage suspected child abuse. This chapter offers practical steps toward developing standards for reporting and procedures for the clinical management of suspected child abuse. This chapter also presents an overview of initiatives to enhance professional training in child abuse and recommends areas for future research on the mandated reporting of suspected child abuse.

## ETHICAL STANDARDS AND MANDATED REPORTING

Professional ethics codes have not been particularly helpful in resolving conflicts created by the differences among standards of confidentiality and legal requirements to report suspected child abuse. Professionals are simply advised to "make known their commitment to the Ethics Code and take steps to resolve the conflict in a reasonable manner" (APA, 1992, p. 1598). Ethics committees, of course, do not advocate breaking the law, and ethics codes do not establish standards for professional behavior outside of the law. Ethics codes and ethical principles are written for a broad spectrum of circumstances rather than for a particular situation, so the nuances of mandated reporting must be seen through a broader lens.

Mandatory reporting laws themselves do not help to guide professional in their decisions to report, because the laws are either too vague or too narrow to be useful as decision criteria. In addition, reporting laws do not translate to standards for professional practice (Finlayson & Koocher, 1991). Professionals are thus often left to define their own personal standards for what constitutes a reasonable suspicion of child abuse. Some commentators and policy analysts have suggested that professionals tend to overreport suspected abuse, and believe that it is better to err on the side of reporting (i.e., Finlayson & Koocher, 1991; C. E. Walker, Bonner, & Kaufman, 1988). In contrast, other commentators advise professionals to use stricter reporting criteria, stressing the negative aspects of breaking confidentiality and cautioning against straining the child protection system (Ansell & Ross, 1990; Besharov, 1990). Although arguments are made for both overreporting and underreporting suspected child abuse, the decision to report ultimately remains with the individual clinician who must interpret the meaning of reasonable suspicion.

## POINTS OF ETHICAL CONSIDERATION IN MANDATED REPORTING

The following 11 ethical points are not meant as standards of practice, but to provide a stance for guiding ethical practices in mandated reporting. Given the breadth of issues to which ethics codes must apply, recommendations tailored to mandated reporting may be useful (see Exhibit 8.1).

*Mandated reporters should have current and accurate knowledge of their state mandatory reporting laws.* Over the last two decades, professionals have

## EXHIBIT 8.1
## Points of Ethical Consideration in Mandated Reporting

Know your state mandatory reporting laws

Provide informed consent with details of limited confidentiality

Remember that disclosures of abuse surpass reporting thresholds

Suspicions based on subtle signs of abuse should not be immediately dismissed

Boundaries of professional competence and roles should be maintained

Parents or guardians should be informed of reports unless doing so would endanger children

Keep detailed records of reports

Follow up reports with child protection workers

Verify cases believed to have been reported by clients, supervisors, colleagues, or others

Discuss ambiguous cases with colleagues

Training in abuse should parallel professional contact with potential abuse

---

become increasingly aware of mandated reporting, and have assumed greater knowledge of their own state laws. Professionals should be familiar with how their state defines child abuse and neglect, as well as the conditions under which reporting is required, time constraints, and procedures for filing verbal and written reports. Professionals should also be familiar with how local child protection systems manage reports of abuse and how legal structures dictate child protection.

*Informed-consent procedures should be used in treatment and research to clearly detail the conditions under which confidentiality is limited.* Clients should be provided with the details of an informed-consent policy that includes the limits of confidentiality at the outset of a professional relationship. Procedures for informing persons of limited confidentiality can be delivered verbally, in writing, or both. In any case, limitations to confidentiality should be described in a way that clients can comprehend. When written informed consent is sought, professionals should verbally discuss with clients the limitations of confidentiality and other important points, to clarify issues and answer questions. Optimally, procedures for informed consent involve a discussion of limited confidentiality and a written statement that clients can take with them.

*Verbal revelations of child abuse should always be reported.* Disclosures of child abuse or neglect by either a child–victim or an adult-perpetrator warrant investigation. It is beyond the role of human service professionals to discern the credibility of a discloser. Disclosures by third parties— persons other than the victim or perpetrator in the case—are not as reliable because of the potential motivations for falsely accusing someone of abuse. Nonetheless, all disclosures and allegations of abuse warrant child protective system investigation.

*Suspected child abuse that arises from behavioral or physical signs of abuse may require greater consideration before reporting.* When signs of abuse do not meet a reporting standard, professionals must decide whether to probe for further information (Pruitt & Kappius, 1992). Professionals who remain ambivalent about reporting subtle signs of abuse should also consult with colleagues or make preliminary contact with the child protection system to discuss the case.

*Professionals should practice only within their areas of competence, and should take care not to overstep their limitations.* Mandated reporters should avoid taking actions that are not part of their usual duties. When professionals feel compelled to go beyond their skills and roles to manage a case of suspected child abuse, it probably indicates that they should report and let child protection workers investigate.

*Parents and guardians should be informed before reporting, unless doing so endangers children.* The negative effects that reporting can have on professional relationships are minimized when the report is placed in the context of a therapeutic relationship. Professionals who believe that informing parents of a report will endanger a child should definitely include such a concern in their report.

*Mandated reporters should document information released in their report.* Records of oral reports as well as copies of written reports are an essential part of reporting. In addition, subsequent contact with the child protection system, the police, or anyone else regarding the reported abuse should be documented.

*Professionals should follow up reports with the child protection system.* Information about the screening, outcome, investigation, and status of a report can be requested from child protection workers. Contact with case workers can occur from the time the report is filed until the case is closed.

*Professionals who do not report because someone else has already reported should follow up to verify that a report was indeed filed.* Verifying that a report was made should involve contact with the child protection system, rather than solely relying on the person who filed the report. Professionals can request that their name be placed on file with the original report to ensure a record of their compliance with the state reporting law.

*Suspected child abuse that does not surpass reporting standards should be discussed with a colleague to achieve an objective perspective on the case.* Professionals who state that they consistently report suspected child abuse are also the most likely to discuss cases of suspected child abuse with colleagues. Seeking the opinion of a second mandated reporter serves as a check against one's own judgments and decisions.

*A professional's training in child abuse should reflect his or her contact with abused children or abusive adults.* All human service providers should be somewhat familiar with child abuse issues and reporting laws. Because abuse can emerge in virtually every clinical setting, a minimal standard of training should be achieved. Providers who have more frequent contact with abuse and abusers should be expected to have more advanced training.

## STANDARDS, DEFINITIONS, AND REPORTING THRESHOLDS REVISITED

There are a few guidelines for managing the duty to report suspected child abuse. Idiosyncratic reporting standards tend to rely on the observation of bruises, welts, and marks; malnutrition; verbal descriptions of violent acts; rejection; humiliation; unsheltered living; and descriptions of sexual abuse (Brosig & Kalichman, 1992a; Finlayson & Koocher, 1991). These observations are clear in terms of their ability to meet reporting requirements because they fit well within the parameters of the legal definitions of abuse. Thus, failure to report in these instances clearly violates reporting laws and exposes professionals to liability for not reporting. For more ambiguous situations, however, such as observing disruptive behaviors, emotional distress, precocious sexual behavior, or disclosures by persons other than victims and perpetrators, the circumstances become farther removed from legal definitions of abuse. Cases that require the most professional judgment are the cases that professionals are least likely to be held accountable for not reporting.

Suspected child abuse is often characterized in the literature by either highly salient and specific indicators of abuse or subtle and nonspecific indicators. This dichotomy is apparent in studies that use contrived scenarios to investigate factors that influence reporting decisions (Finlayson & Koocher, 1991; Kalichman & Craig, 1991). In practice, however, clinical cases are rarely so simple. In fact, suspected child abuse is more likely to result from an accumulation of signs that evolve over time than from a single instance or observation. Subtle signs of abuse, such as changes in a child's behavior or descriptions of their family, can lead professionals to suspect that a child is at risk. They may also open the door to more leads for verifying child abuse.

A child's behavior also carries a different meaning during different periods of child development (Finkelhor, 1984; Wurtele & Miller-Perrin, 1992). For example, a preoccupation with sexual behavior can be considered sexual acting out when it involves a 6-year-old but will be interpreted more normatively when it involves a 15-year-old. Different indicators of sexual abuse, for example, appear at different rates across developmental periods (Friedrich et al., 1992).

# A HIERARCHICAL APPROACH TO MANAGING AMBIGUOUS SUSPICIONS OF ABUSE

Mandated reporters who fail to report signs of abuse that meet legal definitions of child abuse and neglect can be held liable for failure to report. Professional discretion, however, can be exerted within the constraints of the law when the suspected abuse does not meet the legal definitions of abuse. The act of reporting suspicions that do not fit within the legal definitions of abuse is permitted, and perhaps even encouraged, by the law. Reporting laws are designed to free professionals from the burden of investigating their suspicions of abuse. Professionals can, however, always explore vague suspicions within the boundaries of their professional competencies and roles.

The close kinship between mandated reporting and duty to warn suggests that similar decision-making processes may apply in these situations. Southard and Gross (1982) proposed a decision tree applicable to duty-to-warn cases that has value in the context of mandated reporting. Although some of the decisions in duty-to-warn cases do not directly correspond to suspected child abuse, Southard and Gross's schema provides a starting place for adapting a decision tree for child abuse reporting. As shown in Figure 8.1, indicators of abuse that do not warrant reporting can be further explored, discussed with a colleague, or discussed with a child protection worker. At any point in the process, the suspicion can either rise to a level that justifies reporting or can be dismissed.

## Exploring the Situation

Role conflict occurs when professionals act outside of their competence and capacity to investigate child abuse. For example, school psychologists who have no previous contact with a family should not prioritize talking with family members about their suspicions of abuse before reporting. Similarly, therapists should not contact a teacher before they report. Reporting decisions should be based solely on information gathered in the course of professional activities, such as evaluating, teaching, counseling, or conducting research. Within these situations, professionals can further explore their concerns about a child.

Direct questions, such as "Is someone touching you in a way that makes you feel uncomfortable?" or "Did you leave marks on your child after hitting him or her?" can confirm abuse. However, a parent's denial of abuse may merely reflect his or her unwillingness to admit abuse, therefore offering less than conclusive information. Children and adults who respond to direct questions about abuse by becoming quiet or by refusing to answer may be communicating important information. Thus, how pro-

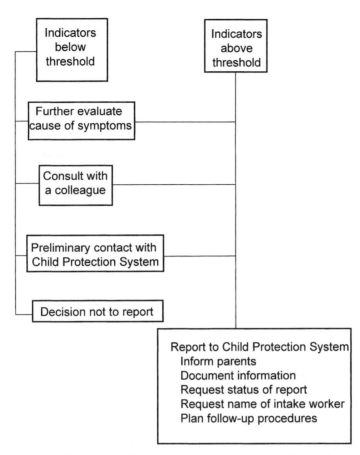

Figure 8.1. Child abuse report decision-making tree. Adapted with permission from Southard and Gross (1982).

fessionals process this information determines the inferences they draw about the situation and their decisions to report.

### Consultation

When an evaluation and exploration of a case remains ambiguous as to whether to report, it is appropriate to consult a fellow mandated reporter. Professionals should identify in advance potential colleagues who they think are qualified to discuss abuse and can offer insight. Seeking advice can also occur in conjunction with case conferences and staff meetings. Through frank discussions, it may become apparent that a case constitutes reasonable suspicion. On the other hand, consultation may also help a professional decide not to report. Once again, when reporting decisions are not reached after consultation, the next course of action is to make preliminary contact with a child protection worker.

## Preliminary Contact

Mandated reporters can contact a child protection worker for feedback on a case before reporting, particularly on whether certain indicators of abuse are reportable. Professionals may discuss cases with an initial intake worker who receives reports, or with a caseworker with whom the professional has had previous experience. Even in the most ambiguous cases, input from child protection workers will most likely resolve the decision to report or not to report suspected abuse.

## Summary

The law does not permit mandated reporters to engage in a decision-making process when there is a reasonable suspicion of child abuse. When professionals have reason to suspect abuse but choose not to report, it is usually due to competing concerns, such as disrupting treatment, maintaining trust, or questioning the child protection system. The process of weighing options in a decision to report is similar to balancing the relative costs and benefits in any uncertain decision (Fischhoff, 1992). Organizing the factors that led to the suspicion in the first place can help professionals judge whether their concerns warrant reporting. Once it is decided to report, professionals should inform parents, organize and document information, and develop communication channels for following up with child protection workers. In some cases it may be appropriate to offer the opportunity for adults to self-report or to ask them to be present while the report is made (Stadler, 1989).

## PROFESSIONAL TRAINING IN CHILD ABUSE AND MANDATED REPORTING

The most common solution offered for dealing with child abuse reporting is training practitioners to recognize child abuse and to know their reporting responsibilities (Besharov, 1988; Faller, 1985). Most service providers lack training in child abuse, including mandated reporting and other ethical issues in treating children (Plante, 1995). Kim (1986) found that more than half of physicians believed that they were not adequately prepared to detect and manage cases of child abuse. Similar findings emerged from studies of schoolteachers (Levin, 1983) and Head Start workers (Nightingale & Walker, 1986). Among practicing psychologists, Kalichman and Brosig (1993) found that most training in child abuse occurred in postgraduate and continuing education workshops. Less than 20% of the psychologists surveyed indicated that they were exposed to issues of child abuse in graduate school. Psychologists sampled from the clinical, psychotherapy, and independent practice divisions of the American Psychological Association were likely to perceive their graduate training in child abuse as poor and viewed their internship training in child abuse as only slightly better (Pope & Feldman-Summers, 1992). Thus, typically, providers who have recently received their degrees have little training and experience in child abuse (Alpert & Paulson, 1990). A survey of clinical, school, and counseling psychology graduate programs found that only 11% offered courses dealing with child abuse, and the three program areas did not differ in the amount of child abuse training students received (Howe, Bonner, Parker, & Sausen, 1992). Because professionals are expected to make reporting decisions throughout their career, it is a cause for concern that professional training is concentrated in *post*degree continuing education (Alpert & Paulson, 1990; Kalichman & Brosig, 1993; J. Wilson, Thomas, & Schuette, 1983).

There have, however, been initiatives directed at increasing graduate training in child abuse. A child abuse training curriculum can be structured to address the major issues that clinicians face while managing suspected child abuse. For example, the Committee on Professional Practice and Standards (1995) of the American Psychological Association identified the following 10 key questions to help frame issues that can form the structure of a training curriculum:

- What constitutes child abuse and neglect?
- Who has to report child abuse and neglect?
- If I report, am I breaking confidentiality?
- Under what circumstances do I have a duty to report child abuse?
- How do I report, and what information am I required to disclose in a child abuse report?
- Will I get in trouble if I do not report child abuse as required under these state laws?
- Will I get in trouble if I do report? Can the person I report sue me?
- Do I have to report every instance of child abuse?
- Do I have to report if the suspected abuser is in treatment or if I believe that reporting would do more harm than good?
- What will be the response to my report?

These questions can be used as a framework for content and discussion topics. The questions can also serve as a springboard for generating discussions.

It is possible to infuse child abuse intervention training into graduate practica, internships, postgraduate fellowships, case conferences, continuing education courses, and workshops. Training can also occur in graduate courses or as a bridge across curricula. With respect to developing courses in child maltreatment, Alpert and Paulson (1990) described a model graduate course on child sexual abuse. Topics included the scope and prevalence of sexual abuse, laws and mandated reporting, the initial and long-term effects of child abuse, developmental considerations, assessment and interviewing techniques, treatment, and prevention. Examples of student assignments, topics and formats for class discussions, and techniques for supervision were also provided. In its document, *A Guide for Including Information on Child Abuse and Neglect in Graduate and Professional Education and Training* (1996), the American Psychological Association specifically suggested that course content address legal involvement in child abuse and neglect:

> Abused children and their families may be involved in the legal system in a variety of ways. Describing these can help students understand the functioning of the legal system in abuse and neglect cases and the influences of their involvement on children and families. Discussions can focus on important conflicts between defendants' rights and victims' rights (e.g., should hearsay testimony be allowed more easily in abuse cases) and between family rights and state rights (e.g., what process must the state complete to remove a child from an abusive home). Furthermore, discussions of the roles of police, prosecutors, social workers, and mental health professionals in abuse cases can provide important information about how they can function smoothly together or work at cross-purposes to each other. (p. 6)

Training can also be tailored to professionals working in particular settings or geared toward a general audience of mandated reporters. Short-term intensive training, such as workshops, can focus on mandated reporting, whereas more in-depth approaches, such as courses, seminars, and practica, may more broadly address the scope of child abuse. Graduate research-methods courses may also cover relevant issues, including detailed procedures for informed consent and the limits of confidentiality. Across training models, mandated reporting should cover legal requirements, maltreatment detection techniques, decision-making processes, and procedures for reporting.

## Legal Requirements

Professionals should be well acquainted with their mandatory reporting laws and state reporting requirements. Familiarity with reporting laws is achieved by reviewing current state statutes, including legal definitions of child abuse and neglect. Specific attention should be paid to *who* is required to report, *what* is required to be reported, and *when* reporting is required. Reporting statutes can be obtained by contacting state child protection agencies (see Appendix C). There are also a number of free booklets and pamphlets available from state agencies that discuss mandated reporting. Because reporting laws are subject to change, mechanisms should be built into continuing education for informing professionals of legislation and policy changes.

Being aware of state statutes, however, is only a starting place for professional training in mandated reporting. Reporting requirements should be placed in the context of local social service systems and resources. For example, legal definitions of child abuse and neglect can be placed in the context of local agency criteria for screening reports. Involving local child protection representatives in training for mandated reporters can enhance understanding of mandated reporting from a community perspective. Social service workers can also help discuss the interface between reporting and child protection. Reporting laws can also be placed in the context of professional ethics. Strategies can be developed to manage issues of confidentiality and trust within the constraints of mandated reporting. Professionals can also be trained to implement informed-consent procedures that include discussions of limited confidentiality.

Failure to report suspected child abuse carries the potential for both criminal and civil actions against mandated reporters, so it is important that professionals be aware of the differences between these two types of liability. Legally, failure to report is a misdemeanor in most states, whereas civil suits are usually based on professional negligence. In addition to legal penalties, licensing boards can sanction professionals for not reporting suspected child abuse. Mandated reporters need to know that they cannot be held liable for reporting suspected abuse, even when reports are not substantiated upon investigation. Finally, professionals should be aware of the requirements that the law places on the agency receiving the report, such as the maximum amount of time allowed for their response to a report and the degree to which law-enforcement agencies can be involved in investigations.

## Child Abuse Detection

Recognizing child abuse requires more than just a knowledge of mandatory reporting laws. Subtle indicators of child abuse are easily missed when professionals are unfamiliar with the signs and symptoms of abuse as they present themselves at different periods of child development. Professionals with limited experience in child abuse and childhood trauma may not recognize emotional responses or behaviors as signs of abuse. Less than obvious signs of abuse can be confused with trauma unrelated to abuse, such as parental and family strife. Professionals unfamiliar with the clinical dimensions of child abuse, neglect, and family constellations associated with child abuse are unlikely to suspect abuse unless it is readily apparent. Thus, decision-making criteria concerning reporting are most effective when they are based on empirically defined descriptors of child abuse and neglect in which clinicians are trained. Knowledge alone, however, only results in checklists of symptoms that are insufficient for accurately detecting child abuse (Finkelhor, 1984).

Professionals not only need to know what to look for in identifying child abuse, but also the methods for critically examining their suspicions of abuse. For example, creative interviewing techniques can help professionals to follow up on their hunches and suspicions within the context of a therapeutic relationship. Drawings and interactive play can facilitate young children's expression of trauma (Wiehe, 1992). Techniques for interviewing children, adults, and families must be sensitive to variations in culture, gender, and development. For example, it is not uncommon for professionals to misinterpret normative child rearing practices from unfamiliar cultural backgrounds as abusive (Grey & Crosgrove, 1985).

In cases of suspected child abuse, clinicians tend to rely more on interpersonal interviews than they do assessment tools, perhaps because many instruments lack reliability and validity (Levy, 1989; Mantell, 1988; C. E. Walker et al., 1988). One standardized assessment instrument developed for child abuse evaluation is the anatomically detailed doll interview. Although using dolls as an assessment technique is controversial, studies suggest that interviews using standardized anatomically detailed dolls demonstrate an acceptable reliability and validity (L. E. Walker, 1988; White, Strom, Santilli, & Halpin, 1986). However, when administered outside of standardized procedures or without sufficient training, doll interviews yield findings that are highly suspect. Therefore, professionals who conduct such interviews must be competent and experienced, or the practice could be considered unethical. Wolfner, Faust, and Dawes (1993) reviewed research on the use of anatomically detailed dolls in assessing child sexual abuse and concluded that (a) interviews with anatomically detailed dolls do not elicit a greater base rate of sexualized play among children who have not been abused, (b) sexualized play with dolls appears more frequent in abused than nonabused children, (c) it is unknown whether the use of anatomically detailed dolls increases the validity of child sexual abuse assessments or investigations, and (d) there is no scientific evidence to support the use of anatomical doll play for diagnosing sexual abuse. This lack of solid evidence in support of doll interviews cautions against their use in evaluating sexual abuse.

Although there are few valid assessment instruments for children, there are several useful models available for conceptualizing and organizing the information that is gathered from interviews. For example, C. E. Walker et al. (1988) developed a scheme for organizing potential risk factors associated with physical and sexual abuse, based on identifiable characteristics of abusers, victims, family members, and social–situational factors. Similarly, Sgroi, Porter, and Blick (1982) constructed a conceptual framework for validating child sexual abuse. This model incorporates behavioral characteristics of sexually abused children and physical symptoms of sexual abuse, both of which are evaluated within a developmental context. Recognizing child abuse also requires developing a framework for interpreting subtle signs of child abuse. This is because most behaviors and emotional reactions carry different meanings at different developmental periods (Kendall-Tackett et al., 1993). The value of empirically derived models is that they serve as a framework for professionals to organize their clinical observations.

There have also been advances in standardized behavioral checklists for recording information about children and adults. One promising assessment tool for sexual abuse is the Child Sexual Behavior Inventory (CSBI; Friedrich, Grambsch, Broughton, Kuiper, & Beilke, 1991; Friedrich et al., 1992). This assessment instrument consists of 35 items representing a range of child behaviors, including sexual self-stimulation, sexual aggression, culturally expected gender role behaviors, and personal boundary violations. Each of the behavioral indicators is rated on a 4-point scale by a parent or caregiver. The instrument was modeled after the Child Behavior Checklist (Achenbach & Edelbrock, 1983), and has demonstrated sound measurement properties of reliability and validity. A strength of the CSBI in evaluating child sexual abuse is its empirical basis for identifying behaviors related to child sexual abuse. However, because the measure is completed by a caregiver, it may have limited use in cases of intrafamilial sexual abuse and with parents who minimize or exaggerate child behavior problems.

With respect to assessing adults suspected of committing abuse, Milner (1986, 1989, 1990, 1991; Milner, Gold, & Wimberley, 1986) developed the Child Abuse Potential Inventory (CAP), a standardized and objective test for screening abusive, or potentially abusive, adults. The CAP consists of 160 items with which respondents can either "agree" or "disagree." Items are grouped on a number of subscales, including several that serve as indicators of a propensity for committing child abuse: parental rigidity, unhappiness, distress, and family problems. Although the CAP has shown great promise, it was not developed to definitively diagnose abusiveness. It should be considered to be only one piece of information when evaluating child abuse.

## Report Decision Making and Procedures for Reporting

Training professionals to recognize and manage child abuse, at least with respect to mandated reporting, requires an explanation of the processes involved in making the decision to report (Handelsman, 1989). Decision making is enhanced when professional training is grounded in well-established decision models. Decision analysis benefits mandated reporting because it applies abstract theoretical principles to practical decision-making problems (Fischhoff, 1992). Such an analytical approach to reporting decisions focuses on five formal steps that are common to human decisions: (a) identifying options, (b) evaluating consequences associated with these options, (c) weighing the alternatives according to their relative importance, (d) assessing the probabilities of consequences, and (e) combining these considerations to arrive at a decision. Using these formal concepts to guide clinical judgment enhances training in mandated reporting decisions.

Training in child abuse should include interactive skills-building activities to bolster clinical decisions regarding child abuse. Case conferences and staff meetings are an excellent forum for critically examining ambiguous and challenging cases and illuminating differential diagnoses. Local experts from children's hospitals, pediatrics departments, and child welfare agencies can share their views and present relevant information. Videotapes depicting clinical interviews with children, perpetrators, and families provide opportunities for focused discussions about indicators of abuse.

Through training, professionals may also learn how to develop their own practice guidelines and strategies for reporting. Procedures discussed earlier, such as informing parents of a report and determining information to release in a report, can be tailored to professional settings. For example, a psychologist working in an interdisciplinary agency may be required to follow internal procedures prior to reporting, such as filing a report with a designated administrator. Likewise, professionals working in residential care facilities will manage reports of suspected maltreatment in the context of treatment center policies (Rindfleisch & Bean, 1988). Strategies for managing limited confidentiality will also vary across situations. Thus, training can be useful for fitting reporting into the demands, policies, and practices that are unique to a given agency.

## MANDATORY TRAINING IN CHILD ABUSE AND REPORTING

It is becoming increasingly common for state licensing boards and other professional regulators to require training and continuing education in managing child abuse (Reiniger, Robinson, & McHugh, 1995). The American Psychological Association's Ad Hoc Committee on Child Abuse Policy recommended that "state licensing boards consider requiring child abuse knowledge base for purposes of licensure and relicensure" (L. E. Walker et al., 1989, p. 11). The committee also recommended that the American Psychological Association require coursework or training experiences on child abuse for graduate program accreditation (p. 11). These two initiatives were thought to serve as effective mechanisms for psychologists to obtain minimal standards of familiarity and knowledge of child abuse and neglect, including mandated reporting.

Training in child abuse issues is now required for professional licensure and relicensure in several states. Courses offered for licensure and relicensure typically cover legal requirements to report, legal definitions of child abuse and neglect, identification of significant indicators of abused and neglected children, characteristics of abusive parents, and procedures for reporting. These courses are, at least in part, a reaction to the magnitude of child abuse and the widespread difficulties that professionals face when interpreting reporting laws.

The movement toward mandatory training in clinical management of child abuse has not been fully embraced by professionals. O'Connor (1989), for example, criticized mandated training for infringing on the rights of professionals and the questionable relevance of such training to all licensed psychologists. Another issue with mandatory training is the increased resistance met by almost any attempt to legislate professional practices. Resistance may even be greater in the case of mandated training in child maltreatment because it is so closely linked to mandated reporting; training can become a mandate to carry out yet another mandate, thus leading to the overregulation of professionals.

Criticisms of mandatory training in child abuse, however, do not negate the need for greater professional competence in managing child abuse. Professional and graduate training programs will likely experience continued pressure to include child abuse assessment training in their curricula. It is likely that accreditation agencies will also continue to develop standards of minimal competence for managing child abuse.

## AVENUES FOR FUTURE RESEARCH

Research in child abuse reporting is disseminated through professional associations and peer-reviewed journals. The literature reviewed here is diverse and, like most areas of research, has several notable limitations. The following section briefly discusses areas for future study. The problems, questions, and hypotheses presented can be molded into viable research agendas that will contribute to the literature on mandated child abuse reporting.

*Future studies in mandated reporting should emphasize ecologically valid methods.* With few exceptions, investigations of reporting suspected child abuse have relied on self-report measures. Examples of more ecologically valid methods of study include case evaluations of reported and unreported suspected child abuse from diverse clinical and research settings. Future studies may therefore build on the clinical evaluation methods of Harper and Irvin (1985), Watson and Levine (1989), and M. Levine, Anderson,

Terretti, Sharma, et al. (1991). Professionals may be interviewed regarding their decision-making processes. Interviews may be structured to elicit information relevant to applied decision analysis, including perceived costs and benefits of reporting and not reporting, weighing potential outcomes, and saliency of reporting criteria. Qualitative as well as quantitative measures can be integrated in attempts to gather a breadth of data that could not be collected through pencil-and-paper surveys alone.

Ecologically valid research, such as in-depth interviews with professionals, case analyses, and direct observation conducted in clinical settings is also needed to evaluate policies and procedures for reporting suspected child abuse. Few models have been developed for managing reports of child maltreatment, and there is no evidence to support any particular procedures. Studies are needed to evaluate the relative effectiveness of reporting policies that are implemented across diverse professional settings. For example, studies can be conducted to evaluate procedures for independent practice as compared with other procedures implemented in facilities that employ multidisciplinary treatment teams.

*The effects of narrow versus broad definitions of abuse and specific versus nonspecific legal requirements for reporting require careful study.* Determining the relative effects of broad and narrow definitions of abuse on reporting is a necessary step toward informed legislative change. Although narrow definitions may result in underreporting and broad definitions may promote overreporting, I know of no study that has sought to verify the relationship between legal definitions of child abuse and reporting decisions. Such studies will clarify the ambiguities in legal definitions of abuse by identifying definitions that facilitate and inhibit accurate reporting. The relative impact of such terms as "reasonable cause to suspect," "knowledge of abuse," and "cause to believe" also remain unstudied.

Future studies on definitions and standards may use a number of different research strategies. Existing legal standards may be investigated through controlled comparisons. For example, treating the definitions or standards as experimental vignettes, professionals could be asked to respond to different definitions of child abuse and standards for reporting on the basis of experimental manipulations (Brosig & Kalichman, 1992b; Kalichman & Brosig, 1992). Such controlled analogue studies would evaluate the influence of specific features of the law. The relative application of legal standards for reporting will also need to be evaluated with regard to their function within various professional settings.

*Mandated reporters often hesitate to report suspected child abuse because they perceive the child protection system as inadequate. Research is needed to further evaluate professional perceptions of child protection workers, as well as how these perceptions influence reporting decisions.* Human service professionals are primarily concerned with the welfare of persons they serve. Therefore, it stands to reason that professionals will hesitate to report to those agencies that they believe are inadequate. Researchers have not yet, however, investigated how closely professional perceptions of local child protection systems match the reality of agencies. The extent to which professional perceptions are based on personal experience with the system (as opposed to second-hand information from fellow professionals) has also not been investigated, to my knowledge.

Studies that address professional perceptions of the child protection system should sample cases from more than one professional setting in more than one state. Diversity in sampling will avoid evaluating professional responses to the idiosyncracies of local systems and child protection resources. Professional perceptions of local child protective systems can also be tested against empirically identified characteristics of the system, such as complaints against agencies, worker caseloads, the availability of intervention resources, and lag times in responding to reports. Research of this type can, therefore, examine the bases for professional perceptions of the child protection system and how these perceptions, both accurate and inaccurate, influence reporting decisions.

*Descriptive research identifying signs of abuse and neglect within developmental periods will improve the rates of both abuse detection and reporting.* Problems in conduct, sexual behavior, emotional disturbances, and physical symptomatology are frequently observed among abused and neglected children (Browne & Finkelhor, 1986; Goldston, Turnquist, & Knutson, 1989; C. E. Walker et al., 1988). Although nonspecific symptoms related to abuse may raise suspicions, these signs frequently fall short of reporting thresholds. Failure to report knowledge of child abuse most likely results from concerns about confidentiality or child protection. Developing sensitive criteria for professionals to use in child abuse detection can reduce unidentified cases of child abuse.

In addition to research on behavioral signs of maltreatment, the nature of disclosures of abuse warrants further study. Although many professionals rely on verbal accounts of abuse in their reporting decisions (Brosig & Kalichman, 1992a; Finlayson & Koocher, 1991), disclosures of abuse from children may be infrequent (Pierce & Pierce, 1985; Reppucci & Haugaard, 1989), and are discounted when recanted (Attias & Goodwin, 1985). Research on base rates of verbal accounts of abuse originating from children, perpetrators, and others could serve to improve professional responses to such disclosures. Empirically defined indicators of child abuse should also fit within the context of child development. Among other purposes, these descriptions could serve as solid ground for the construction of standardized reporting criteria.

*Responses to suspected abuse by researchers have not yet received adequate attention in the literature.* There is a dearth of information concerning mandated child abuse reporting in nonservice delivery contexts, particularly research settings. Few studies have investigated the frequency of suspected child abuse in research settings or the procedures that researchers use for managing suspected child abuse. Issues faced by researchers who suspect that a participant has been abused or who has been abusive may be substantially different from issues in clinical–service delivery settings. Studies are needed to evaluate the frequency of suspected child abuse in research contexts, how researchers manage them, and the degree to which researchers recognize their roles as mandated reporters.

*Research is needed to evaluate the impact of reporting and not reporting on professional services.* Although many human service professionals indicate that they do not report suspected child abuse because they are concerned that reporting will damage professional services, there is little empirical support for their belief. In fact, available evidence tends to support the opposite—that reporting can benefit services (M. Levine, Anderson, Terretti, Steinberg, et al., 1991; Watson & Levine, 1989). Research is therefore needed to identify factors that lead to negative and positive outcomes of reporting. Research is also needed to evaluate procedures for managing limited confidentiality, informing parents or guardians of reports, and discussing reporting in the context of therapeutic relationships.

## CONCLUSIONS

For professionals to serve the public as therapists, evaluators, and educators, and for them to fulfill their social responsibilities as mandated reporters, reporting must be integrated into existing professional roles. Reporting suspected child abuse can be managed within the context of most professional relationships, especially when it is presented as a referral for consultation. Human service professionals routinely refer persons to agencies for specialized care and consultation. But in order for child protective services to be thought of as a referral outlet, there must be a renewed confidence in the system. The current state of crisis that the child protection system is facing (U.S. Advisory Board on Child Abuse and Neglect, 1990) makes it doubtful that professionals will view social service agencies as a viable service for their clients.

One approach to melding mandated reporting with existing professional roles is to develop strategies for mandated reporters to assist families within the child protection system. As mandated reporters, professionals can serve as resources for families and children during child abuse investigations and interventions. Professionals may keep on hand booklets and pamphlets from state and community social service agencies to share with their clients. Professionals may also discuss with families their own experiences with the child protection system, and explore expectations of the child protection process. This type of information can set realistic expectations of the roles and functions of child protection workers. In addition, professionals can make families aware of their rights within the system and the courses of action that are available to them in the event that they are dissatisfied with a caseworker. Whether evaluators, teachers, researchers, or therapists, professionals can deal directly with the distress and anxiety associated with child protection system involvement, and therefore work to apply reporting laws as therapeutically as possible.

# 9

# CHILD PROTECTION POLICY

That the term of a penal statute creating a new offense must be suf-
ficiently explicit to inform those who are subject to it what conduct
on their part will render them liable to its penalties, is a well recognized
requirement, consonant alike with ordering notions of fair play and
the settled rules of law. A statute which either forbids or requires the
doing of an act in terms so vague that men of common intelligence
must differ as to its application violates the first essential of due process
of law. (*Connally v. General Construction Company*, 1926)

Mandatory reporting laws play a direct role in both underreporting
and overreporting suspected child abuse. As discussed previously, reporting
laws are ambiguous in terms of when reporting is required, as well as in
defining child abuse and neglect. Statutory wording is, to a certain degree,
intentionally vague. The language of when reporting is required, including
the terms "reason to believe," "reasonable suspicion," and "reasonable
cause to suspect," are open to interpretation. Similarly, the language of
legal definitions of abuse includes the terms "mental injury" and "harm,"
again allowing judicial discretion. Broad and generalized reporting standards and definitions of abuse limit the overall effectiveness of mandatory
reporting laws. General terms can also lead to overly inclusive reporting
criteria. And although vague language is supposed to capture a maximum
number of abuse cases, it appears that this kind of language is simply too
difficult to interpret, and ultimately leads to noncompliance. The necessity

for laws that are clearly understood is illustrated by the U.S. Supreme Court ruling in *Connally v. General Construction Company* (1926). As stated by J. Jones and Welch (1989) with specific reference to mandated reporting, "it is widely recognized that to observe the law one must first understand what the law is, i.e. the law must be clear" (p. 44).

There is, of course, great danger in blindly increasing the specificity of mandatory reporting laws. In contrast to vague statutory wording, mandatory reporting laws can also be overly narrow and therefore exclusionary. Narrow language tends to be objective and defined in absolute terms. However, narrow statutory language is also more likely to restrict reporting. According to Besharov,

> The dilemma of choosing between general, and therefore somewhat vague, definitions and specific, and therefore potentially over-narrow [*sic*], definitions will be with us for some time. Listing with precise specificity all those actions that constitute child abuse and neglect raises the possibility of inadvertently excluding dangerous situations that should be included. Generalized definitions risk over-broad [*sic*] applications that include behavior that should not be considered abusive or neglectful. (1978, p. 445)

Proposals to change mandatory reporting laws to improve the child protective system have typically reflected three approaches to legislative action. First, it has been suggested that mandatory reporting laws themselves can effectively protect children and require legislative reform. Instead of changing the law, this view recommends that existing systems be supported and that reporting laws be enforced. A second, contrasting position acknowledges the problems posed by child abuse reporting laws and advocates for their clarification, particularly in terms of definitions of abuse and standards for reporting. Finally, a third position is far more critical of reporting laws and calls for reforming the entire reporting system. The following sections review these three levels of proposed legislative change—minimal reform, adaptive reform, and system overhaul.

## MINIMAL REFORM: STRENGTHENING AND SUPPORTING EXISTING SYSTEMS

Even the strongest supporters of mandated reporting are unlikely to offer their unqualified endorsement of existing reporting policies. Arguments against further amendments to mandated reporting laws highlight the fact that reporting statutes have already been subjected to too many amendments and redefinitions. An array of professionals are included on lists of mandated reporters, many of whom share little in common in terms of their interactions with children and families, but who must still respond to the same laws. In addition, definitions of child abuse and neglect have been subjected to redefinitions that broaden their application. It is also feared that further amendments to the law could lead to greater increases in reporting (Besharov, 1990; Lamond, 1989; USDHHS, 1988). From this perspective, mandatory reporting laws currently meet their child protection goals in detecting child abuse.

The perspective that reporting laws do not require reform demands an alternative explanation for why mandated reporters act outside the law or misinterpret their meaning. One explanation is that professionals are not equipped to detect and manage reporting in their professional practice. From this view, professional training should become the focus of initiatives to improve reporting, concentrating on familiarizing reporters with the laws, and increasing their understanding of reporting requirements. As discussed earlier in chapter 8, mandated reporters rarely have training in child abuse assessment, let alone in child abuse reporting. Although most professionals are aware of reporting laws, many human service providers misinterpret legal standards. Thus, training in child abuse assessment and reporting is advocated as a means to correct current reporting problems.

Training in child abuse assessment could be one viable option for improving professional practice and reporting decisions. However, there is mixed evidence to suggest that professionals who lack child abuse training are less inclined to report. For example, Finlayson and Koocher (1991) found that pediatric psychologists with specialized training in sexual abuse were no more likely to report than were respondents with no such training. In contrast, Kalichman and Brosig (1993) identified relationships between specific types of training experiences and reporting history. Among licensed psychologists, those who failed to report suspected child abuse were more likely to obtain postgraduate training in child maltreatment through continuing education and workshops, as compared with psychologists who had consistently reported suspected child abuse. Kalichman and Brosig suggested that the relationship between continuing education and the failure to report reflects the tendency for professionals to seek further training after deciding not to report suspected abuse. Whether providing specific information and skills related to child abuse and reporting in graduate programs and internships would affect the rates of reporting decisions remains an open question (Pope & Feldman-Summers, 1992).

A second factor that may contribute to lower rates of reporting is the child protection system itself. Professionals are required to report suspected child abuse to agencies that they perceive as being at a disadvantage for implementing adequate interventions. In fact, only one in three families where child abuse has been substantiated receive child welfare services (Wang & Daro, 1998). Therefore, consistent with professionals' perceptions, the child protection system is in crisis, and a lack of services and resources raises ethical concerns about reporting (U.S. Advisory Board on Child Abuse and Neglect, 1990). From this perspective, a social commitment to fix the child protective system would build a stronger case for reporting suspected abuse. Similarly, enhancing the trust between mandated reporters and the child protection system will also foster reporting.

One of the most influential frameworks for reforming the child protective system was set forth by the U.S. Advisory Board on Child Abuse and Neglect (1990). In a comprehensive set of recommendations that followed the declaration of child abuse as a national emergency, the members of the board called for the complete reform of state child protection systems. The board appealed to policymakers to lead the restructuring of the child protection system and to reallocate resources to support adequate services. Citizens were called on to provide a unified response to the child abuse crisis. The advisory board identified three major problems associated with the child protective system that required immediate attention: (a) reducing case overloads among child protection workers, (b) addressing the crisis in foster care, and (c) bolstering the system's ability to focus on children. The board also provided recommendations with specific objectives for each of these three problem areas, and outlined a national agenda for reforming child protection systems. The board held that by reforming the child protective system, individuals would be more inclined to report suspected abuse.

## ADAPTIVE REFORM: MODIFYING EXISTING STATUTES

The most common problems with the reporting system are attributed to mandatory reporting laws themselves. Therefore, reforming the reporting system requires advocacy and legislative reform. However, there is little consensus on the degree to which the laws should be revised and how such changes would protect children (Weisberg & Wald, 1984). There are generally four elements of reporting laws that have drawn the most attention with respect to reform: (a) definitions of child abuse, (b) standards for required reporting, (c) immunity for reporters, and (d) abrogating privileged communications.

### Defining Child Abuse and Neglect

Reporting laws define child maltreatment in either broad/general or narrow/restrictive terms. Broad legal definitions of abuse are typically criticized for being so ambiguous as to force professionals to set their own standard for what constitutes suspected child abuse. Otto and Melton (1990) shared this concern when they stated, "Exactly what the professional needs to see or believe in order to report abuse and thereby comply with the reporting statute is not made clear in most statutes" (p. 64). In contrast, narrow definitions run the risk of omitting certain dangerous situations from reporting requirements (Besharov, 1978). Legal definitions of child abuse determine both over- and underreporting, depending on whether definitions are broad or narrow, respectively.

Legal definitions of child abuse do not take into account the same aspects of abuse that clinicians find important in treating child abuse. There are, for example, few behavioral descriptors of abusive acts or symptoms of victimization included in definitions of abuse included in reporting laws. When legal definitions do not include the same signs and circumstances of child abuse as reporting laws, it creates problems for professionals. For example, reporting laws typically define emotional abuse as "mental injury" or "psychological impairment." However, these terms carry little meaning in the context of mental health services, where such terms characterize an entire patient population.

Sexual abuse is typically defined on the basis of acts and behaviors. Regardless of the various types of touching, fondling, or exploitation under consideration, there is no denying that these acts constitute child sexual abuse. Thus, because sexual abuse is defined by clear circumstances and conditions, rather than by signs and symptoms, allegations of child sexual abuse that are made by either children or adults are generally accepted and are more often reported. Child neglect is also defined by the failure to provide basic needs, by the exposure of children to harm, by endangerment, or by prolonged unsupervision (Otto & Melton, 1990; Wald, 1975). This is not to say that sexual abuse and child neglect is easily detected, but they are rarely confused with nonabusive circumstances.

Physical and emotional abuse tend to rely on signs and symptoms for definition. The intent of specifying definitions of physical abuse with such terms as "manifest harm" and "injuries" is to facilitate nondiscriminatory applications of the law and to increase accountability for reporting (Meriwether, 1986). The fact that there are parental acts that are not considered abuse when judged on the basis of parental rights further complicates matters. For example, Besharov (1988) stated that corporal punishment, when reasonable and not excessive, fails to constitute abuse. It is therefore not reportable. Likewise, several states explicitly exclude corporal punishment from definitions of abuse (NCCAN, 1979). These exclusions are consistent with the law when injuries and harm are the focus of legal definitions of physical abuse.

A similar emphasis on signs and symptoms of abuse exists in definitions of emotional abuse. Unlike physical abuse, however, injuries sustained from emotional abuse cannot be seen with the same objectivity and are less clearly linked to parenting behaviors. Although it is widely agreed that mental injury should be defined on the basis of behavioral symptoms exhibited by children, there is little empirical support for such definitions (Corson & Davidson, 1987; Melton & Limber, 1987). Legal definitions of emotional abuse therefore require inclusion of parental behaviors as conditions of abuse, particularly when ridicule, humiliation, and emotional abandonment are known to result in psychological harm (Garbarino et al., 1986).

In summary, those who agree with an adaptive reform perspective on legislative changes in mandatory reporting believe that the law should provide clear and objective definitions of child maltreatment, and specify parental behaviors and child symptoms where appropriate (Otto & Melton, 1990; Wald, 1975). Objectivity in legal definitions is fostered by the use of the empirical literature on child abuse. Early definitions of child abuse were based on legal definitions of child abuse in the empirical literature, which were in turn derived from definitions of physical abuse that relied on Kempe et al.'s (1962) description of the battered child syndrome. These definitions specified radiology findings, bone fractures, and other identifiable injuries. Statutes later included sexual abuse, neglect, and emotional abuse as reportable offences, but their definitions were not informed by objective research. For example, the Child Protection Act of 1974 predated by more than a decade an entire body of empirical work in sexual and emotional abuse (i.e., Finkelhor, 1984, 1986; Garbarino et al., 1986). Amendments to child protection laws have addressed abuse inflicted outside the home, including that committed during foster care, but these changes were also enacted prior to substantive empirical research on these problems.

Although definitions of child abuse and neglect can be revised to provide objective parameters for reporting, most legal definitions will probably retain catchall phrases such as "endangered child," "maltreatment," "refusal to provide care when able to do so," and "physical injury of non-accidental nature." Including these terms encourages professionals to use their discretion in reporting situations before a child suffers abuse. Vague definitions can function in a preventive fashion because they require harm to have occurred before reporting is required (Bourne & Newberger, 1977). Broad and vague definitions of child abuse are useful in judicial rulings because they allow judges to make determinations about cases that do not necessarily fit narrow definitions of abuse.

To conclude, legal definitions of child abuse can be reformed in terms of (a) redefining specific acts, omissions, signs, and symptoms of physical, sexual, and emotional abuse and neglect on the basis of empirical research; (b) implementing periodic reviews of legal definitions of abuse by panels of child maltreatment experts to provide an empirical basis for updating definitions; and (c) retaining catchall clauses for the purpose of inclusiveness.

## Determining When Reporting Is Required

Kempe et al.'s (1962) description of the battered child syndrome led to early definitions of physical abuse. Although Kempe et al. stated that "the report that [the physician] makes should be restricted to the objective findings which can be verified, and where possible, be supported by photographs and roentgenograms" (p. 23), the first reporting statutes did not require any such precision. In fact, reporting laws never mentioned certainty of abuse as a requisite for reporting. The laws were based on the premise that they

> do not require a reporter to know or be certain that a child has been abused or neglected. The degree of certainty most often expressed is "reason to believe" or "reasonable cause to believe or suspect," a standard based on the reasonable person's convictions. (NCCAN, 1979, p. 3)

Including the term "reasonable" in a legal standard allows for objectivity because it can be determined if a reasonable professional with similar training and experience placed in a similar situation would draw the same conclusion (Meriwether, 1986).

The act of using reasonable suspicion as the reporting standard has been criticized for being too vague to interpret and too broad to enforce. Meriwether (1986), for example, pointed out that the "use of broad, and ambiguous language to define reportable abuse may subject the statute to constitutional challenge" (p. 151). Indeed, the language in Michigan's reporting statute formed the basis for just such a challenge in *People v. Cavaiani* (1988), in which a family therapist argued that the reporting statute was unconstitutionally vague and therefore violated First and Fifth Amendment rights to privacy and freedom against self-incrimination. To illustrate, the Michigan statute read,

> A physician or . . . psychologist . . . who has reasonable cause to suspect child abuse or neglect shall make immediately, by telephone or otherwise, an oral report, or cause an oral report to be made, of the suspected child abuse or neglect to the Department. (Michigan Department of Social Services, 1989, p. 2)

In a circuit court, the statute was found unconstitutional by a judge who ruled that the law was void because of its failure to provide "a precise standard for adhering to and enforcing the law" (Denton, 1987b). However, the state of Michigan appealed the decision and brought the case to the Michigan State Supreme Court. As discussed earlier, the case did not proceed because Cavaiani was found not guilty of failure to report and the higher court would hear the case against the statute only if Cavaiani was found guilty. Nevertheless, this case illustrates the problem with vague reporting standards.

Reasonable suspicions of child abuse are typically defined by situations in which a reasonable person would suspect abuse. For example, the California code defines reasonable suspicion when it is "objectively reasonable for a person to entertain such a suspicion, based upon facts that could cause a reasonable person in a like position, drawing when appropriate on his or her training and experience, to suspect child abuse" (California State Statutes, Sec. 11166.a). Under this standard, professionals are to consider the range of potential indicators of abuse and to determine whether the situation warrants reporting. When professionals set their own reporting standards, it is difficult to hold them accountable for their reporting decisions. Establishing more objective standards for defining suspected child abuse could, therefore, clarify what is expected of mandated reporters who might suspect abuse but are unsure if their suspicion warrants reporting.

There is further evidence that mandatory reporting statutes are too broad and that their vagueness interferes with reporting. Among the nearly one in three mandated reporters who have failed to report suspected child abuse, the most common reason for their not reporting is an uncertainty about when reporting is required (Brosig & Kalichman, 1992a). In addition, despite the number of mandated reporters who do not report suspected child abuse, there are few arrests for failure to report. As Meriwether (1986) suggested, the vague wording of mandatory reporting laws interferes with compliant behavior, but it also prohibits law enforcement.

Another aspect of mandatory reporting laws that should be clarified is the source of information that leads to suspected child abuse. Laws that require a report only when a child is the source of the suspected abuse result in a failure to manage cases of abuse revealed through other sources (Brosig & Kalichman, 1992b; Kalichman & Brosig, 1992). The few states that did limit requirements for reporting to those cases of children coming before the mandated reporter have been urged to broaden this standard. The Pennsylvania Department of Public Welfare (1992), for example, had recommended that the state legislature

> amend Section 6311 of the CPSL [Child Protective Services Law] to require mandated reporters to report suspected abuse based on information received without requiring that the child come before the reporter. This change encourages more complete reporting of suspected child abuse and tends to broaden the safety net of services, which may prevent serious or repeated abuse. (p. 19)

In summary, legislative reform to reduce statutory vagueness is most often recommended in two areas: (a) reducing statutory vagueness to provide clearer direction to conform with the law, and (b) eliminating restrictions on the sources of suspicions for triggering a report.

## Immunity for Mandated Reporters

Few policy analysts have recommended the removal of the immunity that is granted by reporting laws to mandated reporters who file in good faith. Immunity is deemed necessary for reporting laws to be effective because immunity removes threats of legal repercussions that would otherwise inhibit reporting (Meriwether, 1986; Schwartz, 1991). All state reporting laws include a statement of immunity, most of which generally indicate the following:

> A person participating in good faith in making of a report, or photographs, or X-rays, or performance of a medically relevant test . . . or aiding and assisting in an investigation of a child abuse report . . . shall have immunity from any liability, civil or criminal, which might otherwise be incurred or imposed. The person shall have the same immunity with respect to participation in good faith in any judicial proceeding resulting from the report or relating to the subject matter of the report. (Iowa Department of Human Services, 1991, p. 30)

Some commentators have argued, however, that providing immunity to mandated reporters is not necessary. Without immunity it would still be necessary to prove a report was malicious, or filed in bad faith, to hold a professional liable for reporting. In essence, there is little added benefit from the immunity clause. Besharov (1978) stated that providing immunity to reporters is technically redundant and that the "presumption of good faith is a public relations provision, designed to soothe potential reporters" (p. 476). Without formal immunity many mandated reporters may not report suspected abuse (Schwartz, 1991).

Besharov (1986a) suggested that reporting laws should be amended to include a second type of immunity for professionals who, in good faith, *do not* report suspected abuse. On the basis of the assumption that mandated reporters are concerned with child welfare and that they have an interest in protecting children from harm, Besharov argued that professionals should be held liable only when they fail to report in bad faith. Such provisions would decrease the number of unnecessary reports because the current standard penalizes negligence for failing to report while granting immunity for frivolous reports. According to Besharov (1986a), some professionals, "fearful of being sued for not reporting . . . play it safe and report whenever they think there is the slightest chance that they will subsequently be sued for not doing so" (p. 29).

There is, however, little evidence to support the influence of immunity on reporting. In fact, contrary to Besharov's (1986a) position, surveys of professionals have shown that concerns about the law and potential liability have little effect on professionals' reporting decisions (Brosig & Kalichman, 1992b). Besharov's ideas on granting immunity to those who do not report have received little attention thus far, but they may be discussed as a solution to the problem of overreporting, if the child protection system remains unable to manage the large volumes of reports.

## Abrogation of Privileged Communications

Professionals who treat perpetrators of sexual abuse have opposed abrogating privileged communication under reporting statutes. Most complaints concern the ways in which abrogating privileged communication interferes with self-referrals of offenders for therapy and reduces disclosure of offenses while in treatment. Coming forward for treatment requires that offenders feel protected from criminal charges (Kelly, 1987; S. Smith & Meyer, 1984; Weinstock & Weinstock, 1989). Clinicians who treat sex offenders argue that requirements to report disclosures of abuse interfere with rehabilitation and actually endanger children (Berlin et al., 1991).

An option to abrogating privileged communication can include "guaranteeing confidentiality" while offenders are in treatment. For example, S. Smith and Meyer (1984) recommended that

> medical privileges and psychotherapist–client privileges should not be lost each time an abuser confesses the abuse to a psychotherapist or physician. To encourage abusers to seek therapy and be open in therapy, they should be assured that their confession of child abuse to a therapist will not be used against them in a criminal case or in child custody proceedings. Destroying the privilege will seldom directly benefit a child, and when there is a possibility of a child custody hearing (e.g., in a divorce action), it makes it extremely difficult for an abuser to seek effective therapy and remain open in the course of therapy. (p. 363)

S. Smith and Meyer (1984) specified circumstances when privileged communication should be dissolved. For example, they suggested that only disclosures made directly by an abuser or an abuser's spouse should remain confidential, whereas information disclosed by any other source should fall outside of the privilege. S. Smith and Meyer also stated that privileged communications should be protected only if treatment is progressing and there is no risk to children. Finally, under all circumstances privileged communications should be immediately dissolved when children are at risk. S. Smith and Meyer's recommendations are aimed at facilitating an environment that promotes open disclosure of offenders in treatment, without increasing risks posed to children.

Although retaining privileged communications under certain circumstances opens the door to self-referred therapy and allows for the necessary openness in treatment relationships, there are reasons why the privilege has not been granted. Working with offenders does not allow for child abuse prevention beyond the treatment itself. Privileged communications for disclosure of abuse also assumes a potential benefit of treatment that will ultimately protect children. With respect to child sexual abusers, the efficacy of treatment for perpetrators is quite low and the probability for repeating an offense remains substantial (Furby, Weinrott, & Blackshaw, 1989). Therefore, the potential costs associated with maintaining privileged communication with adults who abuse children are high.

## OVERHAULING EXISTING SYSTEMS

Amidst suggestions clarifying existing reporting laws, proposals to redesign the mandated reporting system itself have been few. One example, however, was put forward by a political action group called Victims of Child Abuse Legislation, which considers all reporting statutes destructive and intrusive to families and advocates a complete revision of the child protection system so as to remove reporting laws. However, there are no official initiatives to dismantle the reporting system. Rather, efforts are focused on amending existing policies and improving services.

Human service professionals are required to report reasonable suspicions of child abuse, and are therefore given discretion in reporting. However, the law does not stipulate how much discretion is granted in reporting suspected child abuse and whether discretion should vary among mandated reporters. The question posed is whether a child clinical psychologist should be held to the same discretionary standard as a commercial film processor or an X-ray technician, or whether a psychiatrist with 20 years' worth of experience in treating pedophiles should be granted more discretion in reporting sexual abuse than a hospital intern. Zellman (1990, 1992) found that mandated reporters who exercise greater discretion are equally knowledgeable and as well-trained in child abuse as professionals who consistently report every case of suspected abuse. However, reporters who use greater discretion in reporting are more likely to be confident in their reporting decisions and are more often considered a resource by their colleagues for dealing with reporting issues. Zellman also found that reporters who exercise more discretion were more likely to hold negative views of the child protection system. Other research shows that professionals who use greater discretion are more likely to consider the seriousness of abuse and potential effects of reporting on the family when deciding to report suspected abuse (Kalichman & Brosig, 1993).

Research has shown that there is considerable support for increasing the amount of discretion allowed for deciding when to report suspected abuse under mandated reporting (Crenshaw, Bartell, & Lichtenberg, 1994). Emery and Laumann-Billings (1998) suggested that professionals be exempt from reporting less serious cases of suspected abuse when families are in treatment, although their recommendations lacked detail about definitions and implementation (Fischer, 1999). On the basis of Zellman's findings, as well as on findings from other studies, Finkelhor and Zellman (1991) proposed a system of flexible reporting options for mandated reporters with specialized training in child abuse. Finkelhor and Zellman recommended that professionals who are trained in assessing abuse be able to attain a special status within the child protection system. In this system, professionals with demonstrated competence in child abuse detection and intervention would be afforded the opportunity to register themselves with the child protection system and to receive greater latitude in deciding to report suspected child abuse. For example, assuming that there is no immediate danger to children and that therapy would otherwise be compromised, professionals with documented training and experience in treating abusive adults would not be required to report previous acts of abuse that surface in therapy. Discretion granted to mandated reporters under Finkelhor and Zellman's plan would also be limited to circumstances where there has not been serious harm to a child and where a criminal investigation is not warranted. Therefore, cases of severe physical abuse and all cases of sexual abuse would be subject to the usual standards for reporting. Finkelhor and Zellman outlined recommendations for instituting their plan in local child protection agencies, including the training of mandated reporters in child abuse detection and intervention.

Finkelhor and Zellman's (1991) innovative approach to expanding professional discretion in mandated reporting warrants consideration as new solutions are sought for problems of over- and underreporting. To develop such policies, mandated reporters working with the child protection system can establish standards for registered discretionary reporting. Such systems could promote professional training in child abuse evaluation and treatment. Finkelhor and Zellman's ideas offer an option for maximizing the use of limited child protection resources without compromising intervention efforts.

## CONCLUSIONS

Several problems exist with mandatory reporting laws, including legal standards that do not translate to professional settings and vague and imprecise language. In effect, virtually any situation where a child is traumatized may raise a reportable suspicion of child abuse, and, at the same time, only the most severe signs of abuse necessarily meet the reasonable suspicion standard. Thus, the vagueness of reporting laws fosters both over- and underreporting and compromises child protection. Without clear public policies to guide professional behavior, mandated reporters must set their own reporting standards. The mandatory reporting system cannot function in the best interest of children when professionals do not know what or when to report. Clarifying reporting requirements should, there-fore, increase accuracy of reporting and improve compliance with the law.

Statutory reform, however extensive, will not replace the necessity to increase professional training in child abuse assessment and to address the national crisis in the child protection system. When placed in perspective, mandated reporting is only one small part of the social policies that target child abuse. The issue of reporting has captured the attention of human service professionals because it triggers concerns about their roles as man-dated reporters, about ethical practices in their profession, and about pro-tecting children. For mandated reporting to play an effective role in child protection, however, policies will need to address professional responsibil-ities in a language and context that are relevant to professional roles and settings.

# REFERENCES

Achenbach, T. M., & Edelbrock, C. (1983). *Manual for the Child Behavior Checklist and revised Child Behavior Profile.* Burlington: University of Vermont.

Adams, J. A. (1991). Is it (or is it not) sexual abuse? The medical examiner's dilemma. *Child Youth and Family Services, 15,* 129–143.

Adams, J. A., Harper, K., & Knudson, S. (1992). A proposed system for classification of anogenital findings in children with suspected sexual abuse. *Adolescent and Pediatric Gynecology, 5,* 73–75.

Adams, J. A., Phillips, R. N., & Ahmad, M. (1990). The usefulness of coloscopic photographs of suspected child sexual abuse. *Adolescent and Pediatric Gynecology, 3,* 75–82.

Adler, R. (1995). To tell or not to tell: The psychiatrist and child abuse. *Australian and New Zealand Journal of Psychiatry, 29,* 190–198.

Alpert, J. L., & Paulson, A. (1990). Graduate-level education and training in child sexual abuse. *Professional Psychology: Research and Practice, 21,* 366–371.

American Medical Association. (1964). Battered child legislation. *Journal of the American Medical Association, 188,* 136.

American Psychological Association. (1982). *Ethical principles in the conduct of research with human participants.* Washington, DC: Author.

American Psychological Association. (1990). Ethical principles of psychologists (Amended June 2, 1989). *American Psychologist, 45,* 390–395.

American Psychological Association. (1992). *Ethical principles of psychologists and code of conduct. American Psychologist, 47,* 1597–1611.

American Psychological Association. (1996). A guide for including information on child abuse and neglect in graduate and professional education and training. (Available from the American Psychological Association, Public Interest Directorate, 750 First Street NE, Washington, DC 20002)

Ammerman, R. T., Cassisi, J., Hersen, M., & Van Hasselt, V. (1986). Consequences of physical abuse and neglect in children. *Clinical Psychology Review, 6,* 291–310.

Anderson, E., Levine, M., Sharma, A., Ferretti, L., Steinberg, K., & Wallach, L. (1993). *Behavioral Sciences and the Law, 11,* 335–345.

Anonymous. (1992). *Individual conscience and psychologists' responsibility.* Unpublished manuscript.

Ansell, C., & Ross, H. (1990). Reply to Pope and Bajt. *American Psychologist, 45,* 399.

Attias, R., & Goodwin, J. (1985). Knowledge and management strategies in incest cases: A survey of physicians, psychologists, and family counselors. *Child Abuse and Neglect, 9,* 527–533.

*195*

Baily, T. F., & Baily, W. H. (1986). *Operational definitions of child emotional mal-treatment.* (Available from the EM Project, Bureau of Social Sciences, Maine Department of Human Services, Station #11 Main Street, Augusta, ME 04333)

Baird, K. A., & Rupert, P. A. (1987). Clinical management of confidentiality: A survey of psychologists in seven states. *Professional Psychology: Research and Practice, 18,* 347–352.

Beck, K. A., & Ogloff, J. R. (1995). Child abuse reporting in British Columbia: Psychologists' knowledge of and compliance with the reporting law. *Professional Psychology: Research and Practice, 26,* 245–251.

Beeman, D. G., & Scott, N. A. (1991). Therapists' attitudes toward psychotherapy informed consent with adolescents. *Professional Psychology: Research and Practice, 22,* 230–234.

Berkowitz, S. (1991). *Key findings from the state survey component of the study of high risk child abuse and neglect groups.* Rockville, MD: Westat.

Berlin, F., Malin, H., & Dean, S. (1991). Effects of statutes requiring psychiatrists to report suspected sexual abuse of children. *American Journal of Psychiatry, 148,* 449–453.

Bersoff, D. N. (1975). Professional ethics and legal responsibilities: On the horns of a dilemma. *Journal of School Psychology, 13,* 359–376.

Besharov, D. J. (1978). The legal aspects of reporting known and suspected child abuse and neglect. *Villanova Law Review, 23,* 458–520.

Besharov, D. J. (1986a). Unfounded allegations—a new child abuse problem. *The Public Interest, 83,* 18–31.

Besharov, D. J. (1986b, August). Child abuse and neglect: Liability for failing to report. *Trial,* 67–72.

Besharov, D. J. (1987a, November). Policy guidelines for decision making in child abuse and neglect. *Children Today,* 7–10.

Besharov, D. J. (1988). *Child abuse and neglect reporting and investigation: Policy guidelines for decision-making.* Washington, DC: American Bar Association.

Besharov, D. J. (1990). *Recognizing child abuse: A guide for the concerned.* New York: Free Press.

Bollas, C., & Sundelson, D. (1995). *The new informants: The betrayal of confidentiality in psychoanalysis and psychotherapy.* Northvale, NJ: Jason Aronson.

Bourne, R., & Newberger, E. (1977). "Family autonomy" or "coercive intervention?" Ambiguity and conflict in the proposed standards for child abuse and neglect. *Boston University Law Review, 57,* 670–706.

Brahams, D. (1988). Standard of proof in evidence of child abuse. *Lancet, 8580,* 311–312.

Brassard, M. R., & Gelardo, M. S. (1987). Psychological maltreatment: The unifying construct in child abuse and neglect. *School Psychology Review, 16,* 127–136.

Brooks, C. M., Perry, N., Starr, S., & Teply, L. (1994). Child abuse and neglect reporting laws: Understanding interests, understanding policy. *Behavioral Sciences and the Law, 12,* 49–64.

Brosig, C. L. (1992). *Child abuse reporting decisions: The effects of statutory wording of reporting requirements.* Unpublished master's thesis, Loyola University of Chicago.

Brosig, C. L., & Kalichman, S. (1992a). Clinicians' reporting of suspected child abuse: A review of the empirical literature. *Clinical Psychology Review, 12,* 155–168.

Brosig, C. L., & Kalichman, S. C. (1992b). Child abuse reporting decisions: Effects of statutory wording of reporting requirements. *Professional Psychology: Research and Practice, 23,* 486–492.

Bross, D. C. (1983, April). Professional and agency liability for negligence in child protection. *Law, Medicine, and Health Care,* 71–75.

Browne, A., & Finkelhor, D. (1986). Impact of child sexual abuse: A review of the research. *Psychological Bulletin, 99,* 66–77.

Budai, P. (1996). Mandatory reporting of child abuse: Is it in the best interests of the child? *Australian and New Zealand Journal of Psychiatry, 30,* 794–804.

Buie, J. (1989, November). Clinicians don't always tell of suspected abuse. *APA Monitor,* p. 20.

Butz, R. A. (1985). Reporting child abuse and confidentiality in counseling. *Journal of Contemporary Social Work, 66,* 83–90.

Caffey, J. (1946). Multiple fractures in the long bones of infants suffering from chronic subdural hematoma. *American Journal of Roentgenology, 56,* 163–173.

Caldwell, S., English, D., Foote, A., Hodges, V., Nguyen, Q., Pecora, P. J., Pien, D., Stallings, Z., Tong, C., et al. (1992). *An approach to strength and risk assessment with multicultural guidelines.* (Available from Peter J. Pecora, School of Social Work, JH-30, University of Washington, 4101 15th Street NE, Seattle, WA 98195)

California Crime Prevention Center. (1988). *Child abuse prevention handbook.* Sacramento, CA: Author.

California State Department of Social Services. (1991). *The California child abuse and neglect reporting law: Issues and answers for health practitioners.* (Available from California Department of Social Services, Office of Child Abuse Prevention, 744 P Street, M.S. 9-100, Sacramento, CA 95814)

Camblin, L. D., & Prout, H. T. (1983). School counselors and the reporting of child abuse: A survey of state laws and practices. *School Counselor, 30,* 358–367.

Caudill, O. B., & Pope, K. S. (1995). *Law & mental health professionals: California.* Washington, DC: American Psychological Association.

Ceci, S. J., & Bruck, M. (1995). *Jeopardy in the court: A scientific analysis of children's testimony.* Washington, DC: American Psychological Association.

Ceci, S. J., Loftus, E. F., Leichtman, M., & Bruck, M. (1994). The role of source misattributions in the creation of false beliefs among preschoolers. *International Journal of Clinical and Experimental Hypnosis, 62,* 304–320.

Child Abuse Prevention and Treatment Act of 1974, 42 U.S.C., § 5101–5115 (1979, Cum. Supp. 1988).

Colorado Board of Education. (1995). Retrieved June 17, 1998 from the World Wide Web: http://www.cde.state.co.us/board.html

Committee on Professional Practice and Standards. (1995). Twenty-four questions and answers about professional practice in the area of child abuse. *Professional Psychology: Research and Practice, 26*, 377–385.

Compaan, C., Doueck, H. J., & Levine, M. (1997). Mandated reporter satisfaction with child protection: More good news for workers? *Journal of Interpersonal Violence, 12*, 847–857.

Connally v. General Construction Company, 269 U.S. 385 (1926).

Conte, J. R. (1992). Has this child been sexually abused? Dilemmas for the mental health professional who seeks the answer. *Criminal Justice and Behavior, 19*, 54–73.

Conte, J., Sorenson, E., Fogarty, L., & Rosa, J. D. (1991). Evaluating childrens' reports of sexual abuse: Results from a survey of professionals. *American Journal of Orthopsychiatry, 61*, 428–435.

Cook, S. (1991, June). *Role conflict in child protection work: Authority of helper.* Paper presented at the Third Biennial Conference on Community Research and Action, Tempe, AZ.

Corson, J., & Davidson, H. A. (1987). Emotional abuse and the law. In M. R. Brassard, R. Germain, & S. N. Hart (Eds.), *Psychological maltreatment of children and youth* (pp. 185–202). Elmsford, NY: Pergamon Press.

Coulter, M. L., & Chez, R. A. (1997). Domestic violence victims support mandatory reporting: For others. *Journal of Family Violence, 12*, 349–356.

Crenshaw, W., Bartell, P., & Lichtenberg, J. (1994). Proposed revisions to mandatory reporting laws: An exploratory survey of child protective service agencies. *Child Welfare, 73*, 15–27.

Crenshaw, W., Crenshaw, L., & Lichtenberg, J. (1995). When educators confront child abuse: An analysis of the decision to report. *Child Abuse and Neglect, 19*, 1095–1113.

Daro, D., & McCurdy, K. (1992). *Current trends in child abuse reporting and fatalities: The results of the 1991 Annual Fifty State Survey.* (Available from the National Committee for the Prevention of Child Abuse, 332 S. Michigan Ave., Suite 1600, Chicago, IL 60604)

Davidson, H. (1988). Failure to report child abuse: Legal penalties and emerging issues. In A. Maney & S. Wells (Eds.), *Professional responsibilities in protecting children* (pp. 93–103). New York: Praeger.

Dawes, R. (1989). Experience and validity of clinical judgment: The illusory correlation. *Behavioral Sciences and the Law, 7*, 457–467.

DeBell, C., & Jones, R. D. (1997). Privileged communication at last? An overview of *Jaffee v. Redmond. Professional Psychology: Research and Practice, 28*, 559–566.

Deisz, R., Doueck, H. J., George, N., & Levine, M. (1996). Reasonable cause: A qualitative study of mandated reporting. *Child Abuse and Neglect, 20,* 275–287.

Denton, L. (1987a, June). Child abuse reporting laws: Are they a barrier to helping troubled families? *APA Monitor,* p. 3.

Denton, L. (1987b, October). Michigan child report law ruled unconstitutional. *APA Monitor,* p. 23.

Doueck, H. J., & Levine, M. (in press). Reporting clients for child maltreatment: A study of the effect of mandated reporting on social work practice. *Journal of Law and Social Work.*

Doueck, H. J., Levine, M., & Bronson, D. E. (1993). Risk assessment in child protective services: An evaluation of the Child at Risk Field System. *Journal of Interpersonal Violence, 8,* 446–467.

DePanfilis, D., Holder, W., Corey, M., & Oelson, E. (1986). *Child-at-risk field training manual.* Charlotte, NC: ACTION for Child Protection.

Drake, B. (1996). Harassment reports to child protective services: An empirical investigation. *Journal of Social Service Research, 21,* 1–18.

Duhaime, A. C., Christian, C. W., Rorke, L. B., & Zimmerman, R. A. (1998). Nonaccidental head injury in infants: The "shaken-baby syndrome." *New England Journal of Medicine, 338,* 1822–1829.

Eastman, A. M., & Moran, T. J. (1991). Multiple perspectives: Factors related to differential diagnosis of sexual abuse and divorce trauma in children under six. *Child and Youth Services, 15,* 159–175.

Ebert, B. W. (1992). Mandatory child abuse reporting in California. *Forensic Reports, 5,* 335–350.

Eckenrode, J., Munsch, J., Powers, J., & Doris, J. (1988). The nature and substantiation of official sexual abuse reports. *Child Abuse and Neglect, 12,* 311–319.

Eckenrode, J., Powers, J., Doris, J., Munsch, J., & Bolger, N. (1988). Substantiation of child abuse and neglect reports. *Journal of Consulting and Clinical Psychology, 56,* 9–16.

Ellerstein, N., & Canavan, J. (1980). Sexual abuse of boys. *American Journal of Diseases of Children, 134,* 255–257.

Emery, R. E., & Laumann-Billings, L. (1998). An overview of the nature, causes, and consequences of abusive family relationships. *American Psychologist, 53,* 121–135.

Engfer, A., & Schneewind, K. A. (1982). Causes and consequences of harsh parental punishment: An empirical investigation in a representative sample of 570 German families. *Child Abuse and Neglect, 6,* 129–139.

Faller, K. C. (1985). Unanticipated problems in the United States child protection system. *Child Abuse and Neglect, 9,* 63–69.

Finkelhor, D. (1984). *Child sexual abuse: New theory and research.* New York: Free Press.

Finkelhor, D. (1985). Sexual abuse and physical abuse: Some critical differences.

In E. H. Newberger & R. Bourne (Eds.), *Unhappy families* (pp. 21–30). Littleton, MA: PSG Publishing.

Finkelhor, D. (1986). *A sourcebook on child sexual abuse*. Newbury, CA: Sage.

Finkelhor, D. (1987). The sexual abuse of children: Current research reviewed. *Psychiatric Annals: The Journals of Continuing Psychiatric Education, 17*, 233–237, 241.

Finkelhor, D. (1990). Is child abuse being over-reported? *Public Welfare, 48*, 38–41.

Finkelhor, D., & Zellman, G. (1991). Flexible reporting options for skilled child abuse professionals. *Child Abuse and Neglect, 15*, 335–341.

Finlayson, L., & Koocher, G. (1991). Professional judgment in child abuse reporting in sexual abuse cases. *Professional Psychology: Research and Practice, 22*, 464–472.

Fischer, H. (1999). Exemptions from child abuse reporting. *American Psychologist, 54*, 145.

Fischhoff, B. (1992). Giving advice: Decision theory perspectives on sexual assault. *American Psychologist, 47*, 577–588.

Freeman, J. B., Levine, M., & Doueck, H. J. (1996). Child age and caseworker attention in child protective services investigations. *Child Abuse and Neglect, 20*, 907–920.

Friedrich, W. N., Grambsch, P., Broughton, D., Kuiper, J., & Beilke, R. L. (1991). Normative sexual behavior in children. *Pediatrics, 88*, 456–464.

Friedrich, W. N., Grambsch, P., Damon, L., Hewitt, S., Koverola, C., Lang, R. A., Wolfe, V., & Broughton, D. (1992). Child Sexual Abuse Inventory: Normative and clinical comparisons. *Psychological Assessment, 4*, 303–311.

Fryer, G. E., Bross, D., Krugman, R., Denson, D., & Baird, D. (1990). Good news for CPS workers: An Iowa survey shows parents value services. *Public Welfare, 48*, 38–41.

Furby, L., Weinrott, M., & Blackshaw, L. (1989). Sex offender recidivism: A review. *Psychological Bulletin, 105*, 3–30.

Garb, H. N. (1989). Clinical judgment, clinical training, and professional experience. *Psychological Bulletin, 105*, 387–396.

Garbarino, J. (1987). What can the school do on the behalf of the psychologically maltreated child and the community. *School Psychology Review, 16*, 181–187.

Garbarino, J., Guttman, E., & Seeley, J. (1986). *The psychologically battered child*. San Francisco: Jossey-Bass.

Gelardo, M. S., & Sanford, E. (1987). Child abuse and neglect: A review of the literature. *School Psychology Review, 16*, 137–155.

Gelinas, D. (1983). The persisting negative effects of incest. *Psychiatry, 46*, 312–332.

Giovannoni, J. (1989a). Substantiated and unsubstantiated reports of child maltreatment. *Children and Youth Services Review, 11*, 299–318.

Giovannoni, J. (1989b). Definitional issues in child maltreatment. In D. Ciccetti

& V. Carlson (Eds.), *Child maltreatment* (pp. 3–37). New York: Cambridge University Press.

Glosoff, H. L., Herlihy, S., Herlihy, B., & Spence, E. B. (1997). Privileged communication in the psychologist–client relationship. *Professional Psychology: Research and Practice, 28,* 573–581.

Goldston, D. B., Turnquist, D. C., & Knutson, J. F. (1989). Presenting problems of sexually abused girls receiving psychiatric services. *Journal of Abnormal Psychology, 98,* 314–317.

Gomes-Schwartz, B., Horowitz, J., & Cardarelli, A. (1990). *Child sexual abuse: The initial effects.* Newbury Park, CA: Sage.

Goodman, G. S., Bottoms, B. L., Schwartz-Kenny, B. M., & Rudy, L. (1991). Children's testimony about a stressful event: Improving children's reports. *Journal of Narrative and Life History, 1,* 69–99.

Goodwin, J., Sahd, D., & Rada, R. T. (1982). False accusations and false denials of incest: Clinical myths and clinical realities. In J. Goodwin (Ed.), *Sexual abuse: Incest victims and their families* (pp. 17–26). Boston: John Wright.

Graham-Bermann, S. A. (1998). The impact of woman abuse on children's social development: Research and theoretical perspectives. In G. W. Holden, R. Geffner, & E. N. Jouriles (Eds.), *Children exposed to marital violence: Theory, research, and applied issues* (pp. 21–54). Washington, DC: American Psychological Association.

Gray, A. (1987, August). North Carolina experience. In L. Pantano (Chair), *Duty to warn, protect, and report: Criminal and civil implications.* Symposium conducted at the 95th Annual Convention of the American Psychological Association, New York.

Green, A. H. (1983). Child abuse: Dimension of psychological trauma in abused children. *Journal of the Academy of Child Psychiatry, 22,* 231–237.

Green, S. L., & Hansen, J. C. (1989). Ethical dilemmas faced by family therapists. *Journal of Marital and Family Therapy, 15,* 149–158.

Grey, E., & Crosgrove, J. (1985). Ethnocentric perception of child-rearing practices in protective services. *Child Abuse and Neglect, 9,* 389–396.

Gustafson, K. E., McNamara, R., & Jensen, J. A. (1994). Parents' informed consent decisions regarding psychotherapy for their children: Consideration of therapeutic risks and benefits. *Professional Psychology: Research and Practice, 25,* 16–22.

Handelsman, M. H. (1989). Ethics training at mental health centers. *Community Mental Health Journal, 25,* 42–50.

Harper, G., & Irvin, E. (1985). Alliance formation with patients: Limit-setting and the effect of mandated reporting. *American Journal of Orthopsychiatry, 55,* 550–560.

Haughton, P. B. (1977). Child abuse: Early diagnosis and management. In A. Rodriguez (Ed.), *Handbook on child abuse and neglect* (pp. 14–24). Flushing, NY: Medical Examination Publishing Company.

Hedberg, A. (1992, August). *Child abuse reporting—A personal and professional trauma and trial.* Paper presented at the 100th Annual Convention of the American Psychological Association, San Francisco.

Helfer, R. E. (1975). Why most physicians don't get involved in child abuse cases and what to do about it. *Children Today, 4*, 28–32.

Herbert, C. P. (1987). Expert medical assessment in determining probability of alleged child sexual abuse. *Child Abuse and Neglect, 11*, 213–221.

Herrenkohl, E. C., & Herrenkohl, R. C. (1979). A comparison of abused children and their nonabused siblings. *Journal of the American Academy of Child Psychiatry, 18*, 260–269.

Herzberger, S. D. (1988). Cultural obstacles of abuse by professionals. In A. Maney & S. Wells (Eds.), *Professional responsibilities in protecting children* (pp. 33–53). New York: Praeger.

Heymann, G. (1986). Mandated child abuse reporting and the confidentiality privilege. In L. Everstine & D. Everstine (Eds.), *Psychotherapy and the law* (pp. 145–155). Orlando, FL: Grune & Stratton.

Hoffman-Plotkin, D., & Twentyman, C. T. (1984). A multimodal assessment of behavioral and cognitive deficits in abused and neglected preschoolers. *Child Development, 55*, 794–802.

Holden, G. W., Geffner, R., & Jouriles, E. N. (1998). *Children exposed to marital violence: Theory, research, and applied issues.* Washington, DC: American Psychological Association.

Holder, W., & Corey, M. (1986). *Child protective services risk management: A decision-making handbook.* Charlotte, NC: ACTION for Child Protection.

Howe, A. C., Bonner, B., Parker, M., & Sausen, K. (1992, August). *Graduate training in child maltreatment in APA-approved psychology programs.* Paper presented at the 100th Annual Convention of the American Psychological Association, Washington, DC.

Howitt, D. (1992). *Child abuse errors: When good intentions go wrong.* New Brunswick, NJ: Rutgers University Press.

Hutchison, E. D. (1990). Child maltreatment: Can it be defined? *Social Service Review, 38*, 60–78.

Hutchison, E. D. (1993). Mandatory reporting laws: Child protective case finding gone awry? *Social Work, 38*, 56–63.

Illinois Department of Child and Family Services. (1992). *Service delivery: Subchapter a—Procedures 300—Reports of child abuse and neglect.* (Available from Illinois Department of Children and Family Services, Station 75, State Administrative Offices, 406 East Monroe Street, Springfield, IL 62701)

Iowa Department of Human Services. (1991). *Recognizing and reporting child abuse and neglect.* Des Moines, IA: Author.

Jackson, H., & Nuttall, R. (1993). Clinician responses to sexual abuse allegations. *Child Abuse and Neglect, 17*, 127–143.

Jaffee v. Redmond, 135 L. Ed.2d 337, 340, 116 S.Ct. 1923 (1996).

James, J., Womack, W., & Strauss, F. (1978). Physician reporting of sexual abuse of children. *Journal of the American Medical Association, 240*, 1145–1146.

Jones, D. P. H., & McGraw, J. M. (1987). Reliable and fictitious accounts of sexual abuse to children. *Journal of Interpersonal Violence, 2,* 27–45.

Jones, J., & Welch, B. (1989). Mandatory reporting of child abuse: Problems and proposals for solutions. In L. Walker, J. Alpert, E. Harris, & G. Koocher (Eds.), *Report to the APA Board of Directors from the Ad Hoc Committee on Child Abuse Policy* (pp. 44–46). Washington, DC: American Psychological Association.

Judge Baker Children's Center. (1990). *Privacy and confidentiality in mental health services.* Boston: Author.

Kalichman, S. C. (1990). Reporting laws, confidentiality, and clinical judgment: Reply to Ansell and Ross. *American Psychologist, 45,* 1273.

Kalichman, S. C. (1991). Laws on reporting sexual abuse of children. *American Journal of Psychiatry, 148,* 1618–1619.

Kalichman, S. C., & Brosig, C. L. (1992). Practicing psychologists' interpretations of and compliance with child abuse reporting laws. *American Journal of Orthopsychiatry, 62,* 284–296.

Kalichman, S. C., & Brosig, C. L. (1993). The effects of child abuse reporting laws on psychologists' reporting behavior: A comparison of two state statutes. *Law and Human Behavior, 17,* 83–93.

Kalichman, S. C., Brosig, C. L., & Kalichman, M. O. (1994). Mandatory child abuse reporting laws: Issues and implications for the treatment of offenders. *Journal of Offender Rehabilitation, 21,* 27–43.

Kalichman, S. C., & Craig, M. E. (1991). Professional psychologists' decisions to report suspected abuse: Clinician and situation influences. *Professional Psychology: Research and Practice, 22,* 84–89.

Kalichman, S. C., Craig, M., & Follingstad, D. (1988). Mental health professionals and suspected cases of child abuse: An investigation of factors influencing reporting. *Community Mental Health Journal, 24,* 43–51.

Kalichman, S. C., Craig, M. E., & Follingstad, D. (1989). Factors influencing the reporting of father–child sexual abuse: Study of licensed practicing psychologists. *Professional Psychology: Research and Practice, 20,* 84–89.

Keith-Spiegel, P., & Koocher, G. P. (1985). *Ethics in psychology: Professional standards and cases.* New York: Random House.

Kelly, R. J. (1987). Limited confidentiality and the pedophile. *Hospital and Community Psychiatry, 38,* 1046–1048.

Kempe, C., Silverman, F., Steele, B., Droegemueller, W., & Silver, H. (1962). The battered child syndrome. *Journal of the American Medical Association, 181,* 4–11.

Kendall-Tackett, K. A., Williams, L. M., & Finkelhor, D. (1993). Impact of sexual abuse on children: A review and synthesis of recent empirical studies. *Psychological Bulletin, 113,* 164–180.

Kennel, R. G., & Agresti, A. A. (1995). Effects of gender and age on psychologists' reporting of child sexual abuse. *Professional Psychology: Research and Practice, 26,* 612–615.

Kim, D. S. (1986). How physicians respond to child maltreatment cases. *Health and Social Work, 11*, 95–106.

Kinard, E. M. (1985). Ethical issues in research with abused children. *Child Abuse and Neglect, 9*, 301–311.

Kitchener, K. S. (1988). Dual-role relationships: What makes them so problematic. *Journal of Counseling and Development, 67*, 217–221.

Knapp, S. (1983). Counselor liability for failing to report child abuse. *Elementary School Guidance Counseling, 17*, 177–179.

Knapp, S., & VandeCreek, L. (1997). *Jaffee v. Redmond*: The Supreme Court recognizes a therapist–patient privilege in federal courts. *Professional Psychology: Research and Practice, 28*, 567–572.

Koocher, G. P. (1988). A thumbnail guide to "duty to warn" cases. *The Clinical Psychologist, 41*, 22–25.

Koocher, G. P., & Keith-Spiegel, P. (1990). *Children, ethics, and the law.* Lincoln: University of Nebraska Press.

Krugman, R. D. (1990). Physical indicators of child sexual abuse. *Review of Psychiatry, 10*, 336–343.

Lamond, A. (1989). The impact of mandatory reporting legislation on reporting behavior. *Child Abuse and Neglect, 13*, 471–480.

Landeros v. Flood, 551 Calif. P.2d 389 (1976).

Leong, G. B., Eth, S., & Silva, J. A. (1992). The psychotherapist as witness for the prosecution: The criminalization of *Tarasoff*. *American Journal of Psychiatry, 149*, 1011–1015.

Levin, P. G. (1983). Teachers' perceptions, attitudes and reporting of child abuse/neglect. *Child Welfare, 62*, 14–20.

Levine, A., & Levine, M. (1992). *Helping children: A social history.* New York: Oxford Press.

Levine, M. (1993). A therapeutic jurisprudence analysis of mandated reporting of child maltreatment by psychotherapists. *New York Law School Journal of Human Rights, 10*, 711–738.

Levine, M. (1998). Do standards of proof affect decision making in child protection investigations? *Law and Human Behavior, 22*, 341–347.

Levine, M., Anderson, E., Terretti, L., Sharma, A., Steinberg, K., & Wallach, L. (1991). Effects of reporting maltreatment on the psychotherapeutic relationship. In S. Kalichman (Chair), *Mandatory child abuse reporting: A research and policy update.* Symposium conducted at the 99th Annual Convention of the American Psychological Association, San Francisco.

Levine, M., Anderson, E., Terretti, L., Steinberg, K., Sharma, A., & Wallach, L. (1991). *Mandated reporting and the therapeutic alliance in the context of the child protection system.* (Available from the Baldy Center for Law and Social Policy, State University of New York, 511 O'Brian Hall, Buffalo, NY 14260)

Levine, M., & Battistoni, L. (1991). The corroboration requirement in child sexual abuse cases. *Behavioral Sciences and the Law, 9*, 3–20.

Levine, M., & Doherty, E. (1991). The Fifth Amendment and therapeutic requirements to admit abuse. *Criminal Justice and Behavior, 18,* 98–112.

Levine, M., & Doueck, H. J. (1995). *The impact of mandated reporting on the therapeutic process: Picking up the pieces.* Newbury Park, CA: Sage.

Levy, R. J. (1989). Using "scientific" testimony to prove child sexual abuse. *Family Law Quarterly, 23,* 383–409.

Lewis, D. O., Shanok, S. S., Pincus, J. H., & Glaser, G. H. (1979). Violent juvenile delinquents: Psychiatric neurological, psychological, and abuse factors. *Journal of the American Academy of Child Psychiatry, 18,* 307–319.

Liss, M. (1994). Child abuse: Is there a mandate for researchers to report? *Ethics and Behavior, 4,* 133–146.

MacDonald, D., Hill, A., & Li, C. (1993). Confidentiality and the duty to report abuse: A current case study. *Journal of Psychology and Theology, 21,* 119–126.

Macolini, R. M. (1995). Elder abuse policy: Considerations in research and legislation. *Behavioral Sciences and the Law, 13,* 349–363.

Maney, A., & Wells, S. (Eds.). (1988). *Professional responsibilities in protecting children: A public health approach to child sexual abuse.* New York: Praeger.

Mannarino, A. P., & Cohen, J. (1986). A clinical–demographic study of sexually abused children. *Child Abuse and Neglect, 10,* 17–23.

Mantell, D. M. (1988). Clarifying erroneous child sexual abuse allegations. *American Journal of Orthopsychiatry, 58,* 618–621.

Margolin, G. (1998). Effects of domestic violence on children. In P. Trickett & C. Shellenbach (Eds.), *Violence against children in the family and community* (pp. 57–102). Washington, DC: American Psychological Association.

Maryland Social Services Administration. (1988). *Child maltreatment in Maryland.* (Available from Office of Child Welfare, 311 West Saratoga Street, Baltimore, MD 21201)

Mazura, A. C. (1977). Negligence–malpractice–physicians' liability for failure to diagnose and report child abuse. *Wayne Law Review, 23,* 1187–1201.

McCoid, A. H. (1965). The battered child and other assaults upon the family: Part one. *Minnesota Law Review, 50,* 1–59.

McDevitt, S. (1996). The impact of news media on child abuse reporting. *Child Abuse and Neglect, 20,* 261–274.

Meddin, J., & Hansen, I. (1985). The services provided during a child abuse and/or neglect case investigation and the barriers that exist to service provision. *Child Abuse and Neglect, 9,* 175–182.

Melton, G. B., & Corson, J. (1987). Psychological maltreatment and the schools: Problems of law and professional responsibility. *School Psychology Review, 16,* 188–194.

Melton, G. B., & Davidson, H. A. (1987). Child protection and society: When should the state intervene? *American Psychologist, 42,* 172–175.

Melton, G. B., Goodman, G. S., Kalichman, S. C., Levine, M., Saywitz, K. J., &

Koocher, G. P. (1995). Empirical research on child maltreatment and the law. *Journal of Child Clinical Psychology, 24*(Suppl), 47–77.

Melton, G. B., & Limber, S. (1989). Psychologists' involvement in cases of child maltreatment. *American Psychologist, 44*, 1225–1233.

Meriwether, M. H. (1986). Child abuse reporting laws: Time for a change. *Family Law Quarterly, 20*, 141–171.

Michigan Department of Social Services. (1989). *Child protection law*. Lansing, MI: Author.

Miller, R. D., & Weinstock, R. (1987). Conflict of interest between therapist–patient confidentiality and the duty to report sexual abuse of children. *Behavioral Sciences and the Law, 5*, 161–174.

Milner, J. S. (1986). *The Child Abuse Potential Inventory: Manual* (2nd ed.). Webster, NC: Psytec Corporation.

Milner, J. S. (1989). Additional cross-validation of the Child Abuse Potential Inventory. *Psychological Assessment: A Journal of Consulting and Clinical Psychology, 1*, 219–233.

Milner, J. S. (1990). *An interpretive manual for the Child Abuse Potential Inventory*. Webster, NC: Psytec Corporation.

Milner, J. S. (1991). Medical conditions and Child Abuse Potential Inventory specificity. *Psychological Assessment, 3*, 208–212.

Milner, J. S., Gold, R. G., & Wimberley, R. C. (1986). Prediction and explanation of child abuse: Cross-validation of the Child Abuse Potential Inventory. *Journal of Consulting and Clinical Psychology, 54*, 865–866.

Morris, J. L., Johnson, C. F., & Chasen, M. (1985). To report or not to report: Physicians' attitudes toward discipline and child abuse. *American Journal of Disability in Children, 139*, 194–197.

Muehleman, T., & Kimmons, C. (1981). Psychologists' views on child abuse reporting, confidentiality, life, and the law: An exploratory study. *Professional Psychology, 12*, 631–638.

Muehleman, T., Pickens, B., & Robinson, F. (1985). Informing clients about the limits to confidentiality, risks, and their rights: Is self-disclosure inhibited? *Professional Psychology: Research and Practice, 16*, 385–397.

National Association of Social Workers. (1980). *Code of ethics*. Silver Spring, MD: Author.

National Center on Child Abuse and Neglect. (1979). *Child abuse and neglect: State reporting laws*. (Available from the Clearinghouse on Child Abuse and Neglect Information, P.O. Box 1182, Washington, DC 20013)

National Center on Child Abuse and Neglect. (1989). *State statutes related to child abuse and neglect: 1988*. (Available from the Clearinghouse on Child Abuse and Neglect Information, P.O. Box 1182, Washington, DC 20013)

Newberger, E. H. (1983). The helping hand strikes again: Unintended consequences of child abuse reporting. *Journal of Clinical Child Psychology, 12*, 307–311.

Newman, R. (1987). *The psychotherapist's duty to report child abuse and the legislature's duty to strike a better balance.* Unpublished manuscript.

Nightingale, N., & Walker, E. F. (1986). Identification and reporting of child maltreatment by Head Start personnel: Attitudes and experiences. *Child Abuse and Neglect, 10,* 191–199.

Oates, R. K., Forrest, D., & Peacock, A. (1985). Self-esteem and abused children. *Child Abuse and Neglect, 9,* 159–163.

O'Connor, K. (1989, July). Professional conflicts and issues in child abuse reporting and treatment. *The California Psychologist,* 22–23.

Otto, R., & Melton, G. (1990). Trends in legislation and case law on child abuse and neglect. In R. Ammerman & M. Hersen (Eds.), *Children at risk: An evaluation of factors contributing to child abuse and neglect* (pp. 55–83). New York: Plenum.

Paradise, J. E., Rostain, A. L., & Nathanson, M. (1988). Substantiation of sexual abuse charges when parents dispute custody or visitation. *Pediatrics, 81,* 835–839.

Parker, J. F. (1995). Age differences in source monitoring of performed and imagined actions on immediate and delayed tests. *Journal of Experimental Child Psychology, 60,* 84–101.

Paulsen, M. C. (1967). Child abuse reporting laws: The shape of legislation. *Columbia Law Review, 67,* 1–49.

Pecora, P. J. (1991). Investigating allegations of child maltreatment: The strengths and limitations of current risk assessment systems. *Child and Youth Services, 15,* 73–92.

Pennsylvania Department of Public Welfare. (1992). *Child abuse and neglect report.* Harrisburg: Author.

People v. Cavaiani. 172 Mich. App. 706, 432 N.W.2nd. 409 (1988).

People v. Cavaiani. 432 Mich. 835, 434 N.W.2d. 411 (1989).

Pierce, R. L., & Pierce, L. H. (1985). Analysis of sexual abuse hotline reports. *Child Abuse and Neglect, 9,* 37–45.

Plante, T. G. (1995). Training child clinical predoctoral interns and postdoctoral fellows in ethics and professional issues: An experiential model. *Professional Psychology: Research and Practice, 26,* 616–619.

Poole, D. A., & Lamb, M. E. (1998). *Investigative interviews of children: A guide for helping professionals.* Washington, DC: American Psychological Association.

Pope, K. S., & Bajt, T. (1988). When laws and values conflict: A dilemma for psychologists. *American Psychologist, 43,* 828–829.

Pope, K. S., & Brown, L. S. (1996). *Recovered memories of abuse: Assessment, therapy, forensics.* Washington, DC: American Psychological Association.

Pope, K. S., & Feldman-Summers, S. (1992). National survey of psychologists' sexual and physical abuse history and their evaluation of training and competence in these areas. *Professional Psychology: Research and Practice, 23,* 353–361.

Pope, K. S., Tabachnick, B. G., & Keith-Spiegel, P. (1987). The beliefs and behaviors of psychologists as therapists. *American Psychologist, 42*, 993–1006.

Pope, K., & Vasquez, M. (1991). *Ethics in psychotherapy and counseling.* San Francisco: Jossey-Bass.

Pope, K. S., & Vetter, V. (1992). Ethical dilemmas encountered by members of the American Psychological Association: A national survey. *American Psychologist, 47*, 397–411.

Priest, R., & Wilcoxon, S. (1988). Confidentiality and the child sexual offender: Unique challenges and dilemmas. *Family Therapy, 15*, 107–113.

Pruitt, J. A., & Kappius, R. E. (1992). Routine inquiry into sexual victimization: A survey of therapists' practices. *Professional Psychology: Research and Practice, 23*, 474–479.

Racusin, R. J., & Felsman, J. K. (1986). Reporting child abuse: The ethical obligation to inform parents. *Journal of the American Academy of Child Psychiatry, 25*, 485–489.

Reinhart, M. A. (1987). Sexually abused boys. *Child Abuse and Neglect, 11*, 229–235.

Reiniger, A., Robison, E., & McHugh, M. (1995). Mandated training of professionals: A means for improving reporting of suspected child abuse. *Child Abuse and Neglect, 19*, 63–69.

Reppucci, N. D., & Haugaard, J. J. (1989). Prevention of child sexual abuse: Myth or reality. *American Psychologist, 44*, 1266–1275.

Rindfleisch, N., & Bean, G. (1988). Willingness to report abuse and neglect in residential facilities. *Child Abuse and Neglect, 12*, 509–520.

Roane, T. H. (1992). Male victims of sexual abuse: A case review within a child protective team. *Child Welfare, 71*, 231–239.

Rodriguez, M. A., McLoughlin, E., Bauer, H. M., Paredes, V., & Grumbach, K. (1999). Mandatory reporting of intimate partner violence to police: Views of physicians in California. *American Journal of Public Health, 89*, 575–578.

Rosenthal, J. A. (1988). Patterns of reported child abuse and neglect. *Child Abuse and Neglect, 12*, 263–271.

Rycraft, J. R. (1990). Redefining abuse and neglect: A narrower focus could affect children at risk. *Public Welfare, 49*, 14–21.

Salovitz, B., & Keys, D. (1988). Is the child protective service still a service? *Protecting Children, 5*, 17–23.

Saulsbury, F., & Campbell, R. (1985). Evaluation of child abuse reporting by physicians. *American Journal of Diseases of Children, 139*, 393–395.

Schwartz, A. (1991, March). Child abuse—Despite the law it is not reported. *CBA Record*, 24–28.

Sebold, J. (1987). Indicators of child sexual abuse in males. *Social Casework: The Journal of Contemporary Social Work, 20*, 75–80.

Sgroi, S., Porter, F., & Blick, L. (1982). Validation of child sexual abuse. In S.

Sgroi (Ed.), *Handbook of clinical intervention in child sexual abuse* (pp. 39–79). Lexington, MA: Lexington Books.

Shiff, A. R., & Wexler, D. B. (1996). Teen court: A therapeutic jurisprudence perspective. *Criminal Law Bulletin, 32*, 342–357.

Sieber, J. E. (1994). Issues presented by mandatory reporting requirements to researchers of child abuse and neglect. *Ethics and Behavior, 4*, 1–22.

Sink, F. (1988). A hierarchical model for evaluation of child sexual abuse. *American Journal of Orthopsychiatry, 58*, 129–135.

Small, M. A. (1996). Legal psychology and therapeutic jurisprudence. In D. B. Wexler & B. J. Winick (Eds.), *Law in a therapeutic key* (pp. 611–631). Durham, NC: Carolina Academic Press.

Smith, S., & Meyer, R. (1984). Child abuse reporting laws and psychotherapy: A time for reconsideration. *International Journal of Law and Psychiatry, 7*, 351–366.

Smith, T. S., McGuire, J., Abbott, D., & Blau, B. (1991). Clinical ethical decision making: An investigation of the rationales used to justify doing less than one believes one should. *Professional Psychology: Research and Practice, 22*, 235–239.

Southard, M. J., & Gross, B. H. (1982). Making clinical decisions after *Tarasoff.* In B. Gross & L. Weinberger (Eds.), *New directions for mental health services: The mental health professional and legal system* (pp. 93–101). San Francisco: Jossey-Bass.

Stadler, H. A. (1989). Balancing ethical responsibilities: Reporting child abuse and neglect. *The Counseling Psychologist, 17*, 102–108.

State of Washington v. David Motherwell, E. Scott Hedley, and Louis Mensonides. S.Ct. 55875-2 (1990).

Steinberg, K. L., Levine, M., & Doueck, H. J. (1997). Effects of legally mandated child abuse reports on the therapeutic relationship: A survey of psychotherapists. *American Journal of Orthopsychiatry, 67*, 112–122.

Stone, A. A. (1976). The *Tarasoff* decisions: Suing psychotherapists to safeguard society. *Harvard Law Review, 90*, 358–378.

Swets, J. A. (1992). The science of choosing the right decision threshold in high-stakes diagnostics. *American Psychologist, 47*, 522–532.

Swoboda, J. S., Elwork, A., Sales, B. D., & Levine, D. (1978). Knowledge of and compliance with privileged communication and child abuse reporting laws. *Professional Psychology, 9*, 448–457.

Tarasoff v. Board of Regents of the University of California. 551 P.2d 334 (Cal. 1976).

Taylor, L., & Adelman, H. (1989). Reframing the confidentiality dilemma to work in children's best interest. *Professional Psychology: Research and Practice, 20*, 79–83.

Turner, A. (1982). What subjects in survey research believe about confidentiality. In J. E. Sieber (Ed.), *The ethics of social research: Surveys and experiments* (pp. 151–165). New York: Springer-Verlag.

U.S. Advisory Board on Child Abuse and Neglect. (1990). *Child abuse and neglect: Critical first steps in response to a national emergency.* (Available from Switzer Building, Room 2070C, 200 Independence Avenue, S.W., Washington, DC 20201)

U.S. Department of Health and Human Services. (1988). *Study findings: Study of national incidence and prevalence of child abuse and neglect.* Bethesda, MD: Westat.

Van Eenwyk, J. R. (1990). When laws and values conflict: Comment on Pope and Bajt. *American Psychologist, 45,* 399–400.

Wald, M. (1975). State intervention on behalf of "neglected" children: A search for realistic standards. *Stanford Law Review, 27,* 985–1040.

Walker, C. E., Bonner, B., & Kaufman, K. (1988). *The physically and sexually abused child: Evaluation and treatment.* New York: Pergamon Press.

Walker, L. E. (1988). *Handbook on sexual abuse of children.* New York: Springer.

Walker, L. E., Alpert, J., Harris, E., & Koocher, G. (1989). *Report to the APA Board of Directors from the Ad Hoc Committee on Child Abuse Policy.* Washington, DC: American Psychological Association.

Walker, N. E., & Nguyen, M. (1996). Interviewing the child witness: The do's and the don't's, the how's and the why's. *Creighton Law Review, 29,* 1587–1617.

Walters, D. (1995). Mandatory reporting of child abuse: Legal, ethical, and clinical implications within the Canadian context. *Canadian Psychology, 36,* 163–182.

Wang, C. T., & Daro, D. (1998). *Current trends in child abuse reporting and fatalities: The results of the 1997 Annual Fifty State Survey.* Chicago: National Committee for the Prevention of Child Abuse.

Warner, J., & Hansen, D. (1994). The identification of physical abuse by physicians: A review and implications for research. *Child Abuse and Neglect, 18,* 11–25.

Watkins, S. A. (1989). Confidentiality: An ethical and legal conundrum for family therapists. *American Journal of Family Therapy, 17,* 291–302.

Watson, H., & Levine, M. (1989). Psychotherapy and mandated reporting of child abuse. *American Journal of Orthopsychiatry, 59,* 246–256.

Weinstock, R., & Weinstock, D. (1989). Clinical flexibility and confidentiality: Effects of reporting laws. *Psychiatric Quarterly, 60,* 195–214.

Weisberg, R., & Wald, M. (1984). Confidentiality laws and state efforts to protect abused or neglected children: The need for statutory reform. *Family Law Quarterly, 18,* 143–212.

Weissman, H. N. (1991). Forensic psychological examination of the child witness in cases of alleged sexual abuse. *American Journal of Orthopsychiatry, 61,* 48–58.

Wells, S. (1988). On the decision to report suspected abuse or neglect. In A. Maney & S. Wells (Eds.), *Professional responsibilities in protecting children* (pp. 191–202). New York: Praeger.

Wells, S., Downing, J., & Fluke, J. (1991). Responding to reports of child abuse and neglect. *Child and Youth Services, 15*, 63–72.

Wells, S., Stein, T., Fluke, J., & Downing, J. (1989). Screening in child protective services. *Social Work, 34*, 45–48.

Wexler, D. B. (1979). Patients, therapists, and third parties: The victimological virtues of *Tarasoff. International Journal of Law and Psychiatry, 2*, 1–28.

Wexler, D. B. (1993). Applying the law therapeutically. In D. B. Wexler & B. J. Winick (Eds.), *Law in a therapeutic key* (pp. 831–842). Durham, NC: Carolina Academic Press.

Wexler, D. B. (1995). Reflections on the scope of therapeutic jurisprudence. *Psychology, Public Policy, and Law, 1*, 220–236.

White, S., Strom, G. A., Santilli, G. A., & Halpin, B. M. (1986). Interviewing young sexual abuse victims with anatomically correct dolls. *Child Abuse and Neglect, 19*, 519–529.

Wiehe, V. R. (1992). *Working with child abuse and neglect.* Itasca, IL: Peacock.

Wilcoxon, S. A. (1991). Clarifying expectations in therapy relationships: Suggestions for written guidelines. *Journal of Independent Social Work, 5*, 65–71.

Wilkins, M. A., McGuire, J., Abbott, D., & Blau, B. (1990). Willingness to apply understood ethical principles. *Journal of Clinical Psychology, 46*, 539–547.

Williams, H. S., Osborne, Y., & Rappaport, N. (1987). Child abuse reporting law: Knowledge and compliance. *Southern Psychologist, 3*, 20–24.

Willis, C. L., & Wells, R. H. (1988). The police and child abuse: An analysis of police decisions to report illegal behavior. *Criminology, 26*, 695–714.

Wilson, C. A., & Gettinger, M. (1989). Determinants of child abuse reporting among Wisconsin school psychologists. *Professional School Psychology, 4*, 91–102.

Wilson, J., Thomas, D., & Schuette, L. (1983). Survey of counselors on identifying and reporting cases of child abuse. *School Counselor, 30*, 299–305.

Winick, B. J. (1994). The right to refuse mental health treatment: A therapeutic jurisprudence analysis. *International Journal of Law and Psychiatry, 17*, 99–117.

Winick, B. J. (1996). The psychotherapist–patient privilege: A therapeutic jurisprudence view. In B. Wexler & B. J. Winick (Eds.), *Law in a therapeutic key* (pp. 483–497). Durham, NC: Carolina Academic Press.

Wisconsin Department of Health and Social Services. (1985). *Investigation handbook for child protective service workers.* Madison, WI: Author.

Wolfner, G., Faust, D., & Dawes, R. W. (1993). The use of anatomically detailed dolls in sexual abuse evaluations: The state of the science. *Applied and Preventive Medicine, 2*, 1–11.

Wolock, I., & Magura, S. (1996). Parental substance abuse as a predictor of child maltreatment re-reports. *Child Abuse and Neglect, 20*, 1183–1193.

Wulach, J. S. (1993). *Law & mental health professionals: New York.* Washington, DC: American Psychological Association.

Wulach, J. S. (1998). *Law & mental health professionals: New Jersey*. Washington, DC: American Psychological Association.

Wurtele, S. K., & Miller-Perrin, C. L. (1992). *Preventing child sexual abuse: Sharing the responsibility*. Lincoln: University of Nebraska Press.

Zellman, G. (1990). Report decision-making patterns among mandated child abuse reporters. *Child Abuse and Neglect, 14*, 325–336.

Zellman, G. (1992). The impact of case characteristics on child abuse reporting decisions. *Child Abuse and Neglect, 16*, 57–74.

Zellman, G., & Antler, S. (1990). Mandated reporters and child protective agencies: A study in frustration. *Public Welfare, 48*, 30–37.

Zielinski, S. (1992, April). *Clinical perspectives in child abuse*. Paper presented at the Loyola Conference on Child Abuse: Clinical, Ethical, Social, and Legal Dimensions, Chicago, IL.

# APPENDIX A

## Glossary

Many terms commonly used in reference to child abuse may be unfamiliar to mandated reporters. The following glossary presents some of the more frequent terminology found in medical and legal reports and physical descriptions of child abuse and neglect.

ABRASION A wound in which an area of the body surface is scraped of skin, mucous membrane, or both.

ACUTE PANCREATITIS A severe inflammation of the pancreas. When present in children its most common cause is trauma.

ADJUDICATORY HEARING Held by juvenile and family courts to determine the occurrence of abuse or neglect and appropriate state interventions. Terms, definitions, and scope of court functions vary by state.

ALLEGATION OF ABUSE A notification to a child protective services agency of suspected maltreatment of a child.

ALLEGED VICTIM Subject of a report regarding maltreatment that has been made to a child protective services agency.

ANONYMOUS/UNKNOWN REPORTER An individual who reports a suspected incident of child maltreatment without identifying himself or herself, or when the type of reporter is unknown.

ARACHNOID A delicate membrane of the spinal cord and brain that may be damaged due to trauma.

ASPHYXIATION Breathing impaired to the extent of losing consciousness, with potential for brain damage or death. Causes are varied, including strangulation, suffocation, smothering, and smoke inhalation.

ATROPHY Wasting away of body tissues or organs.

AVITAMINOSIS (HYPOVITAMINOSIS) A condition that results from a deficiency of one or more essential vitamins.

BASILAR SKULL FRACTURE A fracture to the base of the brain case, near the nose and ears. Could involve loss of spinal fluid and risk of infection.

BONE SCAN  A nuclear study to diagnose early or minimal fractures.

BONE SURVEY  A total body X-ray to determine fractures without obvious symptoms. Old fractures can be detected with this procedure.

BURNS  Wounds resulting from the application of excessive heat. Degree classifications include 1st degree, or a scorching or painful redness of skin; 2nd degree, or the formation of blisters; and 3rd degree, or the destruction of outer layers of skin.

CALCIFICATION  Formation of bone. Amounts of calcium deposits can be detected by X-ray and used to identify healed fractures.

CALLUS  New meshwork of bone formed during the healing process of a fracture.

CALVARIUM  Domelike portion of the skull.

CELLULITIS  Inflammation of the loose tissue underneath the skin.

CEREBRAL EDEMA (CONTUSION OF THE BRAIN)  Brain swelling, usually associated with bleeding into brain tissue.

CHILD-BASED REPORT  A method of reporting in which each child alleged to be a victim of maltreatment is counted as one report. A child-based report does not include multiple children. Also known as victim based.

CHILD PROTECTIVE SERVICES (CPS)  The social service agency or division of a larger social agency that is charged with receiving reports, investigating, and providing services for child abuse and neglect.

CHILD–VICTIM  A child for whom an incident of abuse or neglect has been substantiated or indicated by an investigation or assessment.

CHILDREN/FAMILIES IN NEED OF SERVICES  A term used by a child welfare agency as a result of an assessment to specify the decision that a child or family is in need of services. This disposition is applicable only in states that have a diversified response system, in which there are other classifications, such as *substantiated*, *indicated*, or *unsubstantiated*.

CLOSED WITHOUT FINDINGS  A disposition that is unsubstantiated because it could not be completed. Reasons for incompletion might include that a family moved out of jurisdiction, that a family could not be located, or that necessary reports were not received within time limits.

COLPOSCOPY  A binocular magnifying device, traditionally used in gynecology and often used in the physical examination of sexual abuse cases.

CONGENITAL  Physical condition present at birth, regardless of etiological cause.

CONTUSION  Wound producing injury to soft tissue without a break in the skin, causing bleeding into surrounding tissue.

COURT ACTION Legal action initiated by a representative of a CPS agency on behalf of a child. This includes, for instance, authorization to place a child, filing for temporary custody, dependency, or termination of parental rights. It does not include criminal proceedings against a perpetrator.

COURT-APPOINTED REPRESENTATIVE A person appointed by the court to represent a child in a neglect or abuse proceeding. This person may be an attorney or a court-appointed special advocate (or both) and is often referred to as a *guardian ad litem*. The court-appointed representative makes recommendations to the court concerning the best interests of a child.

CRANIUM The skull.

DIAPHYSIS The shaft of a long bone.

DISLOCATION The displacement of bone, usually at the joint. May or may not be accompanied by fractures.

DISPOSITION The determination by a social services agency or a court whether evidence is sufficient under state law to conclude that abuse, neglect, or both has occurred. Where state law permits, dispositions may also include the determination that a child is at risk of being abused or neglected, or that additional services are needed.

DISPOSITION HEARING Held by juvenile or family court to determine the placement and services for cases that have proceeded through adjudication.

DIVERSIFIED RESPONSE SYSTEM CPS practice in which an assessment or other response to a report of alleged maltreatment may be made, instead of an investigation. Diversified responses usually result in a determination of needed services.

DRUG-DEPENDENT NEWBORN An infant under 28 days of age exhibiting abnormal growth or neurological signs coupled with strong evidence that the mother was substance abusive during pregnancy.

DURA MATER A tough fibrous membrane that covers the brain and spinal cord.

ECCHYMOSIS The passage of blood from ruptured blood vessels into subcutaneous tissue, marked by purple discoloration of the skin.

EDEMA Swelling caused by an excessive amount of fluid in body tissue. It follows a bump or bruise.

EPIDURAL HEMATOMA Blood that is above the dura (cover of the brain or spinal cord).

EPIPHYSIS Growth center near the end of a long bone, usually wider than the shaft, and separated from the shaft by a growth plate.

EXTRAVASATED BLOOD Discharge or escape of blood into tissue.

FAILURE TO THRIVE (FTT) SYNDROME A child's, height, weight, and motor development are significantly below the average growth rate expected for his or her chronological age. FTT syndrone may result from severe emotional and physical neglect of a child. However, about 30% of cases involve an organic condition. When caused by parental neglect, the symptoms will reverse with proper nurturing.

FAMILY BASED A type of reporting system that counts in a report the family unit involved in a child abuse or neglect allegation, regardless of the number of children involved.

FAMILY PRESERVATION SERVICES Services designed to protect children from harm and to assist families at risk or in crisis, including services to prevent placement, to support the reunification of children with their families, or to support the continued placement of children in adoptive homes or other permanent living arrangements.

FAMILY PRESERVATION/REUNIFICATION Established in law and policy, the belief that children and families should remain together if the safety of children can be ensured.

FONTANEL The soft areas on an infant's skull where bones have not yet grown together.

FOSTER CARE A 24-hour substitute care for all children placed away from their parents or guardians and for whom a state agency has placement and care responsibility. This includes, but is not limited to, family foster homes, foster homes of relatives, group homes, emergency shelters, residential facilities, child care institutions, and preadoptive homes. This is regardless of whether the foster care facility is licensed and whether payments are made by the state or local agency for the care of a child or whether there is federal matching of any payments that are made.

FOSTER PARENT Individual licensed to provide a home for orphaned, abused, neglected, delinquent, or disabled children, usually with the approval of the government or a social service agency. This individual can be a relative or a nonrelative.

FRACTURE A broken bone. There are numerous types of breaks, some of which are indicative of abuse.

BUCKET HANDLE TEARS Total fractures of the wider part of a long bone, between the end and the shaft, such that it is loose and floating.
CHIP FRACTURE A small piece of bone flaked from the major part of the bone.
COMMINUTED FRACTURE Bone crushed into many pieces.
COMPOUND FRACTURE Fragments of bone cut through soft tissue, causing a wound.

CORNER FRACTURE The corner of the wider part of a long bone torn off during wrenching or twisting injuries.

SIMPLE FRACTURE Bone breaks without wounding the surrounding tissue.

SPIRAL FRACTURE Fracture that encircles the bone like a spiral, caused by twisting.

TORUS FRACTURE A folding, bulging, or buckling fracture.

GUARDIAN AD LITEM An attorney or layperson who serves as a child's representative in juvenile or family court. Considers the best interest of a child in an advocacy manner.

GOOD FAITH Standard that applies to determinations for reporting. In general, good faith implies that any reasonable person, given the same information, would draw a conclusion that a child may have been abused or neglected.

HEMATOMA A swelling caused by a collection of blood in an enclosed space (i.e., under the skin or skull).

HEMORRHAGE The escape of blood from the vessels; bleeding.

HYPHENA Hemorrhage within the front chamber of the eye, often appearing as a bloodshot eye. The cause may be a blow to the head or violent shaking.

IMMUNITY Protects reporters from civil lawsuits and criminal prosecution resulting from filing a report of suspected child abuse in good faith.

IMPETIGO A contagious and rapidly spreading skin condition that occurs principally in infants and young children. Characterized by red blisters that develop rapidly into pustules, commonly around the mouth and nose. May be an indicator of neglect and inadequate living conditions.

INDICATED A disposition that concludes that although maltreatment could not be substantiated under state law or policy, there is reason to suspect that a child may have been maltreated or was at risk of maltreatment. This is applicable only in states that distinguish between substantiated and indicated dispositions.

INITIAL INVESTIGATION Face-to-face contact with an alleged victim, when this is appropriate, or contact with another person who can provide information essential to the disposition of the investigation or assessment.

INITIAL SCREENING DECISION The decision by a CPS agency to conduct either an investigation or an assessment of an allegation of child maltreatment. The screening process may include more than one decision.

INTENTIONALLY FALSE An unsubstantiated disposition about which it has been concluded that the person reporting the alleged incident of maltreatment knew that the allegation was false.

INVESTIGATION The gathering of objective information to determine whether a child has been, or is at risk of being, maltreated. Generally includes face-to-face contact with a victim and results in a disposition to substantiate the report.

JUVENILE AND FAMILY COURTS Established to resolve conflicts and intervene in the lives of families in a manner that promotes the best interest of a child.

LACERATION A cut or wound of the skin where the edges are jagged or separated and may require stitches.

MALNUTRITION Failure to receive adequate nourishment. Can result from a lack of food or specific vitamins. Can be a sign of neglect, poverty, or an organic condition.

MARASMUS A wasting away of fat and muscle, associated with inadequate nourishment.

MEDICAL NEGLECT Failure to provide medical care in preventing or treating illness. Can occur as a result of not seeking assistance in cases of emergency or from not following prescribed treatments.

METAPHYSIS Wider part of a long bone between the end and the shaft. It contains the growth zone of the bone.

NEGLECT OF DEPRIVATION OF NECESSITIES A type of maltreatment that refers to a failure of a caretaker to provide needed, age-appropriate care, although he or she is financially prepared to do so.

NONCARETAKERS A person who is not responsible for the care and supervision of a child. Includes school personnel, friends, neighbors, etc.

NOT SUBSTANTIATED Disposition that determines that there is not sufficient evidence under state law or policy to conclude that a child has been maltreated or is at risk of being maltreated. Equivalent terms may be "Unfounded" or "Unsubstantiated."

OCCIPITAL Referring to the back of the head.

OSSIFICATION Formation of bone.

OUT-OF-COURT CONTACTS Contact, which is not part of the actual judicial hearing, between a court-appointed representative and a child–victim. Such contacts enable a court-appointed representative to obtain a firsthand understanding of the situation and the needs of a child, and to make recommendations to the court concerning the best interests of a child.

OUT-OF-HOME CARE Child, foster, or residential care provided by individuals and institutions to children who are placed outside of their families, usually under the jurisdiction of a juvenile or family court.

PERPETRATOR A person who has been determined to have caused or knowingly allowed the maltreatment of a child.

PETECHIA A small spot on a body surface caused by a discrete hemorrhage.

PETITION Document filed with a court to initiate a civil child protection proceeding. Contains all of the detailed allegations of abuse, but not the facts to support abuse.

PHYSICAL ABUSE A type of maltreatment that refers to physical acts that caused or could have caused physical injury to a child.

PIA MATER A fine vascular membrane that envelopes the brain and spinal cord under the arachnoid membrane and dura mater.

PREMATURE A neonate who is less than 2,500 g at birth, unrelated to gestational age.

PREPONDERANCE OF EVIDENCE The burden of proof for civil cases in most states, including child maltreatment proceedings. The standard means that the evidence presented by the attorney for a child protection agency is more credible than the evidence presented by a defendant.

PRIORITY STANDARD The state or local requirements for responding to a report alleging child abuse or neglect based upon the initial screening decision, such as immediate, within 1–2 hr, within 72 hr, etc.

PROPOSED–CONFIRMED Reports where the preponderance of evidence substantiates abuse and identifies a perpetrator.

PROTECTION ORDER Order by a judge to control or restrain the behavior of an alleged abusive adult or any other person who may harm a child or interfere with a disposition.

PSYCHOLOGICAL/EMOTIONAL ABUSE A form of maltreatment that results in impaired psychological functioning and development. It frequently occurs as verbal abuse or excessive demands on a child's performance and may cause a child to have a negative self-image and to display disturbed behavior.

PURPURA A condition caused by hemorrhages into tissues. It is characterized by purplish discoloration running together over any part of the skin or mucous membranes.

RAREFACTION Loss of density, as in a bone that has lost calcium.

RELATIONSHIP OF PERPETRATOR TO VICTIM This refers to the primary role of a perpetrator in relation to a child–victim of maltreatment. The relationship may be established with each child in the investigated report or with one child in the report, regardless of how many children are victims of maltreatment.

REMOVED FROM HOME The removal of the child from his or her normal place of residence to a substitute care setting by a child protective services or social services agency.

RESPONSE TIME The time elapsed between the receipt of a report to an initial investigation.

REVIEW HEARING Held by juvenile or family court to review dispositions and to determine the need to maintain placements. All states require such a reevaluation process of cases, but the time frame for review varies. Federal law requires (for federal funding) a review of cases 18 months after disposition and a continued reevaluation at regular intervals to determine final resolutions of cases.

RETINAL HEMORRHAGE Bleeding that can be seen on the retina, detected by viewing the eye through an opthamoscope.

RICKETS Condition of disturbed bone development due to vitamin D deficiency.

SCREENED OUT The decision by a CPS agency not to conduct an investigation or assessment. This decision may be the result of an inappropriate referral, lack of information, or a decision to refer the report to another agency.

SCREENING AT INTAKE Portion of the case flow from point of contact with a reporter to the time that the report is assigned to a CPS agent, who will investigate or assess the allegation.

SEXUAL ABUSE The employment, use, persuasion, inducement, enticement, or coercion of any child to engage in, or assist any other person to engage in, any sexually explicit conduct or simulation of such conduct for the purpose of producing a visual depiction of such conduct. Also refers to rape, and in cases of caretaker or interfamilial relationships, statutory rape, molestation, prostitution, or any other form of sexual exploitation of, or incest with, children.

SCURVY Condition caused by vitamin C deficiency, characterized by weakness, anemia, spongy gums, and other symptoms.

SOURCE OF REPORT Person who makes a report to a CPS agency alleging child maltreatment.

SUBARACHNOID BLEEDING Bleeding that occurs between the pia and arachnoid membranes covering the brain and spinal cord.

SUBDURAL HEMATOMA A collection of blood beneath the dura (outermost covering of the brain). A hematoma may result from a blow to the head or from shaking.

SUBJECT OF REPORT Child or children about whom a report of abuse or neglect is made.

SUBSTANTIATED A disposition that concludes that the allegation of maltreatment or risk of maltreatment was supported or founded by state law or state policy. This is the highest level of finding by a state agency.

TERMINATION OF PARENTAL RIGHTS HEARING Legal proceeding to free a child from a parents' legal custody, allowing his or her adoption by others. The determination made by the court is that the parents will not be able to provide adequate care for the child in the future, using a legal standard of clear and convincing evidence. This burden of proof is higher than a preponderance of evidence.

TRAUMA An internal or external injury or wound inflicted by an outside force. Usually used to describe an injury due to violence.

WHIPLASH/SHAKEN INFANT SYNDROME Injury to an infant or child resulting from shaking, often as a misguided form of discipline. Common symptoms include bleeding of the head and detached retinas. Repeated occurrences can result in developmental disabilities.

# APPENDIX B

## Directory of Information Resources

**Action for Child Protection**, 4724 Park Road, Unit C, Charlotte, NC 28209 (704) 529-1080.

**Adam Walsh Child Resource Center**, 7812 Westminster Blvd, Westminster, CA 92683-4034 (714) 898-4802; 319 Clematis Street, Suite 409, West Palm Beach, FL 33401-1579 (407) 820-9000; 249 Highland Ave, Rochester, NY 14620-3036 (716) 461-1000; 1400 Pickens Street, Suite 102, Columbia, SC 29201-3465 (803) 254-2326.

**American Bar Association, National Legal Resource Center on Children and the Law**, Suite 200, 1800 M Street, NW Washington, DC 20036 (202) 331-2250.

**American Humane Association, American Association for Protecting Children**, 9725 East Hampton Avenue, Denver, CO 80231 (800) 227-5242.

**American Professional Society on Abuse and Children (APSAC)**, 332 South Michigan Avenue, Suite 1600, Chicago, IL 60604 (312) 554-0166.

**American Public Welfare Association**, 810 First Street NE, Suite 500, Washington, DC 20002 (202) 682-0100.

**Baldy Center for Law & Social Policy**, Division of Children and Law, 511 O'Brian Hall, State University at Buffalo, Buffalo, NY 14260 (716) 645-2102.

**C. Henry Kempe National Center for Prevention and Treatment of Child Abuse and Neglect**, 1205 Oneida Street, Denver, CO 80220 (303) 321-3963.

**Child Welfare League of America**, 440 First Street NW, Suite 310, Washington, DC 20001-2085 (202) 638-2952.

**Childhelp U.S.A.**, 6463 Independence Avenue, Woodland Hills, CA 91367-2617 (213) 347-7280; National Hotline for Counseling and Information (800) 4-A-CHILD.

**Committee for Children**, 172-20th Avenue, Seattle, WA 98122 (206) 322-5050.

**Family Violence and Sexual Assault Institute**, 1310 Clinic Drive, Tyler, TX 75701 (817) 485-2244.

**Films for the Humanities and Sciences**, P.O. Box 2053, Princeton, NJ 08543-2053. (800) 257-5126. (Several educational videotapes available for rental or purchase concerning child physical and sexual abuse.)

**Military Family Resource Center**, Ballston Center Tower Three, Ninth Floor, 4015 Wilson Blvd., Suite 903, Arlington, VA 22203 (703) 696-4555.

**National Center for Missing and Exploited Children**, 2101 Wilson Blvd., Suite 550, Arlington, VA 22201-3052 (703) 235-3900; (800) 843-5678.

**National Center for Prosecution of Child Abuse**, 1033 N. Fairfax St., Suite 200, Alexandria, VA 22314 (703) 739-0321.

**National Child Abuse Coalition**, 733 15th St. NW, Suite 938, Washington, DC 20005 (202) 347-3666.

**National Committee for the Prevention of Child Abuse**, 332 South Michigan Avenue, Suite 1600, Chicago, IL 60604-4357 (312) 663-3520.

**National Crime Prevention Council**, 733 15th Street NW, Room 540, Washington, DC 20005 (202) 393-7141.

**National Network of Runaway and Youth Services**, 1400 I Street NW, Washington, DC 20005 (202) 682-4114.

**National Resource Center on Child Sexual Abuse, National Children's Advocacy Center**, 106 Lincoln Street, Huntsville, AL 35801 (205) 533-KIDS; (800) KIDS-006.

**Parents Anonymous**, National Office, 520 S. LaFayette Park Place, Suite 316, Los Angeles, CA 90057 (213) 388-6685; (800) 421-0353.

**Parents United International**, 232 E. Gish Road, First Floor, San Jose, CA 95112 (408) 453-7611 ext. 124.

**U.S. National Center on Child Abuse and Neglect**, P.O. Box 1182, Washington, DC 20013 (703) 385-7565; (800) 394-3366.

**Washington Risk Assessment Project**, Department of Social and Health Services, Children's Services Research Project, 1602 NE 150th, N/17-2, Seattle, WA 98195.

# APPENDIX C

# Directory of National and State Child Protection Hotlines

This listing of state offices of child protective services is provided as a resource for finding information regarding specific mandatory reporting statutes as well as phone numbers for local reporting agencies.

## NATIONAL CHILD ABUSE HOTLINES

| | |
|---|---|
| Foresters National Abuse Hotline | 800-4-A-CHILD |
| ChildAlert.com | 888-CHILD-ALERT (1-888-244-5325) |
| Child Find of America | 800-426-5678 |
| Missing Children's Hotline | 800-THE-LOST (1-800-843-5678) |
| National Child Abuse Hotline | 800-422-4453 |
| National Child At Risk Hotline | 800-792-5200 |
| National Drug Abuse Hotline | 800-662-4357 |
| National Institute of Drug Abuse Helpline | 800-662-HELP (1-800-662-4357) |
| National Runaway Hotline | 800-231-6946 |
| National Runaway Switchboard | 800-621-4000 |
| National Sexually Transmitted Disease Hotline | 800-227-8922 |
| Nation's Missing Children Organization | 800-690-FIND (800-690-3463) |
| Teen AIDS Hotline | 800-234-TEEN (1-800-234-8336) |
| Vanished Children's Alliance | 800-VANISHED (1-800-826-4743) |
| Youth Crisis Hotline | 800-448-4663 |

These are toll-free numbers for reporting suspected child abuse in selected states. To report in those states not listed or for reporting suspected abuse of a child in a different state, call the National Abuse Hotline at 1-800-4-A-CHILD.

## STATE CHILD ABUSE HOTLINES

| | | | |
|---|---|---|---|
| Arkansas | (800) 482-5964 | Arizona | (800) 330-1822 |
| Connecticut | (800) 842-2288 | Delaware | (800) 292-9582 |
| Florida | (800) 962-2873 | Iowa | (800) 362-2178 |
| Illinois | (800) 252-2873 | Indiana | (800) 562-2407 |
| Kansas | (800) 922-5330 | Kentucky | (800) 752-6200 |
| Massachusetts | (800) 792-5200 | Maine | (800) 452-1999 |
| Michigan | (800) 942-4357 | Missouri | (800) 392-3738 |
| Mississippi | (800) 222-8000 | Montana | (800) 332-6100 |
| North Carolina | (800) 662-7030 | Nebraska | (800) 652-1999 |
| New Hampshire | (800) 894-5533 | New Jersey | (800) 792-8610 |
| New Mexico | (800) 432-2075 | Nevada | (800) 992-5757 |
| New York | (800) 342-3720 | Oklahoma | (800) 522-3511 |
| Oregon | (800) 854-3508 | Pennsylvania | (800) 932-0313 |
| Rhode Island | (800) 742-4453 | Texas | (800) 252-5400 |
| Utah | (800) 678-9399 | Virginia | (800) 552-7906 |
| Washington | (800) 562-5624 | West Virginia | (800) 352-6513 |

# INDEX

Access to services, 157
Adult abuse, 44, 159
Advisory Board on Child Abuse and Ne-
    glect, 4, 12, 184
Affective functioning
    signs of physical abuse, 75
    signs of sexual abuse, 72–73
Age of child, 83
American Academy of Pediatrics, 14
American Humane Association, 13
American Medical Association, 15
American Psychological Association. *See*
    *Ethical Principles of Psychologists
    and Code of Conduct*
Anatomically-detailed dolls, 172
Anonymous report, 147
Anxiety, in abused children, 73
Arizona, 153
Assessment
    abuse allegations seen as psychiatric
        symptoms, 111–112
    child interview, 143–145, 172
    child maltreatment, 20
    continuum of abuse indicators, 79–80
    emotional abuse, 77, 129–130
    investigative actions of practitioners in
        suspected abuse, 116–117, 121
    neglect, 75–76
    parenting, 155
    physical abuse, 74–75
    physical examination, 123
    risk, in investigation of abuse report,
        153–156
    role conflicts for therapists in man-
        dated reporting, 51–53
    screening of abuse reports, 150–152
    sexual abuse, 71–74
    of suspected adults, 173
    training for detection of child abuse,
        171–173
    training in detection of child abuse,
        183

Battered child syndrome, 14, 15, 187
Behavioral indicators

as basis for reporting, 88, 164, 165
    emotional maltreatment, 77
    physical abuse, 74–75
    sexual abuse, 72

California, 16, 44, 188
Case law
    duty to warn, 45
    failure to report, 34–41
Casebook, 95–96
Certainty of abuse suspicions, 26–27, 32–
        33, 63, 65, 71, 80–81, 165
    hierarchical approach to evaluation,
        166–168
    legal requirements for reporting, 187–
        188
    *See also* Threshold models of decision
        making
Child Abuse Potential Inventory, 173
Child Abuse Prevention and Treatment
    Act, 15–16
*Child at Risk Field*, 155
Child maltreatment
    clinical conceptualization, 14
    legal definitions, 16, 20, 184–186
    prevalence, 3–4, 11–12
    reporting trends, 3, 11
    training of clinicians for intervention
        in, 168–170, 174–175
    training of clinicians in detecting,
        171–173
Child pornography, 73–74
Child Protection Act of 1974, 186
Child protective services
    effectiveness, 68–69
    initial screening of reports, 150–152
    investigative procedure, 152–156
    mandated reporting as harmful to, 30–
        31, 87
    rationale for reform, 183–184
    reporter follow-up with, 142, 156, 160,
        164
    reporter relations with/perceptions of,
        160, 177, 178–179, 183–184

Child protective services (*continued*)
   resources for handling case reports,
     141, 160
   resources for intervention, 157, 160,
     177, 183–184
   role conflicts in mandated reporting,
     53
   role of mandated reporting in, 9, 193
Child Sexual Behavior Inventory, 173
Children
   confidentiality issues, 49
   interviewing, 143–145, 172
   memory processes, 144
   recanted allegations, 83
   verbal disclosure of abuse, 82–83
Civil disobedience, 62
Civil liability, 34, 67
Colorado, 29
Competency, practitioner, 52, 164
Confidentiality
   client understanding of limits to, 48–
     51, 92, 108–110
   duty to warn issues, 44–46
   ethical issues in mandated reporting,
     46
   informing of intent to report, 145, 164
   mandated reporting as exception to, 48
   report contents, 148, 149
   of reporter identity, 147
   in research settings, 53–55
   significance of, in mental health pro-
     fessions, 47, 55
   treatment of perpetrators and, 190–191
Connecticut, 149
*Connolly v. General Construction Com-*
   *pany*, 181, 182
Consultation, 63, 164, 167
Content of report, 146–149, 164
Corporal punishment, 118–119, 120, 185
   definitions of maltreatment and, 23
Cost–benefit analysis in reporting decision, 66–69, 80, 92
   case vignette, 105–108
Court-ordered treatment, 59–60, 101


Day care, reporting behaviors in, 4, 12
Decision-making models, 66, 91–93
   evidence-based, 69–71
   hierarchical approach, 166–168
   therapeutic considerations, 104
   threshold model, 79–91
   utility model, 66–69

Decision tree, 166–168
Definitions of maltreatment, 16, 20–26,
     73–74, 76, 176–177, 184–186
Depression in abused children, 73
Disclosure of abuse
   age of child, 83
   from child, 82–83, 163–164
   interviewing children, 143–145
   legal issues in mandatory reporting,
     188
   from perpetrator, 58–60
   recanted allegations, 83
   research directions, 178
   in research setting, 114–116
   self-incrimination issues, 59–60, 100–
     101
   by third party, 110–111
Documentation
   content of report, 146–149, 164
   reporter follow up, 164
Domestic violence, 76–77, 159–160
Duty to warn, 98, 102–103
   as basis of requirement to report abuse,
     43–44, 45
   case law, 45
   ethical issues, 45–46


Elder abuse, 44, 150
Emergency intervention, 152
Emotional maltreatment
   behavioral indicators, 77
   case vignette, 129–130
   definitions, 24–25, 76, 185–186
   domestic violence and, 76–77
   forms of, 76
   prevalence, 4, 12
Epidemiology, 3–4, 11–12
Ethical practice
   basis of mandated reporting, 43–44,
     164
   confidentiality issues, 47–48
   duty to warn, 44–46
   effectiveness of standards for, 162
   ethical beliefs vs., 46
   guidelines, 162–165
   informed consent, 48–51
   mandated reporting and, 16–17, 46–
     47, 61–63, 101
   in research settings, 53–55
   resolving reporting conflicts, 63

role conflicts for mental health professionals, 51–53
*Ethical Principles of Psychologists and Code of Conduct*, 47, 48, 50, 51–53, 61, 148
Evidence-based models of decision making, 69–71
 sexual abuse identification, 71–74

Failure to report
 case law, 34–41
 case vignettes, 105–124
 as civil disobedience, 62
 clinician mistrust of child welfare system, 68–69, 160, 177, 183–184
 conceptualization of reasonable suspicion in, 89, 123, 187–188
 corporal punishment, 118–119, 120
 costs, 67
 determinants of, 81–82, 123–124
 effects of mandated reporting law, 17–18
 estimated prevalence, 4, 12
 immunity for, 189
 intentional failure to discover abuse, 100
 liability, 33–34, 67, 171
 motivation of human service professionals, 14, 67, 124
 specificity of state reporting laws, 27
False positive reports, 85–87, 89, 90
Families
 characteristics associated with increased reporting, 83–84
 informing of intent to report, 145, 146, 164
 risk assessment, 154–155
 sexual abuse indicators, 73
 strengths assessment, 154–155
Fearfulness, in abused child, 73
Federal Certificate for Confidentiality, 55
Federal Child Abuse Prevention and Treatment Act, 20
Fifth Amendment, 59–60, 100–101, 187
Florida, 25

Gender differences in abuse disclosure, 71
Guidelines for reporting
 ethical practice, 162–165

need for, 141–143, 161–162

Help-seeking behaviors
 of abuse perpetrators, 57
 self-disclosure by abuse perpetrators in treatment, 58–59, 145–146
Hospitals
 reporting behaviors in, 4, 12
 reporting procedures in, 111–113, 125–127

Immunity for reporters, 19–20, 189–190
Informed consent
 case vignette, 108–110
 effects on therapy, 57, 101
 ethical practice, 163
 informing of intent to report, 145
 minimizing clinical impact of, 92
 objectives, 48
 professional practice, 48–51
 in research settings, 54, 114–115
 self-disclosure by abuse perpetrators, 58–59
 verbal explanation, 50
 written explanation, 50–51
International practice, 15, 27
Internet, 73–74
Interviewing children, 143–145
 training in, 172
Investigative actions
 child interview, 143–145, 172
 effects on family, 87
 false positive reports, 85–87
 by psychologists, 51–53, 116–117, 121
 reporting threshold and, 89
 *See also* Process of investigation

*Jaffee v. Redmond*, 48

*Landeros v. Flood*, 34
Law
 common features of mandate reporting laws, 18
 ethical practice conflicts, 16–17, 46–47, 61–63
 factors in decision to report, 69
 historical development of mandated reporting, 13–17, 186

Law (*continued*)
    inadequacy of, for guiding professionals, 162
    privileged communication concept, 47–48
    self-incrimination, 59–60, 100–101
    specificity of/vagueness of, 181–182
    therapeutic effects of mandated reporting, 98–100
    therapeutic jurisprudence approach, 97–98
    training of clinicians in, 170
    *See also* Case law; State law
Law enforcement agencies, 69–70, 153, 156

Maine, 57
Malpractice, failure to report as, 34
Mandated reporting
    antitherapeutic applications, 100–101
    client awareness of psychologist's obligations, 49–50
    coercive uses in therapy, 101–102, 113–114
    confidentiality issues, 47–48
    conflicts with professional standards, 16–17, 46–47, 61–63, 101
    degree of certainty required for, 26–27, 32–33, 63, 165
    differences among professions, 191
    duty to warn and, 44–46
    effect on reporting behavior, 17–18, 41, 84
    effects on therapy, 55–61, 66–67
    ethical basis, 43–44
    ethical issues in research settings, 53–55
    exemptions for perpetrators in treatment, 57–58
    historical development, 12–17, 186
    immunity for reporters, 19–20, 189–190
    informed consent issues, 49–51
    legal definitions of maltreatment, 20–26, 176–177, 184–186
    lenient decision criteria, 84–87, 90–91, 92
    objectives, 15, 17, 41, 85–86, 98–99, 134
    obligated persons, 16, 18–20, 53
    opportunities for research in, 176–178
    opposition to, 30–33, 191

perpetrator self-disclosure and, 58–59
    problems of, in mental health settings, 41–42
    reform proposals. *See* Reform proposals
    resolving ethical conflicts, 63
    role conflicts for therapists in, 51–53
    strict decision criteria, 87–91, 92
    therapeutic aims, 98–100
    therapeutic application, 102–104
Maryland, 57–59
Masturbation, 72
Media coverage, 18
Medical professionals
    mandated reporting concerns, 18–19
    mandated reporting requirements, 16, 18
Memory
    recanted allegations, 83
Memory, children's, 144
Mental health professionals
    awareness of reporting law, 19, 162–163
    in child protection system, 179
    investigative role in suspected abuse, 51–53, 116–117, 121
    mistrust of child welfare system, 68–69, 160, 177, 183–184
    opposition to mandated reporting, 30–33
    as perpetrator of abuse, 128–129
    problems of mandated reporting laws, 41–42, 191
    public trust, 68
    reporting behaviors, 4, 12
    *See also* Ethical practice; Training
Michigan, 33, 35–36, 142, 187
Minnesota, 148
Mississippi, 28–29
Mortality, 4, 12
    causes of death, 12

National Center on Child Abuse and Neglect, 15
Neglect
    case vignette, 130–131
    indicators, 75–76
    legal definitions, 20–21, 24, 184–186
    poverty and, 130–131
    prevalence, 3–4, 12
New Jersey, 44
New York, 12, 44

North Carolina, 153

Oregon, 148

Parental rights, 23
  confidentiality in therapy with minors,
    49
  corporal punishment, 185
Pastoral counseling, 40–41
Pennsylvania, 29–30
*People v. Cavaiani*, 33, 34–36, 187
*People v. Gray*, 36–37
*People v. Hedberg*, 37–39
*People v. Stritzinger*, 48
Perpetrator of abuse
  assessment, 173
  help-seeking behaviors, 57
  identification of, reporting and, 116–
    117
  informing of intent of report, 145–146
  liability in self-disclosure, 59–60
  professional colleague as, 128–129
  reporting exemptions for, 57–58, 190–
    191
  self-disclosure related to reporting law,
    58–59
Physical abuse
  behavioral indicators, 74–75
  cognitive deficits associated with, 75
  emotional indicators, 75
  legal definitions, 20, 21, 23–24, 185
  physical indicators, 74
  prevalence, 3, 12
  severity of harm, 21–23
Posttraumatic stress disorder, 77
Poverty, neglect and, 130–131
Preparing to report, 146–148
Prevalence of abuse, 3–4, 11–12
Privileged communication, 47–48
  reform proposals, 190–191
Process of investigation, 142
  burden of proof, 157–158
  findings, 157–159
  goals, 153–154, 157
  home visits, 153
  initial review, 150–152
  interviews, 153
  law enforcement agencies in, 153, 156
  operating standards, 158

prioritizing of reports, 152
reporter involvement, 142, 151–152,
    156, 160, 164
state laws, 152–153
Process of reporting, 146–149
  training in, 173–174
Psychological–emotional abuse. *See* Emo-
    tional maltreatment
Public opinion, 68

Race/ethnicity, 83–84
Reasonable suspicion, 26–27, 32–33, 85–
    86, 88–89, 92, 123, 187–188
Recanted allegations, 83
Reform proposals, 42, 134
  for child protective system, 184
  conceptual approaches, 182, 193
  conditions for mandatory reporting,
    187–188
  defining abuse and neglect, 184–186
  dismantling of reporting system, 191
  immunity for reporters, 189–190
  increased discretion for reporting, 191–
    192
  minimal modification of existing sys-
    tem, 182–184
  modification of existing statutes, 184–
    191
  rationale, 192–193
  treatment of perpetrators, 190–191
Reporting behavior
  base rate of abuse in different settings
    and, 91–92
  case vignettes of reported cases, 125–
    135
  case vignettes of unreported cases,
    105–124
  certainty of abuse suspicions, 26–27,
    32–33, 63, 65, 71, 80–81, 187–
    188
  characteristics of abuse and, 82–84
  characteristics of discretionary report-
    ers, 191
  child abuse training as factor in, 183
  consideration of previous reports, 108
  content of report, 146–149, 164
  cost–benefit analysis in, 66–69, 80, 92
  decision-making models, 66
  decision tree for, 166–168
  delayed action, 118–119
  differences among professions, 19, 159

Reporting behavior (*continued*)
  effects of mandated reporting, 17–18,
    41, 84
  evidence-based models of decision
    making, 69–71
  family characteristics and, 83–84
  high-threshold, 87–91, 92
  of human service professionals, 4, 12,
    14, 62, 77–79, 159
  identification of perpetrator as factor
    in, 116–117
  immunity law and, 189–190
  increasing clinician discretion, 191–
    192
  informing perpetrator of intent to re-
    port, 145–146
  institutional factors, 69–70, 71, 121–
    122, 125–127
  legal definition of maltreatment and,
    26, 184–185
  legal knowledge and, 84
  low-threshold, 84–87, 90–91
  need for guidelines, 141–143, 161–162
  perception of confidentiality issues and,
    55
  physical signs of abuse and, 82
  of police, 69–70
  reporting on colleague, 128–129
  reporting when not mandated, 125–
    127
  research opportunities, 176–177, 178
  role conflicts for therapists, 51–53
  specificity of reporting law, 181–182,
    188
  statutory language on conditions for re-
    porting and, 29–30, 188
  therapeutic aims, 99–100, 102–104
  therapeutic considerations, 42, 43, 55–
    61, 67
  threshold models of decision making,
    77–91
  utility model of decision making, 66–
    69
  verbal disclosures from child and, 82–
    83, 163–164
  without seeing alleged victim, 132
  *See also* Failure to report
Research practice
  case vignette of abuse suspicion, 114–
    116
  ethical issues in mandated reporting,
    53–55
  informed consent, 54, 55

research opportunities in child abuse
    intervention, 176–178
Risk assessment, 152, 153–156
Role conflicts for mental health profes-
    sionals, 51–53


Self-disclosure by abuse perpetrators, 58–
    60, 100–101, 145–146, 190
Self-incrimination, 59–60, 100–101, 187
Severity of harm, 21–23
  as factor in decision to report, 69, 86
Sexual abuse
  behavioral signs, 72
  emotional signs, 72–73
  family indicators, 73
  gender differences in disclosure, 71
  legal definitions, 20, 24, 73–74, 185
  physical signs, 24, 71–72
  prevalence, 3–4, 12
  self-disclosure by abuse perpetrators in
    treatment, 58–59
  training of clinician's for intervention
    in, 170
Society for the Prevention of Cruelty to
    Children, 12
South Carolina, 23
State law
  antitherapeutic values in, 100–101
  coercive uses in therapy, 101–102
  conceptualization of reasonable suspi-
    cion, 26–27, 32–33, 88–89, 92
  conditions for mandatory reporting,
    27–30, 32–33, 187–188
  confidentiality of mandated reporter,
    147
  content of report, 146–147
  definitions of maltreatment, 20–26,
    184–186
  historical development, 15, 16
  immunity for reporters, 19–20, 189–
    190
  mandated training, 174–175
  penalties for failure to report, 33–34,
    67
  persons required to report abuse, 18–
    19
  process of investigation, 152–153
  professional's familiarity with, 19, 162–
    163
  reporting on perpetrators in treatment,
    57–58

therapeutic values in, 100
training of clinicians in, 170–171
as unconstitutionally vague, 33
*State Licensing Board v. Johnson*, 39–40
*State of Washington v. Motherwell, Hedley, and Menosnides*, 40–41
Strengths assessment, 154–155
Study of National Incidence and Prevalence of Child Abuse and Neglect, 4, 12
Substance use, 84
Suspicion
  degree of certainty required for reporting, 26–27, 32–33, 63, 65, 71, 80–81, 165, 187–188
  hierarchical approach to evaluation, 166–168
  legal conceptualizations, 26–27, 32–33
  lenient decision criteria, 84–87, 90–91, 92
  strict decision criteria, 87–91, 92
  threshold models of decision making, 77–91

*Tarasoff v. Board of Regents of University of California*, 45, 98, 102–103
Therapeutic jurisprudence, 97–98
  applications, 98, 102–104
  evaluation of mandated reporting laws, 98–102
  objectives, 97–98
Therapeutic relationship
  with abuse perpetrators, 60
  avoidance of abuse topics in therapy, 100
  coercive uses of mandated reporting, 101–102, 113–114
  confidentiality in, 47, 134
  effects of mandated reporting, 31–32, 43, 55–57, 60–61, 66–67, 99–101
  informed consent and, 49, 92, 101
  investigative role of practitioners in suspected abuse, 51–53

Threshold models of decision making, 77–79
  certainty of suspicions in, 80–81
  continuum of abuse indicators in, 79–80, 84
  determinants of reporting behavior, 81–84
  empirical support, 80–81
  high-threshold reporting behavior, 87–91, 92
  low-threshold reporting behavior, 84–87, 90–91, 92
Training, 62–63, 141, 168–170, 193
  adequacy, 161
  curriculum, 169
  in detecting child maltreatment, 171–173, 183
  for discretionary reporting privileges, 191–192
  goals, 164–165
  to interview children, 144, 172
  in legal environment, 170–171, 183
  mandated, 174–175
  in report decision making, 173–174, 183
  in reporting process, 174, 183
  setting-specific, 174

Unsubstantiated reports, 31, 85–86, 89, 157–158
  characteristics of, 158–159
  prevalence, 100, 157
Utility model of decision making, 66–69

Verbal disclosures from child, 82–83, 163–164, 178
Victims of Child Abuse Legislation, 191

Wisconsin, 27–28
Witnessing violence, 76–77
Written reports, 149

# ABOUT THE AUTHOR

**Seth C. Kalichman, PhD,** is an assistant professor in the Department of Psychiatry and Mental Health Sciences at the Medical College of Wisconsin. Dr. Kalichman has published several empirical studies, review articles, and book chapters concerning professional decisions to report cases of suspected child abuse. With the assistance of his colleagues and students, Dr. Kalichman introduced the use of experimentally controlled case vignettes to investigate factors influencing professionals' decisions to report suspected abuse. His research on child abuse reporting has been published in *Professional Psychology: Research and Practice, Child Abuse and Neglect, American Journal of Orthopsychiatry, Law and Human Behavior, and Law and Policy.* He has served on the American Psychological Association's Working Group on Legal Issues Related to Child Abuse and Neglect and has been an expert court witness.

Dr. Kalichman received his PhD in Clinical-Community Psychology from the University of South Carolina. His research and clinical interests span several areas, including psychological interventions and public policy related to child abuse, psychological characteristics of sexually violent adults, and psychosocial interventions for AIDS prevention and treatment. His work in these diverse areas stems from his commitment to applying psychological principles to solve serious social problems.

## DATE DUE

| | | | |
|---|---|---|---|
| AG 21 '04 | | | |
| AP 19 05 | | | |
| | | | |
| | | | |
| | | | |
| | | | |
| | | | |
| | | | |
| | | | |
| | | | |
| | | | |
| | | | |
| | | | |
| | | | |
| | | | |
| | | | |
| | | | |